CW01359969

Corporate Risk Management for Value Creation

Corporate Risk Management for Value Creation

A guide to real-life applications

By Thomas-Olivier Léautier

Published by Risk Books, a Division of Incisive Financial Publishing Ltd

Haymarket House
28–29 Haymarket
London SW1Y 4RX
Tel: +44 (0)20 7484 9700
Fax: +44 (0)20 7484 9800
E-mail: books@incisivemedia.com
Sites: www.riskbooks.com
　　　www.incisivemedia.com

© 2007 the Author, all rights fully reserved.

ISBN 978 1 904339 83 0

British Library Cataloguing in Publication Data
A catalogue record for this book is available from the British Library

Publisher: Clare Beesley
Commissioning Editor: Steve Fairman
Designer: Rebecca Bramwell

Typeset by Mizpah Publishing Services Private Limited, Chennai, India

Printed and bound in Spain by Espacegrafic, Pamplona, Navarra

Conditions of sale
All rights reserved. No part of this publication may be reproduced in any material form whether by photocopying or storing in any medium by electronic means whether or not transiently or incidentally to some other use for this publication without the prior written consent of the copyright owner except in accordance with the provisions of the Copyright, Designs and Patents Act 1988 or under the terms of a licence issued by the Copyright Licensing Agency Limited of 90, Tottenham Court Road, London W1P 0LP.

Warning: the doing of any unauthorised act in relation to this work may result in both civil and criminal liability.

Every effort has been made to ensure the accuracy of the text at the time of publication, this includes efforts to contact each author to ensure the accuracy of their details at publication is correct. After the no responsibility for loss occasioned to any person acting or refraining from acting as a result of the material contained in this publication will be accepted by the copyright owner, the editor, the authors (or the companies they work for) or Incisive Media Plc.

Many of the product names contained in this publication are registered trade marks, and Risk Books has made every effort to print them with the capitalisation and punctuation used by the trademark owner. For reasons of textual clarity, it is not our house style to use symbols such as ™, ®, etc. However, the absence of such symbols should not be taken to indicate absence of trademark protection; anyone wishing to use product names in the public domain should first clear such use the product owner.

Contents

About the Author ix

Preface and acknowledgements xi

1 Introduction 1
1.1 The risk management paradox 1
1.2 The value of risk management 4
1.3 Objectives and structure of this book 7
    1.3.1 Book's objectives 7
    1.3.2 Book's outline 8
    1.3.3 Topics not covered by this book 9
    1.3.4 Flow of the text 10
1.A A few words on probabilities 11
    1.A.1 Sample space and random variables 11
    1.A.2 Discrete random variables 12
    1.A.3 Continuous random variables 17
    1.A.4 The "square root of time rule" 18
    1.A.5 Covariance revisited 19
    1.A.6 The meaning of correlation coefficients 20

PART I: THE "WHAT" OF RISK MANAGEMENT

2 Value creation from risk management 27
2.1 The universe of risks 28
2.2 Providing financial flexibility at minimum cost 29
    2.2.1 Understanding financial flexibility 29
    2.2.2 Modelling financial flexibility 31
    2.2.3 Examples of the value of financial flexibility 36
    2.2.4 Four financial flexibility levers 38
2.3 Enhancing capital allocation and performance management 41
    2.3.1 Context 41
    2.3.2 Capital allocation 43
    2.3.3 Performance management 46
2.4 Maximising operational and strategic flexibility 48
    2.4.1 Operational flexibility 49
    2.4.2 Strategic flexibility 50
2.5 An integrated approach to risk management 51
    2.5.1 Risk management process 51
    2.5.2 A typology of risk management strategies 52
    2.5.3 Updating the risk management strategy 57
    2.5.4 Allocating capital on a risk-adjusted basis 59

2.6	Concluding remarks	59
2.A	Modigliani-Miller irrelevance results	60
	2.A.1 Irrelevance of capital structure	60
	2.A.2 Irrelevance of risk transfer practices	61
	2.A.3 Limitations to Modigliani-Miller results	64
2.B	Risk typologies	65
2.C	Mapping to "standard" value creation channels	65
2.D	Valuation fundamentals	67
	2.D.1 Financial metrics used for valuation	67
	2.D.2 Cost of capital	70
	2.D.3 Free Cash Flow (FCF) and Economic Profit (EP) valuation approaches	73
2.E	Calculations for examples 2.1 and 2.5: the pharmaceutical company	75
	2.E.1 No purchase case	75
	2.E.2 Purchase case	75
	2.E.3 Volatility management technology	76
	2.E.4 Uncertain investment opportunity	77
2.F	Calculations for example 2.2: the oil company	77
	2.F.1 The no-sale case	77
	2.F.2 The sale case	78
	2.F.3 Risk management technology	78
2.G	Risk adjustment	79
2.H	Calculation for example 2.4: the option value	80

3	**A review of risk management practices**	**83**
3.1	Managing with volatility: Enterprise Risk Management	84
3.2	Measuring volatility: Value at Risk, Cash Flow at Risk, Economic Capital	85
	3.2.1 Value at Risk	86
	3.2.2 Cash Flow at Risk	92
	3.2.3 Economic Capital	95
3.3	Managing volatility: hedging and derivatives	96
	3.3.1 Which firms hedge using derivatives?	97
	3.3.2 Hedging and value creation	99
3.4	What comes next?	103

PART II: THE "HOW" OF RISK MANAGEMENT

4	**Enterprise risk analysis**	**107**
4.1	Outside-in risk analysis	108
	4.1.1 Overall approach	108
	4.1.2 Constant volatility profitability	112
	4.1.3 Mean reverting profitability	113
	4.1.4 Diffusion-like profitability	121
	4.1.5 Invested capital growth distribution	121
	4.1.6 Distribution of future OCF	124

	4.2	Inside-out risk analysis	126
		4.2.1 Price risk	127
		4.2.2 Counterparty risk	142
		4.2.3 Operations risk	147
		4.2.4 Business risk	149
		4.2.5 Risk aggregation – hunting for correlations	154
	4.3	Multi-period analyses	154
	4.4	Specificity of enterprise risk analysis	156
		4.4.1 The peculiar analytics of enterprise risk management	156
		4.4.2 The black swan paradox	157
	4.A	Coal-fired plant profit under emission trading	159
	4.B	The aluminium smelter example	159
5	**Risk capital**		**163**
	5.1	The basic model	164
		5.1.1 Derivation	164
		5.1.2 Discount rate for the insurance payments	166
		5.1.3 Trading example	167
		5.1.4 Industrial example	167
		5.1.5 Bernoulli example	168
	5.2	Investment capital and risk capital	169
		5.2.1 Source and adequacy of risk capital	169
		5.2.2 Resulting cost of capital	170
	5.3	One-period project valuation and performance measurement	173
		5.3.1 Bernoulli example	173
		5.3.2 Trading example	174
	5.4	Risk capital for a multi-period firm	176
		5.4.1 General framework	177
		5.4.2 Bernoulli example	179
		5.4.3 Aluminium producer example	183
	5.5	Link with Economic Capital	186
		5.5.1 How do these measures compare numerically?	186
		5.5.2 Which measure to use?	187
	5.6	Concluding remarks	188
	5.A	Derivation of the β of the insurance payments	189
6	**Risk management strategy**		**191**
	6.1	A simplified risk management analysis framework	192
		6.1.1 Main elements of the framework	193
		6.1.2 Optimal investment decision	197
	6.2	Optimal risk management strategy	199
		6.2.1 Optimal capital structure	199
		6.2.2 Optimal hedging ratio	201
	6.3	Monte Carlo simulations	203
		6.3.1 Main inputs into the analysis	204
		6.3.2 No-uncertainty benchmark	205

	6.3.3	Uncertain profits only	206
	6.3.4	Uncertain profits and investment opportunities	206
6.4	Changes in the firm's business environment		209
	6.4.1	Characteristics of investment opportunities	210
	6.4.2	Characteristics of profitability	212
	6.4.3	Cost of capital environment	213
6.5	Concluding observations		214
6.A	Derivations of the optimal risk management strategy		215
	6.A.1	First-order derivative with respect to initial leverage	215
	6.A.2	First order derivative with respect to hedging ratio	219
	6.A.3	Second order derivatives	220
	6.A.4	Impact of hedging ratio on $\Pr(\Omega^{FC})$	222
	6.A.5	Impact of leverage ratio on $\Pr(\Omega^{FC})$	223

7 Conclusion — 225
  7.1 Being a Chief Risk Officer — 226
  7.2 The path forward — 228

Bibliography — 231

Index — 237

About the Author

Thomas-Olivier Léautier is a professor at University of Toulouse Graduate School of Management and a Research Director at the Institut d'Economie Industrielle. He teaches risk management in the finance and strategy masters programs and conducts research, in particular, risk management.

Formerly, Thomas-Olivier was director of risk measurement and control at Alcan, Inc., a global aluminium and packaging group. There, he set up the risk management function, responsible to identify and quantify risks throughout the company, and develop risk management strategies. He previously held positions at McKinsey and Company where he led the development of the risk management practice for non-financial institutions, and at the World Bank where he was a regulatory economist in the Latin America infrastructure division.

Thomas-Olivier Léautier gained a PhD in economics from M.I.T, in 1997, a MS in Transportation also from M.I.T in 1995, a MS from Ecole Nationale des Ponts et Chaussées in 1995, and a MS in applied Mathematics from Ecole Polytechnique in Paris in 1991.

To Frannie, Oriane-Zénaïde and François-René

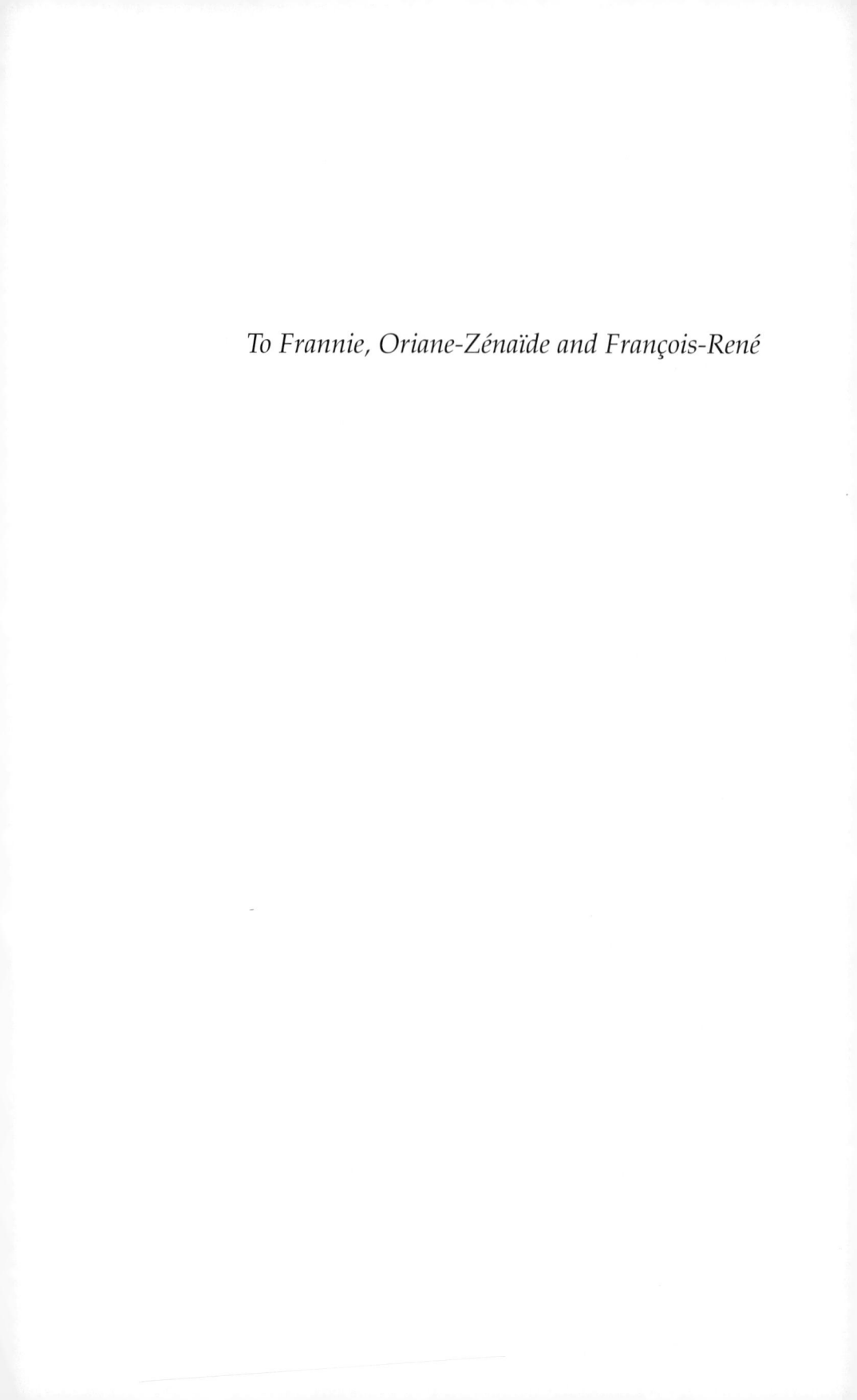

Preface and acknowledgements

Most first books are largely autobiographical. This recounts the path I have travelled over the last ten years as a risk management professional, first advising corporations as a consultant, then putting the advice into practice as I set up the risk measurement group at Alcan, a global aluminum and packaging company, then more recently as a researcher and professor at the University of Toulouse.

As a practitioner, I have felt the rich theoretical apparatus was not directly relevant to the practical issues I was facing. I have also experienced significant discrepancies between theory and practices, even supposedly "best practices". I have therefore devoted considerable time and effort reading, modelling, and trying to reconcile theory and practice. This book is the result of that quest. I hope it will help my fellow risk management professionals in their work.

I have been privileged to have the opportunity to be inspired by outstanding people throughout my career. My PhD advisers at MIT Bengt Holmström and Jean Tirole (who later jointly made critical contributions to risk management), and Paul Joskow have shaped my approach to research, and given me the confidence to pursue an inquiry until I was satisfied.

My colleagues in the risk management practice at McKinsey and Company, in particular Claude Généreux, Arno Gerken, Eric Lamarre, Raoul Oberman, and Hervé Touati, have helped me shape my thinking through numerous discussions and client engagements.

At Alcan, Geoffery Merszei, Dick Evans and Michael Hanley have guided me and encouraged me to be bold as we shaped the risk management function, while Mark Chistolini has been an invaluable thought-partner, sharing his decades of experience. Karim Drira then Benoit Sorel have spent countless hours developing the quanitative financial models supporting our risk management strategy, while Mylène Cochet has typed the first version of this text.

Finally, Geneviève Gauthier, who teaches quantitative finance at HEC Montréal, has sharpened my understanding of the mysteries of stochastic processes and Monte Carlo simulations.

In addition, I have benefitted from the advice of many risk management professionals – too many to mention individually here – who have shared their experience and views with me.

I have also been blessed with two oustanding reviewers: Frannie, my wife, has gone through numerous iterations of this text, and made invaluable suggestions. Corey Copeland read an earlier version and encouraged me to continue this task.

Finally, I would never have completed that undertaking without the support of my family: Frannie, and Oriane-Zénaïde and François-René, our children, who have gracefully accommodated the rigours of a slow writer's schedule.

Thanks to all of you, who have contributed so much to this effort.

1

Introduction

1.1 THE RISK MANAGEMENT PARADOX

Risk management is arguably among the oldest professions on earth. As shown in Peter Bernstein's magisterial essay,[1] mankind has for centuries developed philosophical approaches to comprehend risks arising from uncertain futures, mathematical techniques to measure them, and strategies to manage them, from religious practices to derivatives usage. In parallel, corporations have also developed and applied approaches to manage risks to their future cash flows.

Significant progress has been recently accomplished, at least for corporations. The last decade has seen three significant and mutually reinforcing advances in corporate risk management: first, the theoretical foundations for managing risks have been firmly established.[2] This advance is critical as it reverses the previously held view that "firms should not attempt to manage volatility, since investors can replicate on their own any risk management decision made by the firm".

Second, enhanced computational capabilities and theoretical work by finance scholars enable companies to actually estimate volatility of cash flows and returns.[3] This again is critical: since firms are now able to adequately measure their risk, they can evaluate the impact of different risk management strategies.

Third, a series of significant trading losses (eg, Mettallgesellschaft (1993–1994), Barings (1995), Sumitomo (1996), Long Term Capital Management (1998), Amaranth (2006)) and compliance failures (eg, Enron (2001), WorldCom (2002), Parmalat (2003), Ahold(2003)) have increased the focus of senior executives and Boards of Directors on risk management. This has been – as will be discussed below – a mixed blessing.

Taken together, these three advances constitute an "S-curve" for risk management. As a result, risk management is now established as an important business function. Surveys of senior executives attest to the growing importance of risk management for financial and non-financial firms. Most large corporations have a dedicated risk management organisation and a risk management process. An abundant literature has flourished, from academic articles to practitioners' magazines and handbooks. At least two professional organisations have been created.[4] Specific training programs in risk management are offered. A specific professional qualification, Financial Risk Manager (FRM), similar to the more established Certified Financial Analyst (CFA), has been established.

The usage of risk management products is now widespread. The 1998 Wharton/Canadian Imperial Bank of Commerce survey of Financial Risk Management by US non-financial firms reports that 50% of respondents to the 1998 survey use derivatives, *versus* 35% in 1994. More recently, the International Swap Dealers Association (ISDA) reports that 92% of Fortune 500 companies use some derivatives: 92% for interest rates, 85% for currencies, 25% for commodity prices. Additionally, significant innovation has taken place in the design of risk management products, that now extend well beyond standard forward contracts.[5]

Additionally, all aspects of risk management are progressively converging. In the 1980s, property loss risk was most likely to be managed by the insurance group, interest rates and exchange rates risks by the treasury group, and commodity prices risk by various businesses. Today, many corporations are adopting Enterprise Risk Management (ERM), an integrated approach to managing their risks, breaking old silos.[6]

The risk management paradox is that, despite these monumental advances, the value-creation potential from risk management is still largely untapped.

Two main reasons account for this paradox. First, the focus of most corporate "risk management" programs is in fact *risk measurement and control, not risk management*. As illustrated in Example 1, most programs are defensive: ensuring compliance with rules and regulations (eg, the Sarbanes-Oxley Act for public companies listed the US, the Basel Committee on Banking Supervision international capital framework for financial institutions known as Basel II, see Example 1.1 below), or protecting against possible large trading losses. A joint survey of executives conducted in 2004 by the Conference Board and Mercer Oliver Wyman[7] finds that the top primary drivers for implementing ERM are related to compliance – not value creation: corporate governance requirements (66%), regulatory pressures (53%), and Board requests (51%).

While most risk management programs refer to maximising the value of the corporation as one of their objectives, few explain how it will be achieved in practice.

Example 1.1 *Websites of leading risk management consulting firms attest to the focus on compliance. For example, the Enterprise Risk Services practice of a leading audit firm highlights themes such as capital markets, control assurance, environment and sustainability, internal audit, regulatory consulting, security and privacy services, and does not mention once value creation or enhanced shareholder returns.*

Similarly, the list of recent engagements displayed by a leading risk management consulting firm includes: Economic Capital for a major northern European institution (Basel II compliance), disclosure and Basel II for a German universal bank, group risk for bancassurance for a European bancassurer ("deep A/LM measurement"), risk assessment for North American regional bank, investment portfolio risk for Asian statutory board, and credit model enhancement for a major Asia Pacific-based bank (Basel II compliance). The focus of these engagements is on measurement, often driven by the need to comply with the Basel II regulation, not on value creation.

Obviously, risk control (ie, compliance and loss avoidance) creates significant value for shareholders. Massive value-destroying bankruptcies such as Enron, Worldcom, and Parmalat could have been avoided, or their cost reduced, had higher compliance standards been enforced. Similarly, tighter risk control over trading activities would have prevented trading losses at Barings and Sumitomo. However, risk management creates value over and above compliance and loss avoidance, as will be discussed next.

Second, a gap remains between increasingly clear theoretical/academic predictions and increasingly extensive practitioners activity. Risk management professionals cannot rely on a body of commonly accepted practical tools and frameworks, such as the Net Present Value (NPV) rule for project valuation to develop essential recommendations, such as the selection of a hedging ratio (see Example 1.2). I provide such frameworks in this book.

> **Example 1.2** *The selection of an optimal hedging ratio is a fundamental – and highly practical – risk management question: commodity companies must decide which share – if any – of their production they want to sell forward, global companies must decide how much of their currency exposure to cover, what mix of floating vs. fixed debt they want to hold, etc.*
>
> *The theoretical literature offers limited practical help. A first group of articles determines the hedging ratio as a function of the cost of asymmetric information between insiders/owners and outsiders/financiers.[8] This is a powerful theoretical insight, but exceedingly hard to apply directly. Another group of articles computes the hedging ratio for a given shape of a firm's "utility function" and for a given coefficient of risk aversion.[9] Again, this is difficult to implement.*
>
> *Many risk managers are therefore attempting to establish their firm's "risk appetite", and then use that notion to determine hedging ratios. Most find this process extremely difficult, and resort to imprecise notions such as "balancing risk and rewards".*

1.2 THE VALUE OF RISK MANAGEMENT

The primary message of this book is: *managing risks means maximising value from the volatility inherent in a firm's business environment, and not – as is too often practised – minimising that volatility.* Contrary to most executives' emotional response, risk (or volatility) is not bad per se. In fact, uncertainty often creates opportunities, for those who know how to harness it. Firms can create value from managing risk primarily through three channels, as illustrated in Figure 1.1.

First, risk management enables firms to secure the financial flexibility they require to reach their growth aspirations, at minimum cost, even when faced with adverse business conditions. We will see in Chapter 6 that financial flexibility can increase the value

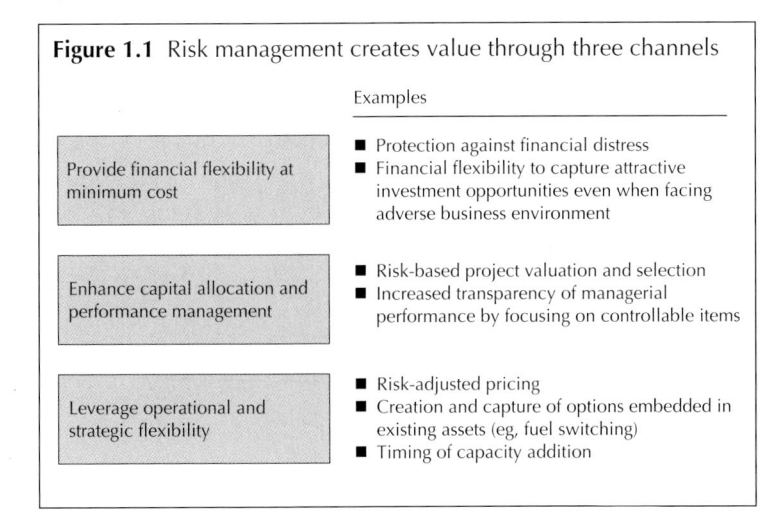

Figure 1.1 Risk management creates value through three channels

	Examples
Provide financial flexibility at minimum cost	■ Protection against financial distress ■ Financial flexibility to capture attractive investment opportunities even when facing adverse business environment
Enhance capital allocation and performance management	■ Risk-based project valuation and selection ■ Increased transparency of managerial performance by focusing on controllable items
Leverage operational and strategic flexibility	■ Risk-adjusted pricing ■ Creation and capture of options embedded in existing assets (eg, fuel switching) ■ Timing of capacity addition

created by a firm by up to 10–20%. The value of financial flexibility is well established in the academic literature,[10] however it has to be fully translated in business practices.

Second, risk management enables firms to make better decisions. By incorporating risk in their projects and business valuation, firms can select and structure better investments. By adjusting performance for risk, firms uncover the true value created by different businesses. Over recent decades financial firms have made significant advances in that direction. This constitutes an untapped source of value for non-financial firms as well.

Finally, risk management enables firms to leverage the operational flexibility (eg, risk-based pricing, multicommodity arbitrage) and strategic flexibility (eg, the right to expand capacity on a site, or the right to produce a sequel to a movie, to be exercised only when market conditions are favourable) embedded in their portfolio of assets and businesses. This notion has been developed in the academic and practitioners' literature,[11] but is still unevenly applied by most firms. The value creation potential is significant: for capital-intensive industries, strategic flexibility can increase asset value by 10–15%.

Since these levers are additive, rigorous, value-focused, implementation of a risk management program could raise the value created by firms by up to 20–35%. Empirical results from recent academic studies[12] find that use of risk management tools is associated with an average 6% increase in firms value created, which is

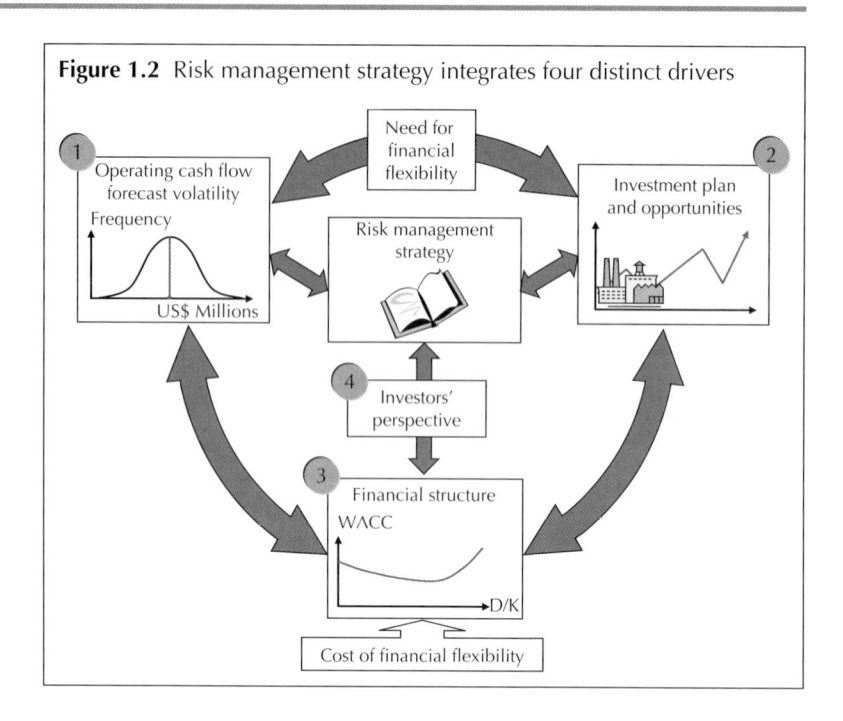

Figure 1.2 Risk management strategy integrates four distinct drivers

- (1) Operating cash flow forecast volatility
- Need for financial flexibility
- (2) Investment plan and opportunities
- Risk management strategy
- (4) Investors' perspective
- (3) Financial structure WACC
- Cost of financial flexibility
- D/K

consistent with a 20–35% increase for best-practice risk managers. For example, BHP-Billiton, a leading natural resources company, attributes part of its spectacular turnaround in recent years to disciplined risk management.[13]

A second – and related – message runs throughout this book: *a firm's risk management strategy is determined by the overall corporate strategy*. Risk management provides a crucial link between assets and strategy on the one hand, and capital structure on the other hand. It can be viewed as the "glue" that holds the two sides of the balance sheet together. As illustrated on Figure 1.2, a firm's risk management strategy is determined by the integration of four drivers: (1) cash flow volatility and (2) investment opportunities jointly determine the need for financial flexibility. Then, (3) the cost of capital environment determines the cost of providing financial flexibility through capital structure. Finally, (4) investors' perspectives inform which risk transfer decisions are possible.

The risk management strategy is dynamic and strategic: it incorporates the *present*: volatility of cash flows given the current business/assets portfolio, current financial structure, but also *the future*: growth aspirations and investment plans. The risk management strategy answers the question: "what mix of equity, risk transfer and portfolio composition is best for our firm to achieve its strategic aspirations?" It stands in contrast with the more static and defensive approach to risk management that answers the question: "what mix of equity, risk transfer and portfolio composition is consistent with our target credit rating?".

For example, a firm that relies on a large research and development (R&D) program to reach its ambitious growth targets will have to adopt a much more conservative risk management strategy (including – but not limited to – lower cash flow volatility) than a firm with lower investment needs/growth target. For this reason, Merck, a pharmaceutical company embarked on an ambitious currency hedging program in the early 1990s. Similarly, high-growth IT companies often have very little debt, and are often aggressive hedgers.

Another example: the link between risk management strategy and growth aspiration explains the apparent paradox that a Special Purpose Vehicle (SPV) that holds only one asset can be more leveraged than the parent company, even for the same volatility level. Surely, the more diversified parent company should be able to support a higher leverage. While that observation is true, it ignores strategic considerations: there is no growth potential in the SPV, hence lower need for flexibility. The SPV can therefore afford a less conservative risk management strategy.

Investors' perspectives can also play a significant role. We will see in Chapters 2 and 6 that most commodities companies (eg, oil, metals and mining, etc) could benefit from lower cash flow volatility, obtained through forward sales of their products. However, that would not satisfy shareholders, who value the optionality of a long commodity position (at least towards the top of the commodity cycle). This leads commodities companies to adopt a costlier risk management strategy involving more equity and less hedging.

1.3 OBJECTIVES AND STRUCTURE OF THIS BOOK
1.3.1 Book's objectives
This book describes how firms can use risk management to maximise their value, by blending conceptual insights with practical applications.

First, it reviews and synthesises the insights from a rich and growing academic literature on risk management. Secondly, it expands several of these insights to make them applicable for practitioners using risk management for value creation. All analyses are cast in terms of Economic Profit or Shareholder Value Added, a metric commonly used by corporations. It then shows how these insights have been applied in practice. All of the processes described have been tested and implemented at Alcan, a leading global aluminium and packaging company, where I have had the privilege of setting up the corporate risk measurement and control group.

This book is written for executives and finance professionals who want a simple yet rigorous introduction to risk management, and its link to value creation. Hopefully, it will contribute to an evolution in the focus of corporate risk management programs towards value creation.

1.3.2 Book's outline

This book is structured in two parts: part one is the *"what"*, that tells the story at a high level, through examples and with few analytics. It is intended as a reference for executives, board members, and finance professionals with an interest in risk management.

Chapter 2 discusses the three avenues through which risk management creates value: providing financial flexibility at minimum cost, enhancing capital allocation and performance management, and leveraging strategic and operational flexibility. It also introduces the four levers that firms can use to achieve their desired financial flexibility level: capital structure, risk transfer, portfolio composition, and operations.

Chapter 3 provides a focused survey of risk management practices. Rather than covering the entire universe of risk management activities, this survey concentrates on three themes: (1) ERM, an integrated approach to manage risk that has gained widespread acceptance in recent years, (2) the various risk metrics used by firms, from Value at Risk (VaR) to Economic Capital and (3) the usage of and value created by corporate hedging programs.

Part two is the *"how"*, that goes into more detail in the implementation of risk management to create value. It is intended as a practical guide for finance professionals tasked with implementing a risk management program.

Chapter 4 focuses on the risk measurement process, and describes a two-step approach to evaluate a company's risk. As a first step, volatility of future cash flows can be estimated outside-in, by drawing statistical inferences from historical cash flows. An inside out analysis constitutes the second step: (1) risks are disaggregated, (2) each risk is evaluated independently, and (3) risks are re-aggregated, taking correlations into account. The second step is complementary to the first one, as it allows a firm to understand the drivers of the volatility estimated in the first step, and to design effective risk management strategies.

Chapter 5 develops a unified risk metric. It is a generalisation of risk capital, a very powerful concept proposed for financial institutions by Robert Merton and André Perold.[14] Risk capital presents two advantages over other measures of risk (eg, Economic Capital used today by most financial institutions): first, it constitutes a metric common to all of risk management activities (financial risk management, insurance, etc), hence is consistent with the recent convergence of risk management practices. Second, it includes the truly worst loss, while other metrics limit the worst loss to a given probability. Chapter 5 then shows how risk capital can be used for risk-adjusted project valuation and performance management.

Chapter 6 presents a simple example where the optimal risk management strategy is determined. The analytical framework builds from leading academic models,[15] and modifies them to make them applicable to a firm's reality. It represents a stylised version of the process that a firm would follow to determine its risk management strategy – and that Alcan followed.

Finally, the concluding Chapter 7 discusses two issues of relevance to Chief Risk Officers (CROs): first, I share my views on what makes a CRO successful, based on my experience (successes and failures), as well as numerous discussions with other CRO. Then I depict a possible path forward for corporate risk management.

1.3.3 Topics not covered by this book

This book does not offer an exhaustive treatment of all important issues pertaining to risk management. I am sure that readers will find many omissions. I have identified three.

First, I do not cover in detail the recent international capital framework for banks issued by the Basel Committee on Banking supervision, known in the industry as Basel II. This text does not meet the needs of CROs of financial institutions interested in a perspective on Basel II implementation, or its advantages and shortcomings.

Since I strive to provide a business-oriented, rigorous yet fairly non-mathematical treatment of risk management, this text does not cover the rich mathematical treatment of risk management and corporate finance. Instead, I provide the interested readers with references that I found most useful.

Finally, I feel risk related to stakeholders, sometimes referred to as Corporate Social Responsibility risk, deserves a fuller treatment. I have found very few solid analyses of this risk, hence have opted not to discuss it in detail. I do believe it is a promising avenue of future research.

1.3.4 Flow of the text

As mentioned earlier, this book is written primarily for practitioners. Therefore, I have strived to keep the main text short and non-technical. Most references are included in the footnotes. I provide many examples, mostly derived from my professional experience.

The more technical material in each chapter is presented in the appendices, to avoid breaking the flow of a first reading. In addition to calculations pertaining to results presented in a specific chapter, these appendices include more general material. This chapter's appendix includes a few elements of probability and statistics. Chapter 2's appendix covers standard corporate finance results, such as the Modigliani–Miller irrelevance theorems, as well as a brief overview of corporate valuation, that constitutes the framework of the risk analysis. These appendices attempt to summarise in one place key results I found helpful as a practitioner. However, they do not replace the more comprehensive texts I have included as reference.

APPENDIX

1.A A FEW WORDS ON PROBABILITIES

I discuss below a few results that I find particularly useful for risk managers, in particular: (1) the expression of the variance of a portfolio, which is probably the single formula I used most as a practitioner, (2) the "square root of time" rule, and (3) correlations, which are often used, and sometimes misunderstood.

Multiple excellent probability and statistics textbooks exist. This appendix follows closely the exposition of Chapter 2 from Alvin Drake's superb introductory text.[16]

1.A.1 Sample space and random variables

We start with a few definitions:

Definition 1.1 Sample space: *the finest-grain, mutually exclusive, collectively exhaustive listing of all possible outcomes of a model of an experiment.*

Our first experiment is the toss of a coin. The sample space is the set {head, tail}: there is no finer grain description of the possible outcomes, it is mutually exclusive (one cannot be head and tail), and collectively exhaustive (all possible outcomes are included).

Our second experiment is the value of the EUR/USD tomorrow. The sample space is the set of all positive numbers: the exchange rate cannot be negative, and it can become very high.[17]

Throughout this appendix, the sample space is denoted Ω.

Definition 1.2 *A random variable is a function which assigns a value to each sample point in the sample space of an experiment.*

As customary, we distinguish between discrete and continuous random variables. Discrete random variables take only experimental values selected from a set of discrete numbers. The toss of a coin is such a variable, as it can take only two values. Continuous random variables may take on experimental values anywhere within continuous ranges. The exchange rate is one such example.

We first present the main results using the notation of discrete random variables, then generalise them to continuous random variables.

1.A.2 Discrete random variables

Probability mass function

Definition 1.3 *For every x_0 in its sample space, the probability mass function (PMF) for discrete random variable x, denoted $p_x(x_0)$, is the probability that the experimental value of random variable x obtained on a performance of the experiment is equal to x_0.*

If our coin is fair, we have:

$$\Pr(head) = \Pr(tail) = 0.5$$

Joint probability mass function

Consider now two discrete random variables, x and y. We extend the previous definition as follows:

Definition 1.4 *For every (x_0, y_0) in the sample space, the joint PMF for discrete random variables x and y, denoted $p_{x,y}(x_0, y_0)$, is the probability that the experimental values of random variables x and y obtained on a performance of the experiment are equal to x_0 and y_0 respectively.*

For example, consider as two random variables the outcome of two successive tosses of a coin. The sample space is:

$$\Omega = \{(head, tail), (head, head), (tail, head), (tail, tail)\}$$

If the coin is fair:

$$\Pr(head, tail) = \Pr(head, head) = \Pr(tail, head) = \Pr(tail, tail) = 0.25$$

We immediately have:

$$\begin{cases} \sum_{x_0} \sum_{y_0} p_{x,y}(x_0, y_0) = 1 \\ \sum_{y_0} p_{x,y}(x_0, y_0) = p_x(x_0) \\ \sum_{x_0} p_{x,y}(x_0, y_0) = p_y(y_0) \end{cases}$$

Conditional probability and independence

Consider again two random variables x and y. One is often interested in the distribution of x for a given value of $y = y_0$.

Definition 1.5 *For every (x_0, y_0) in the sample space, the conditional PMF of $x = x_0$ given $y = y_0$, denoted $p_{x/y}(x_0/y_0)$, is the conditional probability that the experimental value of random variable x is x_0, given that, on the same performance of the experiment, the experimental value of random variable y is y_0.*

We immediately have:

$$p_{x/y}(x_0/y_0) = \frac{p_{x,y}(x_0, y_0)}{p_y(y_0)} \quad \text{and} \quad p_{y/x}(y_0/x_0) = \frac{p_{x,y}(x_0, y_0)}{p_x(x_0)}$$

Denote y the first toss of a coin, and x the second toss of the same coin. If the coin is fair, we have for example:

$$p_{x/y}(x = head / y = tail) = \frac{p_{x,y}(head, tail)}{p_y(tail)} = \frac{0.25}{0.5} = 0.5$$

The definition can be extended to include any conditioning event A:

$$p_{x,y}(x_0, y_0 / A) = \begin{cases} \frac{p_{x,y}(x_0, y_0)}{\Pr(A)} & \text{if } (x_0, y_0) \in A \\ 0 & \text{otherwise} \end{cases}$$

Finally, independence of random variables is a critical notion. Intuitively, random variables are independent if the realisation of one variable does not depend on the realisation of the other. Formally:

Definition 1.6 *Random variables x and y are independent if and only if*

$$p_{y/x}(y_0/x_0) = p_y(y_0)$$

for all possible values of x_0 and y_0.

One can easily verify that two random variables are independent if and only if:

$$p_{x,y}(x_0, y_0) = p_y(y_0) \cdot p_x(x_0)$$

13

Our two tosses of the coin are independent: the outcome of the first does not affect the outcome of the second. This can be true, even if the coin is not fair.

Expectation
Definition 1.7 *Let $g(x)$ be any single-valued function of x. Then, $E[g(x)]$, the expectation, or expected value, of $g(x)$ is defined by:*

$$E[g(x)] = \sum_{x_0} p_x(x_0) \cdot g(x_0)$$

Note that:

$$E[x+y] = \sum_{x_0}\sum_{y_0} p_{x,y}(x_0, y_0) \cdot (x_0 + y_0)$$
$$= \sum_{x_0}\sum_{y_0} p_{x,y}(x_0, y_0) \cdot x_0 + \sum_{x_0}\sum_{y_0} p_{x,y}(x_0, y_0) \cdot y_0$$

Recalling that $\sum_{y_0} p_{x,y}(x_0, y_0) = p_x(x_0)$ and $\sum_{x_0} p_{x,y}(x_0, y_0) = p_y(y_0)$, we have:

$$E[x+y] = \sum_{x_0} p_x(x_0) \cdot x_0 + \sum_{y_0} p_y(y_0) \cdot y_0$$
$$= E[x] + E[y] \qquad (1)$$

The expectation of a sum of random variables is *always* equal to the sum of expectations.

Conditional expectation
For any single-valued function of x $g(x)$ and any subset $A \subset \Omega$, we can define the conditional expectation as:

$$E[x/A] = \sum_{x_0 \in A} p_x(x_0/A) \cdot g(x_0) = \sum_{x_0 \in A} \frac{p_x(x_0)}{\Pr(A)} \cdot g(x_0)$$

If we denote $\bar{A}$ the complement of A in Ω, we have:

$$E[x] = E[x/A] \cdot \Pr(A) + E[x/\bar{A}] \cdot \Pr(\bar{A})$$

This relation is used in Chapter 6.

Variance
Definition 1.8 *The variance of a discrete random variable, denoted var(x) is the expectation of the function $g(x) = (x - E[x])^2$:*

$$var(x) = E[(x - E[x])^2]$$

Specifically:

$$var(x) = \sum_{x_0} p_x(x_0) \cdot (x_0 - E[x])^2$$

Simple algebra shows that:

$$var(x) = E[x^2] - (E[x])^2$$

We often use the standard deviation of a random variable, denoted σ_x:

$$\sigma_x = \sqrt{var(x)} = \sqrt{E[x^2] - (E[x])^2}$$

Covariance and correlation
Definition 1.9 *Let x and y be two random variables. The covariance of x and y denoted cov(x, y) is defined by:*

$$cov(x, y) = E[(x - E[x]) \cdot (y - E[y])] \quad (2)$$

Simple algebra shows that:

$$cov(x, y) = E[x \cdot y] - E[x] \cdot E[y] \quad (3)$$

We immediately observe that the variance of x is the covariance of x with itself:

$$var(x) = cov(x, x)$$

We also observe that, for any random variables $x, y,$ and z, we have:

$$cov(x + y, z) = cov(x, z) + cov(y, z)$$

We often use the correlation between random variables, denoted $\rho_{x,y}$, which is the covariance, normalised for the individual variances:

$$\rho_{x,y} = \frac{cov(x,y)}{\sigma_x \cdot \sigma_y}$$

One can verify that:

$$-1 \leq \rho_{x,y} \leq 1$$

Variance of a sum of random variables

Since the next result is critical for corporate risk managers, we present its complete derivation here. We have:

$$\begin{aligned} var(x+y) &= E[(x+y)^2] - (E[x+y])^2 \\ &= E[x^2 + 2xy + y^2] - \left(E[x] + E[y]\right)^2 \\ &= E[x^2] + 2 \cdot E[x \cdot y] + E[y^2] - E[x]^2 - 2 \cdot E[x] \cdot E[y] - E[y]^2 \\ &= \left(E[x^2] - E[x]^2\right) + \left(E[y^2] - E[y]^2\right) + 2 \cdot \left(E[x \cdot y] - E[x] \cdot E[y]\right) \\ &= var(x) + var(y) + 2cov(x,y) \end{aligned}$$

Introducing standard deviations and correlations:

$$\sigma_{x+y}^2 = \sigma_x^2 + \sigma_y^2 + 2 \cdot \rho_{x,y} \cdot \sigma_x \cdot \sigma_y \qquad (4)$$

Equation (4) is used extensively in risk analysis, as it shows the impact of adding one risk factor to another. One common mistake is simply to add standard deviations. From Equation (4), one sees that:

$$\sigma_{x+y} \leq \sigma_x + \sigma_y$$

The equality occurs only when $\rho_{x,y} = 1$.

Adding one risk factor sometimes reduces the overall risk profile. Consider for example the case where risks are perfectly negatively correlated: $\rho_{x,y} = -1$, then:

$$\sigma_{x+y}^2 = \sigma_x^2 + \sigma_y^2 - 2 \cdot \sigma_x \cdot \sigma_y$$
$$= (\sigma_x - \sigma_y)^2$$
$$< \sigma_x^2$$

1.A.3 Continuous random variables

The probability that a continuous random variable is exactly equal to one value is in general equal to zero. Therefore, one needs to slightly amend the definitions:

Probability density function for a continuous random variable
Definition 1.10 *For any $a \leq b$, the probability density function (PDF) of continuous random variable x is the function $f_x(\cdot)$ such that:*

$$\Pr(a \leq x \leq b) = \int_a^b f_x(x_0) dx_0$$

Cumulative distribution function
Definition 1.11 *For every x_0 in its sample space, the cumulative density function (CDF) for a continuous random variable x, denoted $p_{x \leq (x_0)}$, is the probability that the experimental value of random variable x obtained on a performance of the experiment is smaller or equal to x_0:*

$$p_{x \leq (x_0)} = \Pr(x \leq x_0) = \int_{-\infty}^{x_0} f_x(u) du$$

Joint probability density function
Consider now two continuous random variables, x and y. We extend the previous definition as follows:

Definition 1.12 *For every set A in the sample space, the joint probability density function (PDF) for continuous random variables x and y, denoted $f_{x,y}(x_0, y_0)$, is such that:*

$$P(A) = \Pr((x, y) \in A) = \iint_A f_{x,y}(x_0, y_0) dx_0 dy_0$$

As is the case for discrete random variables, we have:

$$\begin{cases} \iint_\Omega f_{x,y}(x_0, y_0) dx_0 dy_0 = 1 \\ \int_{-\infty}^{+\infty} f_{x,y}(x_0, y_0) dx_0 = f_y(y_0) \\ \int_{-\infty}^{+\infty} f_{x,y}(x_0, y_0) dy_0 = f_x(x_0) \end{cases}$$

Expectation
Definition 1.13 *Let $g(x)$ be any single-valued function of x. Then, $E[g(x)]$, the expectation, or expected value, of $g(x)$ is defined by:*

$$E[g(x)] = \int_{-\infty}^{+\infty} f_x(x_0) \cdot g(x_0) \cdot dx_0$$

We observe that:

$$E[x+y] = E[x] + E[y]$$

With this definition, all previous results apply.

1.A.4 The "square root of time rule"
Consider T random variables, $x_1, \ldots, x_T$, independently and identically distributed with mean μ and standard deviation σ, and denote $X = \sum_{t=1}^{T} x_t$ the sum of these T random variables. After a bit of algebra, Equations (1) and (4) yield:

$$E[X] = T \cdot \mu \quad \text{and} \quad \sigma_X = \sqrt{T} \cdot \sigma$$

The expectation grows with the number of variables, while the standard deviation grows with the square root of the number of variables.

Suppose now that x_t is the logarithmic return on a (portfolio of) asset(s), defined as $x_t = \ln(p_t/p_{t-1})$ where p_t is the value of the asset at date t. Independently and identically distributed returns is consistent with the "efficient markets" hypothesis: all information available at date t is incorporated in the price p_t, and new information arising at date $(t+1)$ is uncorrelated with previous information.

$X_T = \ln(p_T/p_0)$, the logarithmic return over the period $t = 0$ to $t = T$, is then the sum of per period returns:

$$X_T = \ln\left(\frac{p_T}{p_0}\right) = \ln\left(\frac{p_T}{p_{T-1}} \cdot \frac{p_{T-1}}{p_{T-2}} \cdot \ldots \cdot \frac{p_1}{p_0}\right)$$

$$= \sum_{t=1}^{T} \ln\left(\frac{p_t}{p_{t-1}}\right) = \sum_{t=1}^{T} x_t$$

The previous result applies, and in particular *the standard deviation of the return over a period is proportional to the square root of the length of the period*. This is the "square root of time" rule that is extensively used in Chapter 3.

1.A.5 Covariance revisited

Denote x a continuous random variable, and y a discrete random variable:

$$y = \begin{cases} 1 & \text{with probability} \quad \phi \\ 0 & \text{with probability} \quad 1 - \phi \end{cases}$$

We have:

$$E[y] = \phi \cdot 1 + (1 - \phi) \cdot 0 = \phi$$

Then:

$$E[xy] = E[xy \,/\, y = 0] \cdot \Pr(y = 0) + E[xy \,/\, y = 1] \cdot \Pr(y = 1)$$
$$= \phi \cdot E[x \,/\, y = 1]$$
$$= E[x] - (1 - \phi) \cdot E[x \,/\, y = 0]$$

Then, using the definition of covariance given by Equation (3):

$$cov(x, y) = E[x] - (1 - \phi) \cdot E[x/y = 0] - \phi \cdot E[x]$$
$$= (1 - \phi) \cdot (E[x] - E[x/y = 0])$$

This result is used in Chapter 6. We immediately observe that if the random variables are independent ($E[x] = E[x/y = 0]$), their covariance is equal to zero.

1.A.6 The meaning of correlation coefficients

Correlations coefficients are sometimes interpreted erroneously. From Equation (2), we have:

$$\rho_{x,y} = \sum_{x_0} \sum_{y_0} P_{x,y}(x_0, y_0) \cdot \left(\frac{x_0 - E[x]}{\sigma_x} \right) \cdot \left(\frac{y_0 - E[y]}{\sigma_y} \right)$$

For any random variable z, we introduce $\tilde{z}$ normalised random variable:

$$\tilde{z}_0 = \frac{z_0 - E[z]}{\sigma_z}$$

Denote A the set of states of the world such that x_0 and y_0 are on the same side of their average: $\tilde{x}_0 \cdot \tilde{y}_0 \geq 0$, and $\overline{A}$ the other states of the world. We then have:

$$\rho_{x,y} = \sum_{x_0, y_0 \in A} P_{x,y}(x_0, y_0) \cdot |\tilde{x}_0 \cdot \tilde{y}_0| - \sum_{x_0, y_0 \in \overline{A}} P_{x,y}(x_0, y_0) \cdot |\tilde{x}_0 \cdot \tilde{y}_0|$$

The correlation measures the "excess mass" between A and $\overline{A}$. A positive correlation indicates that the first term is larger than the second in the above expression. This arises if x and y are either (1) more often than not on the same side on their average, and/or (2) further away from their average when they are on the same side of their average than when they are on opposite sides.

Consider for example the price of aluminium in *USD/ton* and the exchange rate *USD/CAD* (the value of one *CAD* in *USD*).

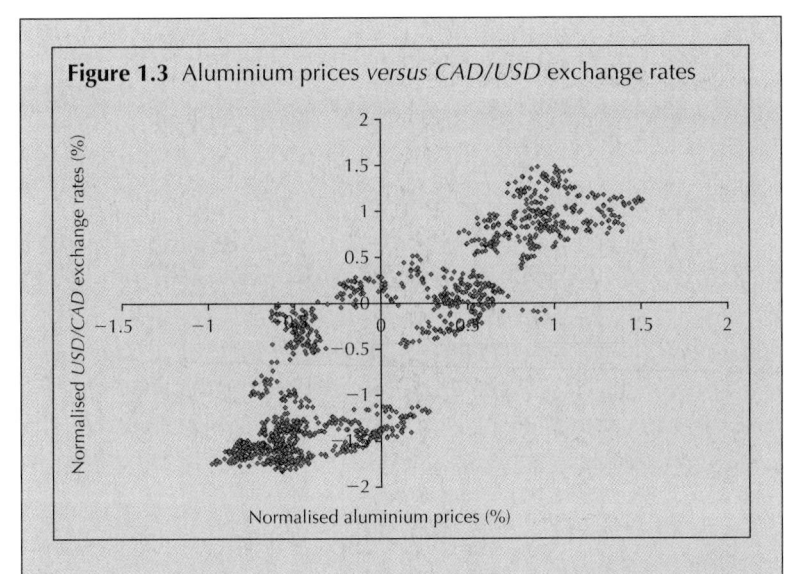

Figure 1.3 Aluminium prices *versus* CAD/USD exchange rates

[Scatter plot: x-axis labeled "Normalised aluminium prices (%)", y-axis labeled "Normalised USD/CAD exchange rates (%)"]

Between January 2001 and May 2005, both prices have been strongly positively correlated: the correlation coefficient between daily prices is $\rho_p = 80\%$. The Canadian dollar (CAD), like the Australian dollar (AUD), are known as commodity currencies: since Canada exports multiple commodities, demand for the Canadian dollar is higher when commodity prices are higher. This is illustrated on Figure 1.3, which plots normalised aluminium prices on the *x-axis* and normalised USD/CAD exchange rates on the *y-axis*. We observe that when the aluminium price is above (below) its average over the period, so is likely to be the CAD.

Price correlation is the economically relevant information for corporate risk analysis. For example, the revenues of an aluminium producer located in Canada are high when the aluminium price is high, while its operating costs (expressed in USD) are high when the USD/CAD exchange rate is high. Therefore, a strong positive price correlation indicates that, when revenues are high, operating costs are also very likely to be high. This creates a natural hedge.

The correlation between returns is much lower. Over the same period, it is only $\rho_r = 12\%$. This is illustrated on Figure 1.4, which plots normalised aluminium price returns on the *x-axis* and normalised USD/CAD exchange rate returns on the *y-axis*.

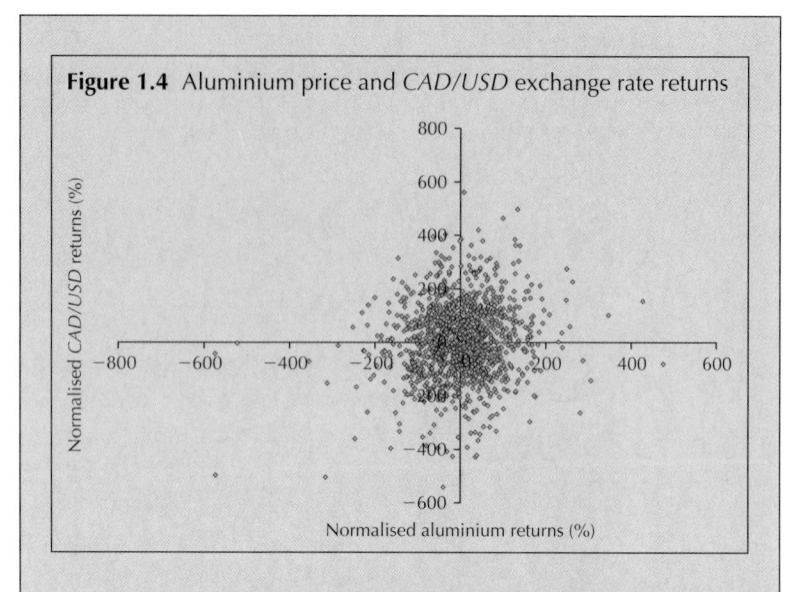

CORPORATE RISK MANAGEMENT FOR VALUE CREATION

Figure 1.4 Aluminium price and *CAD/USD* exchange rate returns

On a day when the aluminium price goes up, the *USD/CAN* is slightly more likely to also go up, but not very much so. While this is the economically relevant information for traders and asset managers, it is much less so for corporate risk managers.[18]

1 Bernstein (1996).
2 Tirole (2006) provides an insightful discussion of the theory of corporate finance, and the role of risk management in value creation.
3 Numerous textbooks exist. For example Hull (2003) provides an overview of many risk models.
4 The Global Association of Risk Professionals (GARP, www.garp.com), founded in 1996, and around 20,000 members strong, and the more recent Professional Risk Managers' International Association (PRMIA, www.prmia.org), founded in 2002.
5 For example Shimpi (2001) provides a description of many such innovative products.
6 See for example Culp (2002) for a description of the convergence process.
7 Gates and Hexter (2005).
8 See for example the seminal article by Bengt Holmström and Jean Tirole (2000).
9 For example Bessembinder and Lemmon (2002), Aid *et al.* (2006), and Baldursson and von der Fehr (2006).
10 See for example the seminal article by Froot *et al.* (1993).
11 See for example Dixit and Pindyck (1994), and Copeland and Antikarov (2003).
12 For example, Allayanis and Weston (2001).
13 See *Wall Street Journal* article, April 2006.
14 Merton and Perold (1993).
15 In particular, Froot *et al.* (1993), Froot and Stein (1998), Holmström and Tirole (2000) and Rochet and Villeneuve (2006).
16 Drake (1967).

17 We ignore here the fact that exchange rates do not have an infinite number of decimals. Mathematically, the sample space is therefore a subset of the positive real numbers.
18 Returns correlations are mathematically relevant for corporate risk managers. Most stochastic models for commodity prices are in fact stochastic models of returns. Therefore, corporate risk managers need to evaluate returns correlations to develop these models.

Finally, price and returns correlations are not independent, rather they are related by (sometimes complex) mathematical relationships.

Part 1

The "What" of Risk Management

2

Value Creation from Risk Management

The academic consensus on how risk management actually creates value is around ten years old, and is the outcome of 50 years of debates amongst academics and practitioners.

As with much modern finance theory, it starts with the famous Modigliani-Miller irrelevance propositions (1958, 1963): in perfect capital markets, risk management and capital structure are irrelevant for firms, as investors can replicate on their own any choice made by the firm. If a firm has too little debt for a particular investors' liking, they can borrow to buy more shares to achieve their target leverage. If an investor does not want a particular exposure, they can hedge it themselves in the futures market. If a particular risk is not directly hedgeable, it can be diversified away in a portfolio of stocks. Therefore, the (expected) value of a firm is solely determined by the (expected) value of the cash flows generated by its assets. The last 50 years have seen a rich debate establishing exceptions to Modigliani-Miller theorems. This is the story told in this chapter.

We first set the stage: Section 2.1 proposes a definition of risk and a classification of types of risks. We then turn to the three value creation channels: financial flexibility (Section 2.2), capital allocation and performance management (Section 2.3) and operational flexibility (Section 2.4). Section 2.5 presents an integrated risk management process and a typology of risk management strategies. Section 2.6 presents concluding remarks.

This chapter includes a sizeable appendix. Appendix 2.A presents heuristic proofs of the Modigliani-Miller irrelevance propositions, and discusses their limitations. Appendix 2.B maps the classification of risks introduced in this chapter to risk typologies introduced by various authors/organisations. Appendix 2.C maps the value channels discussed in this chapter with the classification found in most corporate finance textbooks. Appendix 2.D presents a very brief summary of valuation techniques.

Finally, Appendices 2.G, 2.E, 2.F and 2.H present derivations supporting the examples discussed in the main text.

2.1 THE UNIVERSE OF RISKS
We first start by defining risk.

Definition 2.1 *Risk is the variability in the value of a firm (or a project).*

Risk is simply the acknowledgement that the future – hence the profitability – of an endeavour, is variable. Contrary to most managers' emotional response, risk is not negative per se. For example, the risk that the oil price goes up to US$100/bbl is positive for oil companies. What is negative, however, is accepting misunderstood risks or mispricing risks.

Every risk management text proposes a typology of risks. This one is no exception. We propose four broad categories of risk: price risk, counterparty risk, operations risk, and business risk. This typology is consistent with other classifications introduced in particular for financial institutions (reviewed in Appendix 2.B), and modified to better meet the needs of non-financial firms.

Price risk is the variability in cash flows created by variability in prices, including exchange rates, interest rates, and commodity prices. In most instances, price risk is "linear": it is the exposure to a price times the variability in that price.[1] Price risk is sometimes called "market" risk or "financial" risk.

Counterparty risk is the variability in cash flows created by the variability in counterparties' performance against their obligation to the company. It includes receivables risk, but also supplier default risk. The latter does not give rise to a receivable on the firm's balance sheet, hence is sometimes overlooked in credit risk policies. However, it can create more volatility than receivables.

For this reason, I prefer the term "counterparty" risk "to credit" risk.

Operations risk is the variability in cash flows created by failure in the firm's operations and processes. This risk is often split between two subcomponents: (1) plant risk, the failure of a piece of equipment such as a power plant turbine, and (2) process risk, the failure of a process (eg, deal confirmation or account payable).

Business risk is the variability in cash flows created by variability of margins and production volumes. This can be further subdivided in a variety of categories. It is helpful to distinguish between (1) short-term risk, mostly created by competitive pressures in the current industry structure, and (2) long-term strategic risk, created by shifts in industry structure (eg, transformational technology, regulatory change, etc).

Corporate Social Responsibility (CSR) risk is an important component of business risk. For example, a firm that suffers a negative reputation shock is likely to see demand for its products decline, or may have difficulties attracting and/or retaining talented employees, thereby reducing its future profitability. Similarly, poor CSR practices may contribute to strikes that reduce production.

Of course, some events may straddle multiple categories. If a supplier fails to deliver a commodity, the firm has then to replace it on the open market: the counterparty risk leads to a price risk. Similarly, if a plant produces a faulty product that harms customers, these are likely to bring a lawsuit against the manufacturer: the operations risk leads to a litigation risk.

Having set the stage, we now examine each value creation channel in turn.

2.2 PROVIDING FINANCIAL FLEXIBILITY AT MINIMUM COST

We first describe in general terms how financial flexibility adds to firms' value. We then discuss how financial flexibility can be modelled. Finally, we review the various levers firms can use to achieve their desired level of financial flexibility.

2.2.1 Understanding financial flexibility

Financial flexibility is the firm's ability to finance its operations or investments even when facing adverse cash flow shocks. Financial flexibility is critical to firms' achieving their value creation objectives.

A firm may have to pass on value-creating opportunities (on a stand-alone basis), because it does not have the financial flexibility to pursue them (an issue known as the under-investment problem). A firm may have to dispose of value-creating assets to restore its financial health. At the extreme, a value-creating firm may have to file for bankruptcy due to a liquidity shortage. While each of these situations is obviously different, they are in fact the different sides of the same coin: the firm is financially constrained.

If financial markets had perfect knowledge of a firm's operations, firms would have unlimited financial flexibility: as long as its projects/businesses are value-creating, investors would be willing to fund them. However, substantial empirical evidence documents these imperfections, and recent theoretical models provide some fundamental justification, which are reviewed below.

Empirical evidence

Examples of firms that had to sell value-creating businesses (sometimes the entire firm) to manage liquidity constraints are numerous. A few recent examples include:

❑ Following the crisis that engulfed the US power industry in 2001, US independent power producers in 2002–2003 had to sell power generation assets below, what they viewed as, their fair value, to raise cash required to meet debt obligations.
❑ In 1994, Metallgesellschaft had to liquidate its oil derivatives portfolio, for the liquidity requirements were too high. While no consensus has emerged, it has been argued that the derivatives portfolio was in fact value-creating, and that Metallgesellschaft sold it below its value solely to manage a liquidity constraint, thereby destroying value for its shareholders.[2]

Empirical evidence of the under-investment problem is also strong:

❑ An academic study of 1,300 non-financial firms[3] confirms that investments are dramatically curtailed when internal funds are falling short: firms in the top quartile in cashflow volatility in their industry are 19% below the mean level of capital expenditure for their industry, while firms in the bottom quartile of their industry in terms of cash flow volatility are 11% above the mean.

❑ Another study reports that for every US$1 reduction in capital, firms reduce their investment budget by approximately 35%.[4]
❑ I have personally observed situations where value-creating acquisitions were not pursued, for they would weaken the financial situation of the firm.

Theoretical justification
Recent advances in finance theory provide an intellectual foundation for the value of financial flexibility. Misaligned incentives between equity holders (owners), bond/debt holders (creditors), and managers, combined with information asymmetries between managers (insiders) and equity and debt holders (outsiders) constitute the micro foundation for the value of financial flexibility.

The logic is as follows: capital providers realise that insiders need incentives to perform, hence, they are not willing to finance value-creating projects if the financial structure does not provide for these incentives. At the limit, as in the stylised model described by Jean Tirole[5], misaligned incentives and asymmetry of information lead to credit rationing: lenders simply refuse to lend, no matter what rate is offered by the owner/manager. The availability of internal funds reduces the need for external financing, hence increases the likelihood that value-creating investments will be financed.

2.2.2 Modelling financial flexibility
Once we have established the empirical and theoretical foundations for the value of financial flexibility, the remaining task is to build a financial model to determine the desired level of financial flexibility, ie, the risk management strategy. This is described in Chapter 6. In this section, we discuss the main features of the model: we first provide an overview of the structure of the model, then discuss its three key ingredients.

Model overview
The first ingredient of the risk management model is the fact that the timing and magnitude of investment opportunities facing firms are unknown, ie, that investment opportunities can be viewed as random variables.

The second ingredient of the risk management model is the fact that the cost of capital is U-shaped with respect to the debt to assets ratio (finance professors talk about the "convexity" of the cost of capital, which we will use in the remainder of the text, as it is shorter than "U-shaped-ness"). As a firm's leverage increases its cost of capital first decrease, then increases.

The final ingredient of the model is known as the "pecking order hypothesis": firms finance themselves by using internal funds first, then by issuing debt, then only as a last resort by issuing equity.

With these ingredients, the logic is then as follows: if a firm is hit by (possibly successive) cash flow shocks, it issues debt to cover its cash shortfall (pecking order hypothesis), which at some point increases its cost of capital (U-shaped cost of capital). As the leverage increases, the firm becomes more financially fragile: continued cash flow shocks become more and more costly, and at the limit could push the firm into bankruptcy. At this point, the firm will have to pass investment opportunities, even if they are profitable on a stand alone basis (this is Example 2.1 below). Furthermore, it may have to sell profitable assets to raise cash, repay debt, and "rebuild its balance sheet" (this is Example 2.2 below).

What can the firm do to avoid entering that spiral? Adding equity to the capital structure is the simplest approach to increase financial flexibility. However, since debt is tax-advantaged, it is also costly. Firms can then reduce the volatility of cash flows, possibly purchasing costly risk transfer instruments. These are the costs of financial flexibility. The optimal risk management strategy is such that the incremental cost and incremental benefits of financial flexibility are precisely equal.

Random investment opportunities
Of course, every large firm follows a capital budgeting process, where investment opportunities and capital needs are listed, and where an investment plan and the adjacent capital plan are developed. These are the anticipated investment opportunities.

In parallel, firms face unanticipated investment opportunities. For example, a firm is unlikely to perfectly anticipate if/when an "adjacent" firm becomes weak, and a potential take-over target.

Figure 2.1 U-shaped cost of capital

- Taxes
- Cost of financial distress
- Information asymmetry

Potential 30 bbps WACC reduction for same credit rating

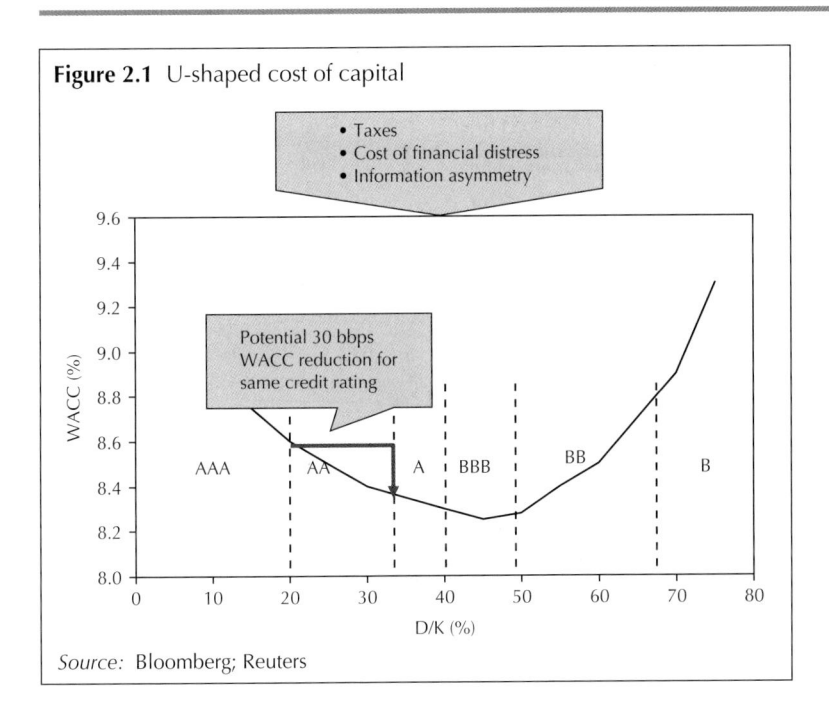

AAA · AA · A · BBB · BB · B

WACC (%) vs D/K (%)

Source: Bloomberg; Reuters

Similarly, a power development company cannot anticipate which among the projects it develops will secure the required approvals and come to fruition in a short period of time, hence requiring significant capital deployment. Similarly, oil companies can estimate the breakeven oil price that justifies investing in its various fields or technologies (eg, oil sands in Canada were vastly out-of-the-money at US$20/bbl are now fully in-the-money). However, since oil prices are random, investment opportunities are also random.

U-shaped cost of capital
The cost of capital is U-shaped with respect to the leverage ratio. Start with all-equity financing, on the left of Figure 2.1. Increasing the leverage has two effects: (1) it substitutes debt for equity, and (2) it increases the tax shield, as interest payments are tax-deductible in most jurisdictions. The first effect has no impact on the cost of capital: the cost of equity increases with the leverage, precisely to offset the higher share of debt. An increase in the tax shield is value-creating, as long as the tax shield is lower than the tax liability.[6]

33

However, at a certain point, as leverage increases and financial ratios (eg, interest coverage) weaken, the probability of bankruptcy increases, and cost of debt and the opportunity cost of equity, hence the average cost of capital, start to increase. Furthermore, falling below a certain credit rating creates additional costs, for example, the inability to access the market for very short-term lending (Commercial Paper in North America, and Billets de Trésorerie in France, both cheap and highly liquid sources of short-term financing), or the need to collateralise all lending.[7]

The shape of the U varies by company, and also across time. Corporations with a long track record of financial discipline may benefit from goodwill from credit rating agencies, and will benefit from a higher credit rating than other firms, even though their financial metrics are weaker (in other words, they will face a flatter U). At the time of this writing in 2007, capital is abundant, and the U is relatively flat.

"Pecking order" theory of financing
The "pecking order" theory is the final critical ingredient to the value of financial flexibility.[8] As was observed by Donaldson in 1961, firms prefer to finance investments with internal funds rather than external funds. Among external funds, firms tend to issue the safest security first: straight debt, then convertible bonds, then equity as a last resort.

If firms were indifferent to their source of financing in the presence of U-shaped cost of capital, they would select the cost-of-capital-minimising leverage, and issue debt and equity in the appropriate proportions to meet their financing needs, or retire debt and repurchase equity in the appropriate proportions to use their excess cash. For example, if a firm needs US$2 billion and the cost-minimising leverage is 50%, it would simply issue US$1 billion debt and US$1 billion equity. The pecking order theory suggests this is not the case. It may seem counter-intuitive at first: one of the advantages of being publicly traded is that firms can issue stocks. However, it is consistent with empirical evidence as well as predictions from theoretical models, as we discuss below.

A well-established empirical fact is that internal funds (ie, retained earnings) constitute the primary source funding for firms: one academic study[9] reports it accounted for around 67% of financing for US firms during the period 1970–1985. Similarly, another academic study[10] report that the fraction of gross fixed-capital formation raised via equity (including initial and seasoned equity offerings) in 1999 was only 12% in the US, 9% in the United Kingdom and France, 8% in Japan and 6% in Germany.

Multiple reasons jointly account for the "pecking order" theory.

As can be seen from Figure 2.1, debt is cheaper than equity on the left of the cost-minimising leverage, when the incremental tax shield more than offsets the increase in cost of equity. Issuing debt (ie, moving to the right on Figure 2.1) is therefore preferred to issuing equity (ie, moving to the left).

That is no longer true to the right of the of the cost-minimising leverage, where issuing debt in fact increases the cost of capital more than would issuing equity. Four main reasons explain the "pecking order" on the right of the minimum.

First, issuing seasoned equity generates substantial transaction costs, estimated on average at 7.1% of the proceeds in one recent academic study,[11] while issuing debt is usually much cheaper.

Second, since managers are reluctant to issue equity when they believe it is undervalued, equity issuance sends a signal to investors that managers believe the stock is overvalued, hence, should be accompanied by a share price fall. This is confirmed empirically: academic studies[12] find that seasoned equity offerings usually yield a permanent fall in the stock price of about 3%. Additionally, there is substantial empirical evidence that firms issue shares at high prices and repurchase them at low prices. In other words, firms are good at timing the market for their own shares.

Third, issuing equity to face adverse cash flow shock often reduces the value of existing equity, hence is met with reluctance by existing stockholders. First, it mechanically dilutes existing stockholders. Second, it makes debt safer, hence transfers wealth from stockholders to debt holders (by improving their risk-return profile). This transfer is more important the closer the firm is to financial distress. This effect also contributes to the fall in stock price upon new equity issuance.

Finally, equity issuance increases the scrutiny over managers, and more generally over the firm's operations and plans. This is particularly true if the firm is "weak": new equity investors may demand costly concessions from the existing shareholders and managers (sit on the board, broad restructuring initiatives, change in plans, etc).

As Donaldson observed,[13] one perverse implication the pecking order theory is:

> "the reluctance of firms to issue equity appears to be greatest when firms need equity capital the most"

The examples below use a strong version of pecking order, which is that firms never issue equity.

2.2.3 Examples of the value of financial flexibility

As discussed, a firm that suffers from insufficient financial flexibility may miss profitable investment opportunities, as in Example 2.1 below.

Example 2.1 *A pharmaceutical company has US$8 billion invested in its core business, returning 11%. Its current cost of capital is 10%. The firm contemplates a US$2 billion investment in a growth business, which generates a 13% return. However, financing the investment has an 80% chance of raising the cost of capital to 12%. Should the firm undertake this profitable investment?*

If the firm does not invest, the value created by its core business is US$800 million (all calculations are presented in Appendix 2.E). If it invests, the expected value created falls to −US$120 million: when the cost of capital is raised to 12% – which occurs 80% of the time post-investment – the (large) core business is value destroying, hence the expected value post-investment is negative. Since the purchase destroys value on average, the firm does not invest in the growth business, even though it is highly profitable on a stand alone basis. The pharmaceutical company is financially constrained.

Suppose now a volatility reduction technology reduces the risk of increasing the cost of capital post-investment to 20%. The expected value created post-investment grows to US$1,020 million: the large core business is value destroying much less often (on average, it is value-creating), hence the expected value post-investment is positive. The risk management technology relaxes the financial constraint and enables the firm to capture the investment opportunity.

The value of volatility reduction is therefore the difference between the expected value created with the volatility reduction technology (and the investment) and without the volatility reduction technology (and no investment): $\Delta VC = US\$1{,}020m - US\$800m = US\$220m$.

Similarly, a firm close to financial distress will consider selling assets, leading it to part with value-creating assets, as in Example 2.2 below.

Example 2.2 *A diversified oil company has US$10 billion invested in two businesses: US$8 billion in a downstream business generating 11% return on capital, and US$2 billion in an upstream business returning 14%. Its cost of capital is currently 10%. The firm faces significant cash flow risks, which imply that there is an 80% chance of the cost of capital increasing to 12%. The firm has an opportunity to sell its upstream business. Doing so would allow the firm to partially repay its debt, hence reduce the probability of an increase in its cost of capital to 20%. Paying down debt would raise the cost of capital to 10.5%. Should the firm sell the business, even though it is highly profitable?*

In the no-sale case, the expected values are US$7,625 million for the downstream business US$2,425 for the upstream business, and US$10,050 million for the entire firm (all calculations are presented in Appendix 2.F). The firm creates almost no value, given the high probability of a cost of capital increase, which would lead to value destruction on its large downstream business.

On the other hand, the sale reduces the probability of value destruction in the downstream business, and raises the expected value of this business to US$8,170 million. If a buyer offers more than US$1,880 million, the value to the owners will be higher when selling than when keeping the downstream business (US$8,170 million + US$1,880 million ≥ US$10,050 million). Since the minimum value is lower than the book value – and the enterprise value – of the upstream business, a buyer is likely to offer an adequate price. The firm will therefore sell the business, even though it is highly profitable on a stand alone basis. The firm is financially constrained.

Suppose now the firm has access to a volatility reduction technology that reduces the probability of increasing the cost of capital to 20%. The upstream business is now worth US$2,710 million, the downstream business US$8,500 million, and the entire firm US$11,210 million. Selling the downstream business would lead to an expected value for the downstream business of US$8,170 million, hence the minimum sale

> price is equal to US$3,040 million (US$11,210 million − US$8,170 million). While a buyer may offer to pay 10% above the enterprise value for the downstream business, it is not certain.
>
> We can estimate the value of the volatility reduction technology. Suppose that, without volatility reduction, a buyer offers only the "indifference" price for the downstream business, and that with the volatility reduction no buyer offers a price above the "indifference" price. This constitutes a very unfavourable set of assumptions, hence produces an upper bound for the value of the volatility reduction technology.
>
> Without the volatility reduction technology, the firm sells the downstream business, and creates US$170 million in value for its shareholders (US$8,170 million enterprise value minus US$8,000 million invested capital). With the volatility reduction technology, the firm keeps the downstream business, and the value created grows to US$1,210 (US$11,210 million enterprise value minus US$10,000 million invested capital). The volatility reduction technology creates US$1,040 million (US$1,210 million − US$170 million). A share of the value comes from the reduction in the cost of capital, but the bulk comes from holding on the very profitable upstream business.

Example 2.2 tells a variation on a well-established story: "reducing cash flow volatility reduces the expected cost of financial distress". In this case, the firm does not suffer the direct cost of financial distress, as it does not go into bankruptcy. However, it does face a higher cost of capital, which is a precursor to financial distress. Example 2.1 tells a more recent story, relevant for many more firms than the first one: "reducing cash flow volatility increases the flexibility to capture attractive opportunities".

Both examples show that the value of risk management does not come from volatility reduction alone. For this reason, firms that attempt to determine their risk appetite in abstraction of their growth aspirations cannot find a satisfactory answer.

The value at stake can be significant: the simple model developed in Chapter 6 shows that an effective risk management strategy can increase expected value created by a firm by up to 20%.

2.2.4 Four financial flexibility levers

Once the strategy has been defined, firms pursue two avenues to reach their desired financial flexibility: (1) adopt a "conservative" capital structure, and (2) reduce cash flow volatility. Three levers are available for the second objective: portfolio selection, risk transfer, and operations management.[14]

Capital structure is probably the most commonly used financial flexibility lever. Equity protects from the downside, and increases the ability to borrow, should the need arise. For example, oil companies' executives used to structure their balance sheet to sustain US$10 per barrel for 2–3 years in a row. Many industrial companies maintain a conservative financial structure as one of their key levers to achieve their corporate goals.

However, as discussed before, equity is costly. A conservative financial structure could rapidly become a lazy one. For this reason, firms also reduce volatility of their cash flows.

When feasible, volatility reduction provides two benefits: first, it increases the financial flexibility by reducing the probability of adverse shocks to operating cash flow, at lower cost for the firm than equity. As Justin Pettit, a very experienced corporate finance expert, once put it:

> "Hedging is tax-advantaged equity".

Everything else being equal, lower cash flow volatility is also associated with lower cost of borrowing. One study[15] reports that higher credit rating is associated with lower volatility of cash flow from operations, Net Income, and EBITDA. For example, volatility of cash flow from operations is less than 10% for double A-rated companies, and around 25% for double B-rated companies. The same study reports that, in a linear regression of credit ratings against multiple variables, volatility of Funds from Operation/Sales is found to have a negative and statistically significant impact on credit rating.

Another academic study of 1,300 non-financial firms[16] reaches similar conclusions:

> Cash flow volatility is positively related to a firm's cost of accessing external capital. Specifically, higher cash flow volatility is associated with worse S&P bond ratings, higher yield-to-maturity.

Firms can use three levers to reduce cash flow volatility.

Portfolio composition allows the firm to manage its cash flow volatility over the medium- to long-term. First, business portfolio diversification increases financial flexibility. A critical driver of the debt credit rating of a company is its size:[17] a larger company will have more opportunities to diversify its risk. Some credit rating agencies go one step further, that explicitly take into account the number of different businesses and regions a firm is involved in when setting ratings.

Second, a firm can systematically structure its portfolio of businesses to create "natural hedges". An electric power producer selling its output in an open wholesale market is exposed to fluctuations in wholesale power prices. By acquiring an electric power retail company, or by signing long-term contracts, the electric power producer significantly reduces its cash flow volatility (provided it manages the credit risk appropriately). Similarly, Airbus, an European-based aircraft manufacturer, sells airplanes (determined) in USD, while most of its costs are (determined) in EUR, creating significant cash flow volatility (and at current exchange rates, a competitive disadvantage). Relocating production facilities to USD-regions to increase the share of USD-determined costs, structurally reduces cash flow volatility.

Risk transfer is more a short- to medium-term volatility management tool.[18] Risk can be transferred through three channels: (1) insurance, (2) derivatives, and (3) contractual agreements with suppliers, consumers, and more generally partners. Insurance and derivatives are now well-known risk transfer instruments. Contractual agreements can also provide significant risk mitigation benefits. For example aluminium companies sometimes purchase electric power at a price indexed to the aluminium price quoted in USD. This provides them with a very good hedge against the fluctuations in aluminium price, and transfers the risk to the electric power supplier. Since electric power companies purchase equipment made in part of aluminium, this mechanism offers them a (limited) hedge as well.

Currency choice can reduce risks, sometimes creating a win-win for both parties. For example, if two large multinational companies with the same functional currency (eg, USD) contract for delivery of goods and services in a third country, they may find it preferable to contract in their functional currency rather than in the local currency.[19]

Operations management is also a critical volatility-reduction tool, that can have impact in the short-, medium- and long-term. For example, a financial firm can develop procedures to reduce the impact of operational risk. A manufacturing firm can increase its maintenance budget to reduce the impact of plant failure. A contrarian example comes from British Petroleum, that appears to have reduced its maintenance budget over the last ten years, which has contributed to the explosion at a Texas refinery in March 2005.[20] All firms can implement environment, health, and safety programs aimed at improving the working conditions of employees, hence reducing the impact of injuries, absenteeism, etc.

2.3 ENHANCING CAPITAL ALLOCATION AND PERFORMANCE MANAGEMENT

2.3.1 Context

The underlying logic is straightforward: by correctly accounting for the risks of assets and businesses (new and existing), firms allocate their capital to the opportunities that offer the highest ex ante risk-adjusted returns, hence increase their *ex post* observed return. The challenges to effective risk adjustment lie in implementing the logic.

The first challenge is practical: identify and quantify risks in a project or venture. Fortunately, as mentioned in Chapter 1, increased computing power and financial modelling advances make it easier to perform this task. Various approaches available to firms are reviewed in Chapter 4.

The second challenge is more conceptual: what is the appropriate financial framework for risk adjustment? Corporate finance theory recommends taking the risks into account through the cost of capital used to discount future cash flows generated by the assets. Furthermore, it separates risks into two categories: (1) firm-specific, and (2) non-diversifiable, ie, correlated to the market, and argues that, since investors can diversify or "neutralise" firm-specific risks in a portfolio of stocks, they are willing to pay only for non-diversifiable risk. This forms the basis of the Capital Asset Pricing model (CAPM). Therefore, as the non-diversifiable risk of a project or asset increases, its cost of capital increases, and its value (the discounted sum of its cash flows) decreases.

While this approach is sound, practitioners face three issues when implementing it. First, the risk taken may vastly exceed the "physical" capital invested. Consider for example a financial institution building a trading portfolio that requires about US$5 million of physical capital, but where potential losses could exceed hundreds of millions of dollars. Obviously, requiring a 10% or even a 20% return on the US$5 million invested – the direct application of finance theory – does not adequately remunerate the risk taken. While this concern has arisen historically in financial institutions, similar situations can now be found in non-financial institutions (eg, potential liabilities associated with new product developments and launching could vastly exceed the "physical" cost of product development).

Practitioners are concerned with the full risk, not only the non-diversifiable risk. Consider for example a financial institution deciding to allocate its capital among two trading strategies: Strategy A (eg, building a portfolio of weather derivatives) has significant upside and downside potential, and is perfectly uncorrelated with the market, while Strategy B (eg, building a portfolio of stocks) has a much lower downside potential, and is strongly correlated with the market. No matter how large the worst-loss from strategy A, the CAPM prices that risk lower than that of strategy B. Therefore, if both strategies have the same expected profitability, the financial institution will allocate more capital to strategy A. This of course is counter-intuitive, and does not feel right to bank managers.

The logic underlying the CAPM is that managers are "transparent" and value projects as if they were diversified shareholders. As discussed in Section 2.2, this is not always true in practice, hence managers care about the full losses.

To address these two issues, financial institutions have developed over the last ten years an entirely different approach to risk-adjustment relying primarily on VaR, that measures the worst possible loss of a business, under normal market conditions, at a given confidence level, over a given horizon. Using VaR as measure of risk created by a business, financial institutions have developed various Risk-Adjusted Profitability Metrics such as RARoC (Risk-Adjusted Return on Capital) and RoRAC (Return on Risk-Adjusted Capital).[21] The risk management profession is therefore facing the paradox that the most advanced risk management professionals (ie, the financial institutions) are developing risk-adjustment approaches that differ significantly from the standard corporate finance approach.

The third issue in implementing the standard corporate finance approach lies with estimating the appropriate cost of capital. Consider now an upstream oil company evaluating the acquisition of a network of gas stations. Which cost of capital should it use?

First, it should not use its own average cost of capital, as it reflects only exploration and production risk. It will probably then use comparables, ie, the cost of capital a "pure play" gas station operator. However, the risks vary greatly from one business to the next, as the stability of the regulatory environment, competition intensity, and political climate vary. Perfect comparables do not always exist, and the company will have to make imperfect adjustments.

We propose in this book an alternative approach to risk adjustment, that solves these three issues, while being consistent with standard finance theory. This approach builds on risk capital, initially introduced in Robert Merton and André Perold[22]: the smallest amount of capital that could notionally be invested in an insurance contract to make the investment in the project risk-free. By construction, risk capital includes the full possible loss, hence resolving the second issue discussed above. Risk adjustment then proceeds as follows.

If the risk capital is lower than the investment capital, which is the case for most non-financial projects/businesses, Chapter 5 shows how to incorporate risk capital in estimating the cost of capital, by combining the Capital Asset Pricing Model and the Black-Scholes-Merton option pricing model. This resolves the third issue discussed above. We can then use the Discounted Cash Flow (DCF) technique to value projects/investments.

If risk capital is higher than the investment capital, which is the first issue discussed above, we then subtract the risk capital to the project/investment profit, to estimate the true profitability. This approach is particularly well-suited for trading activities: we show in Chapter 5 that the risk-adjusted value is simply the trading margin less the risk capital. Adopting this approach reduces the misalignment of incentives between traders and capital providers discussed in Section 2.3.3.

2.3.2 Capital allocation

Risk adjustment

As discussed above, a thorough risk assessment (following the procedure described in Chapter 5) allows the firm to determine the appropriate cost of capital, hence the value of the project.

This choice is illustrated in Figure 2.2. The vertical axis represents the returns (eg, expected value created per unit of invested capital), and the horizontal axis represents the risks (eg, risk capital

Figure 2.2 Risk-based capital allocation

Project A is preferred, even if project B generates higher expected return

X-axis: Risk (%) eg, risk capital/invested capital
Y-axis: Return (%) eg, E(VC)/invested capital

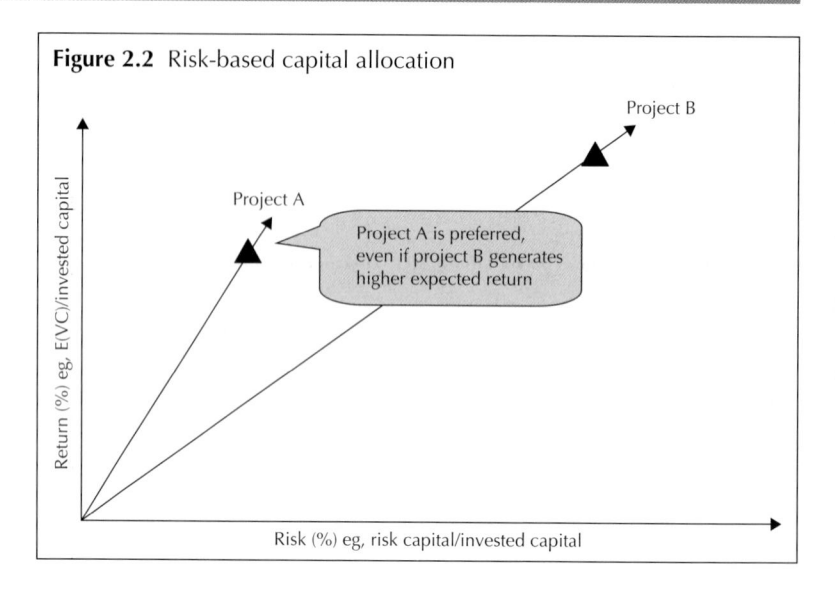

per unit of invested capital). Two projects are evaluated. B has higher returns and higher risk than A. The slope of the line between the origin and a project measures the percentage increase in return for 1% increase in risk. It is a crude but graphical approach to risk adjustment. On a risk-adjusted basis, the capital constrained firm will then select project A, despite higher expected returns from project B.

For example, Business B could be the "investment bank" arm of a universal bank that is likely to generate higher absolute returns on invested capital than the "commercial bank" (Business A). However, on a risk-adjusted basis, the commercial bank may offer a higher return than the investment bank.

This applies to non-financial firms as well. In the late 1990s, many US electric power utilities have invested in domestic unregulated power generation (Business B), lured by the prospect of unregulated – hence uncapped – returns. Since then, many have found that these returns have not materialised, and that, on a risk-adjusted basis, the regulated – but safe – returns of the traditional utility business (Business A) were preferable for shareholders. Electric power companies that used to advertise their share of earnings coming from unregulated business have now come full circle, and reassure investors that their earnings are safely regulated!

Similarly, US and European utilities have invested in regulated electricity assets in privatising developing countries (Business B), where expected returns were higher than in their domestic market (Business A). In many instances, country risk has taken its toll, and these utilities are focusing their capital on their domestic market again. While hindsight is always perfect, a more rigorous ex ante risk-return analysis would have led to higher *ex post* returns on the capital then deployed.

Once the ranking of projects/ventures has been established, if the firm faces no capital constraint, it will accept all those with positive risk-adjusted value. If the firm – more realistically – faces capital constraints, it will select the projects/ventures with highest risk-adjusted value. In both cases, risk-adjustment will yield to better capital allocation.

Risk-adjusted profit determination

Risk-adjustment may impact the valuation in another way, as the risk-adjusted cash flows may turn out to be different than expected, as shown in Example 2.3 below.

> **Example 2.3** *Consider a technology company weighting the introduction of a new device, for example an MP3 player. The first risk is sales volume. Specifically, suppose the company believes there is 50% chance it will sell 5 million units, and a 50% chance it will sell 15 million units. On average, the company expects to sell 10 million units. The second risk is profitability. Markets studies show that there is a 50% chance it can achieve a US$15/unit profitability, and a 50% chance it can achieve only US$5/unit profitability, leading to a US$10/unit expected profitability. The analysts therefore conclude the expected profit is US$100 million.*
>
> *That number turns out to be wrong if profitability and margins are correlated. That would be the case if entry by a competitor was driving both sales and volume. For example, if the sales volume and margins are perfectly negatively correlated (ie, the profitability is US$5/unit when the competitors enter), the expected profitability in only US$75 million (derivations are presented in Appendix 2.G). Incorporating the volatility appropriately results in a 25% difference in expected profitability!*

2.3.3 Performance management

Risk management enhances performance management in two ways: first, firms can explicitly adjust the observed (or expected) performance for the risks taken to achieve that performance. Second, firms can (*ex post*) filter out some of the noise in a team's performance. We discuss both effects in turn.

Risk-adjusted performance

Traders' compensation provides a classical case where risk-adjusted performance management makes all the difference. Risk taken by traders is "invisible" ex ante and even sometimes *ex post*, if the gamble has been successful. In his classic essay "Fooled by Randomness", Nassim Taleb[23] tells the tale of John, the high yield bond trader, who had a very successful seven-year run on Wall Street trading high yield corporate bonds. However, this run ended

> "during the summer of 1998, with the meltdown of high-yield bond values ... John had earned for the employers, New York investment banks, around US$250 million in the course of the seven years. He lost more than US$600 million for his last employer in barely a few days."

Of course, as long as the market was going his way, John was highly regarded by his employer, constantly promoted, and very generously rewarded (his net worth went to US$16 million). The employer was simply not aware of the magnitude of the risks taken.

This is the classical example of misaligned incentives between the principal (the bank) and her agent (the trader): traders have a tendency to pursue high risk/high return strategies, to maximise their highest possible compensation, since their downside is limited to loss of employment (in fact, even after a bad episode, they can still find employment at another trading firm). On the other hand, the downside is (almost) unlimited for the capital providers of the trading company.

By explicitly incorporating risks taken in the measure of performance, the capital providers can better align the traders' incentives with their own, hence push them towards higher risk-adjusted returns strategies. The adjustment takes place ex ante at the capital allocation stage, as discussed in the previous section, but also *ex post*, when the realised profits are adjusted for risk taken. For example, if the realised profit is US$100 million, and the bank determines that the risks taken cost US$50 million, the risk-adjusted profit on which compensation is based is only US$50 million.

Over the last ten years, trading firms have recognised the need to properly account for and control risk taken in trading operations. Rigorous processes, built on sophisticated mathematical techniques, have been developed and implemented. Yet, the list of massive trading losses keeps growing, from Sumitomo in 1996 to Amaranth during the summer of 2006, suggesting that trading businesses do not yet fully price risks in their capital allocation and performance management processes.

"Noise"-adjusted performance

Enhanced performance management is not limited to trading. It is by now well established that managers' performance should be evaluated on controllable items only. Filtering out noise, such as foreign exchange fluctuations, provides a clearer read on the performance of the manager, hence it allows the firm to design more effective compensation mechanisms. Commodities companies constitute the classical case example: over the last five years, high oil prices have lead to record profits for oil companies. However, these high profits do not necessarily indicate management performance has been stellar. Similarly, low oil prices in the late 1990s led to low profits for these same oil companies. Again, one could not infer that these companies were poorly managed then. To evaluate the true performance of oil companies' managers, one would need to somehow filter out the impact of oil prices.

An academic study[24] quoted in the magazine "The Economist", suggests that current practices do not perfectly correct for movements in uncontrollable factors:

> "In the oil industry they found that chief executives' pay always benefit when the price is high, but does not necessarily suffer correspondingly when the price is low. Across a large collection of companies, they looked at the effect of changes over which managers have no control, such as shifts in exchange rates. They found that the typical firm rewards its chief executive as much for luck as it does for good performance".

For this reason, many firms have internal mechanisms to risk-adjust the performance of their divisions: some firms use internal risk transfer (eg, internal hedging), while others adjust the realised performance to set managers' compensation. Both approaches have their pros and cons: hedging produces "clean" financial results, ie, the actual financial results reflect the actual "noise-adjusted" performance. However, as reviewed in Chapter 3, hedging involves substantial transaction costs, and new accounting rules (eg, FASB 133, IAS 39) make it more difficult to match the hedges against the exposure in the financial results.[25] Furthermore, firms sometimes cannot hedge the exposure that is the largest contributor to "noise": for example, BP will not hedge its exposure to oil price to enhance the readability of its managers' performance, as it would conflict with shareholders' objectives.

Ex post performance adjustment has no accounting impact, hence lower implementation cost during the performance period (often the year), and does not conflict with shareholders' objectives. However, the adjustment process at year-end is sometimes cumbersome.

There is a fine balance here: firms do not want operational managers to focus too much on uncontrollable items, such as commodity prices, yet they do not want these managers to be fully insulated from commodity price fluctuations. For example, a petroleum refinery manager should not be directly accountable for the wide fluctuations in oil prices, however, the plant should be managed to best take advantage of these fluctuations, through its refining mix, maintenance plan, etc. Similarly, managers cannot be held accountable for fluctuations in exchange rates, but should take them into account in their business decisions. For example, Airbus, a European aircraft manufacturer who sells in USD planes manufactured (primarily) in Europe is hurt from a higher EUR compared to the USD. While Airbus shareholders cannot blame current managers for the exchange rate, they expect these managers to actively explore various sourcing mechanisms to reduce its exposure (eg, determine the price of some components in USD when feasible).

2.4 MAXIMISING OPERATIONAL AND STRATEGIC FLEXIBILITY

Most contracts and assets include explicit or hidden optionality. Systematically exploiting this optionality requires including risk

VALUE CREATION FROM RISK MANAGEMENT

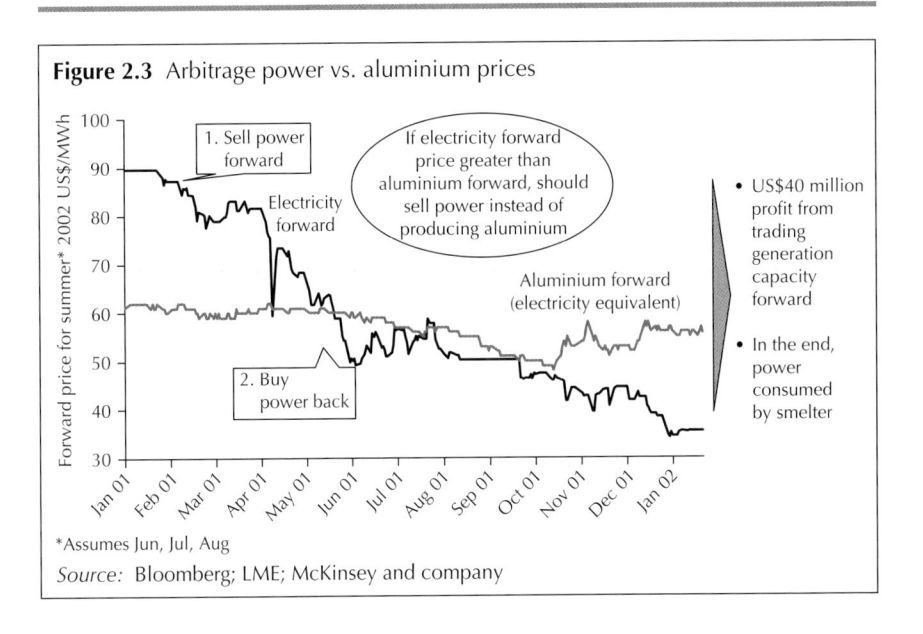

Figure 2.3 Arbitrage power vs. aluminium prices

[Chart showing forward price for summer* 2002 US$/MWh from Jan 01 to Jan 02, with electricity forward and aluminium forward (electricity equivalent) curves. Annotations: "1. Sell power forward", "2. Buy power back", "If electricity forward price greater than aluminium forward, should sell power instead of producing aluminium", "US$40 million profit from trading generation capacity forward", "In the end, power consumed by smelter"]

*Assumes Jun, Jul, Aug
Source: Bloomberg; LME; McKinsey and company

management into many business decisions, from structuring purchase or sales contracts to negotiating construction deals. It constitutes a true mindset-shift: viewing risks as opportunities as well as threats. It can create significant value for firms. As this theme is highly situation-specific, it is not developed extensively in this book. Rather a few examples are provided in this section.

2.4.1 Operational flexibility

Consider first a supply contract, for example a one-year oil supply contract, that provides flexibility in the volume purchased in any given month. The purchase price is agreed to be a public index price for the month of delivery, plus possible transportation charge, taxes and rebates. A savvy buyer will buy more during the months where price is low, store the oil, buy less during the months where the price is high, and use her stocks to meet her needs. Of course, the buyer may misjudge the market, and end up paying more than the average price over the year. However, exploiting the volume option can create significant value. Purchasing and pricing decisions provide multiple examples of risk management decisions.

Consider now a conversion asset, for example an aluminium smelter. This plant is in fact a (call) option on the spread between the aluminium price and the electric power price, as illustrated in Figure 2.3.

The plant should run only when the aluminium price exceeds the electric power price (including other variable costs, and startup and shutdown costs). The value of the option increases with the volatility in power prices and aluminium prices. Aluminium companies are now negotiating resale rights in electric power supply agreements and flexibility in labour contracts – when feasible – to capture that opportunity.

Similarly, electric power plants are an option on the spread between the price of electric power and the price of fuel. The value of the option is small for base load assets, such as coal-fired and nuclear power plants: the option is always "in the money". However, the value of the option is significant for marginal assets. This has dramatic implications for asset valuations. Old peaking assets deemed worthless in the regulated era (up to the early 1990s) revealed their value as deregulation happened. Players who correctly valued the operational flexibility gained handsomely.

2.4.2 Strategic flexibility

Most executives and finance professionals are familiar with the concept of strategic flexibility, or real option.[26] Again, the logic is straightforward: investing in a project sometimes gives the right to make an additional investment. For example, a movie producer financing one movie has the option, should the movie be successful, to produce sequels. The true value of the project is therefore the sum of the value of the first phase, and the value of the option to execute the second. Again, the challenge lies in the implementation, precisely in correctly depicting the multiple states of the world to correctly evaluate the value of the option. The tools of risk management, in particular Monte Carlo simulations, apply perfectly.

Strategic flexibility can add significant value to a project, as illustrated on Example 2.4 below.

> **Example 2.4** *A firm contemplates a US$1 billion investment with expected (after tax) return of 10%. The firm's cost of capital is 8%. The expected value created by the investment is roughly US$250 million (2% spread over US$1 billion, discounted at 8%). Suppose now that the project return's standard deviation is 4%, and that the firm has the option to execute the project in two phases: invest US$500 million, immediately, and invest another US$500 million only if the market*

> *conditions are such that the return is above 6%. The expected value created by the project is then US$290 million (calculations are presented in Appendix 2.H). Flexibility adds 16% to the value created by the project.*

Of course, the value of real options vary widely. Furthermore, capturing the value requires solid execution. Real option practitioners[27] agree that structuring and exploiting real options in investment plans can increase value created by up 30%.

2.5 AN INTEGRATED APPROACH TO RISK MANAGEMENT
Every company develops its own approach to risk management. This section describes one such possible approach.

2.5.1 Risk management process
As for risk categories, every risk management book has a definition of risk management. Here, we use the notion in its broadest sense:

Definition 2.2 *Risk management is a business process aimed at maximising value from volatility in the firm's environment.*

Risk management is defined here as a business process, not merely as a function aimed at monitoring compliance of traders with policies and guidelines. Value creation is the over-arching objective of the risk management process.

Risk management and strategy are intimately linked: the strategy development process identifies and quantifies opportunities, while the risk management process (1) estimates risks around these opportunities, and (2) develops the risk management strategy required to support the overall strategy.

As most business processes, risk management has four steps: measurement, strategy development, execution and monitoring, illustrated in Figure 2.4.

Risk measurement is a technical activity. For this reason, firms usually create a centre of excellence that develops the appropriate models and techniques. Risk measurement requires aggregation of risks across the firm (across the types of risks, and across the businesses). The centre of excellence often builds the aggregated risk profile. Risk measurement is described in greater detail in Chapter 4.

Risk management strategy is developed by the senior management team (often a Risk Management Committee, a group of senior

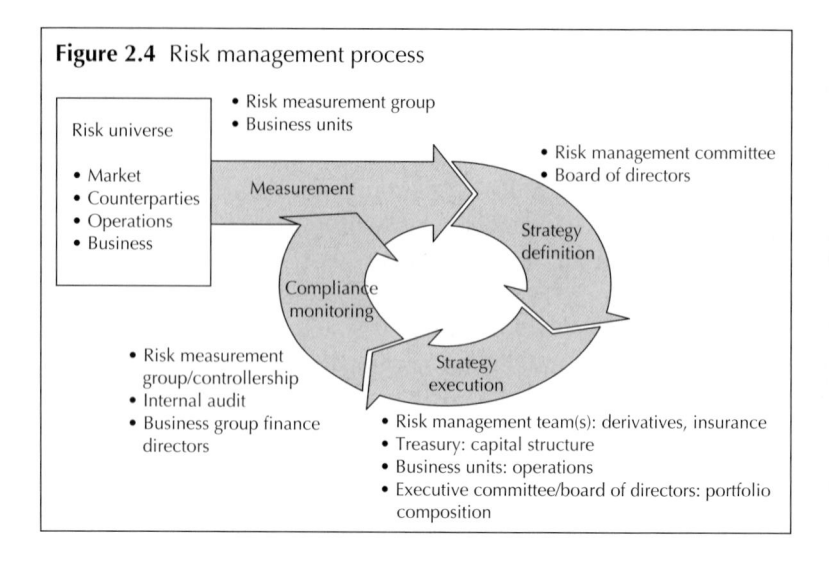

Figure 2.4 Risk management process

Risk universe
- Market
- Counterparties
- Operations
- Business

Measurement
- Risk measurement group
- Business units

Strategy definition
- Risk management committee
- Board of directors

Strategy execution
- Risk management team(s): derivatives, insurance
- Treasury: capital structure
- Business units: operations
- Executive committee/board of directors: portfolio composition

Compliance monitoring
- Risk measurement group/controllership
- Internal audit
- Business group finance directors

executives including the CRO, the Chief Financial Officer (CFO), the Treasurer, sometimes the Chief Executive Officer (CEO) and other senior business leaders), and approved by the board of directors.

While measurement requires centralisation, and strategy development is mostly top-down, *strategy execution* is a distributed process: not only the finance function, but also business leaders effectively manage risks.

Finally, *execution monitoring* completes the loop. Finance professionals in the businesses, internal and external auditors, and the risk measurement team perform that role.

2.5.2 A typology of risk management strategies

As mentioned earlier, a firm's risk management strategy integrates the volatility of cash flows, but also the firm's cost of capital environment, its overall strategy, and perspectives from its investors, as illustrated on Figure 2.5, already discussed in Chapter 1.

To define their risk management strategy, firms therefore need to answer two related questions: (1) how conservative should their risk management strategy be?; and (2) which mix of instruments should they use? While the precise answers are firm-specific, theoretical models (such as the one presented in Chapter 6) as well as practical experience suggest the following general guidelines.

VALUE CREATION FROM RISK MANAGEMENT

Figure 2.5 Drivers of risk management strategy

Risk management strategy integrates 4 distinct drivers

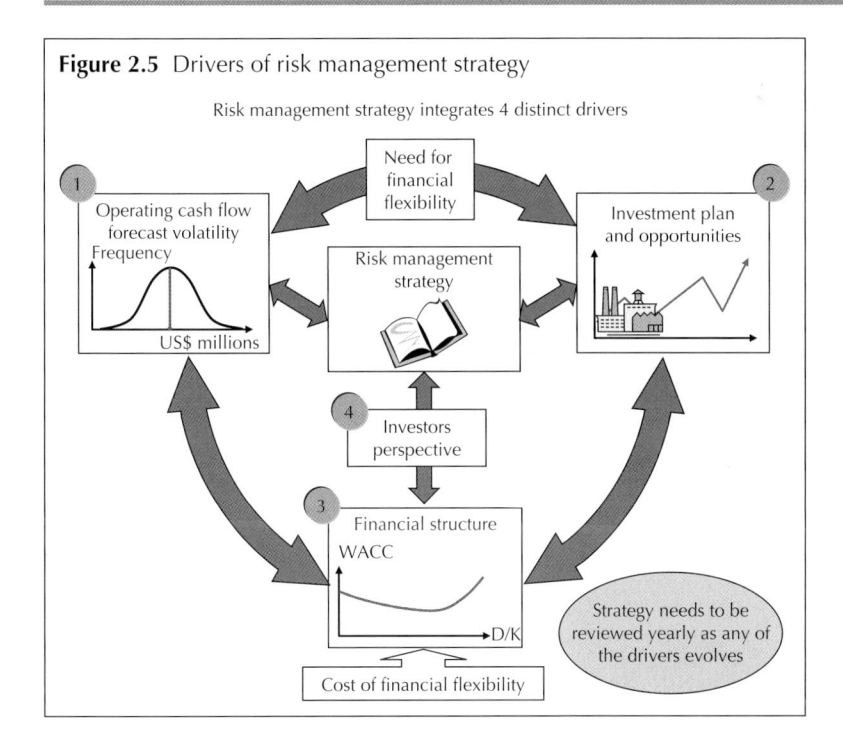

- (1) Operating cash flow forecast volatility Frequency — US$ millions
- Need for financial flexibility
- (2) Investment plan and opportunities
- Risk management strategy
- (4) Investors perspective
- (3) Financial structure WACC — D/K
- Cost of financial flexibility
- Strategy needs to be reviewed yearly as any of the drivers evolves

How conservative should the risk management strategy be?
The answer to the first question has some intuitive elements: everything else being equal, a firm's risk management strategy should be more conservative if: (1) the (potential) volatility of its cash flow is higher, and (2) its growth aspirations are higher, as illustrated in Figure 2.6 on the next page.

This is illustrated in Example 2.5 below.

Example 2.5 *Consider again the pharmaceutical company in Example 2.1. As we have seen in Example 2.1, if the investment opportunities is certain, the firm is willing to pay a premium to ensure that, should these opportunities materialise, it will be able to capture them.*

As we have seen in Example 2.1, if the investment opportunity is certain, $\Delta V^{VM} = US\$220$ million. If the pharmaceutical company believes the investment opportunity has only a 50% chance of occurring, then $\Delta V^{VM} = US\$110$ million.

53

Figure 2.6 How conservative should the risk management strategy be?

Growth aspiration	Moderately conservative	Very conservative
High	Retail, large pharmaceuticals, consumer products	Small medical devices, hi-tech
Low	**Less conservative** Manufacturing, one-asset firms, utilities	**Moderately conservative** Commodity companies, airlines
	Low	High
	(Potential) cash flow volatility	

Which mix of instruments should firms use?
The answer to the second question depends on the impact of available risk transfer instruments on financial flexibility, but also on investors' appetite for the exposure.

Impact of available risk transfer instruments on financial flexibility.
Specifically, the risk management strategy depends on the correlation between cash flow and growth opportunities.

Consider an industry where, statistically, growth opportunities arise precisely when cash flows are lowest (negative correlation). Firms in such a situation would benefit more from hedging. In fact, the model presented in Chapter 6 suggests that in some instances, they should over-hedge, and create a negative exposure (eg, an aluminium company should sell more than its production forward).

Consider another type of industry, where, historically, investment opportunities arise when cash flows are highest (positive correlation). This relationship creates a natural hedge: when cash flow is low, investment opportunities are unlikely. Therefore, firms in that industry will not use hedging (if and when available) to achieve their desired financial flexibility. The model in Chapter 6, suggests these firms should in fact increase their exposure to benefit from the diversification effect (the company should buy additional exposure forward).

The correlation obviously varies across industries, and is not always easy to determine. Consider the oil industry. Two opposite effects are at play: when oil prices are high, previously out-of-the-money fields/technologies become in-of-the-money, hence capital requirements increase. This suggest a positive correlation between cash flows and investment opportunities.

On the other hand, when oil prices are low, assets and companies are cheaper, and sometimes undervalued. Capacity expansion is cheaper, as construction firms have slack. Furthermore, if one believe that commodity prices are cyclical, this is precisely the time to invest in new capacity, so that it can benefit from the full upside part of the cycle. This would suggest that cash-flows and investment opportunities are negatively correlated.

I believe that the second effect dominates, and that true investment opportunities are at the bottom of the cycle for the oil industry and for other commodity industries, but this has to be carefully assessed for every industry.

Investors' appetite for exposure. Firms are limited by investors' preferences in their risk transfer choices.

As previously discussed, corporate finance theory suggests that investors do not value firm-specific risk (called idiosyncratic risk). For example, an investor purchasing shares in Alcoa, an aluminium producer, does not value Alcoa's aluminium exposure or more precisely values it only in proportion of its correlation to the market. The underlying logic is that the investor can undo Alcoa's aluminium exposure by selling a portfolio aluminium forward contracts. Similarly, if an investor wanted aluminium exposure, she could simply purchase a portfolio of aluminium forward contracts.

In practice, however, investors, in particular institutional investors, are restricted in their investment choices. For example, some pension funds are limited to stocks and bonds, and cannot trade commodity forward or indices. In other instances, tax treatment may favour the purchase of a local stock over a portfolio of commodities. For this reason, many investors purchased Alcoa's stock to gain exposure to aluminium prices as commodities rallied in 2005–2006.

Investors' views on firm-specific risk appear inconsistent across time. Consider two investors' surveys commissioned four years apart by a metal and mining company. In the first one, commissioned in 2001 at the trough of the commodity price cycle, investors claimed not to purchase the stock for the underlying metal exposure but for a solid operating and capital management performance. In the second one, commissioned in 2005, at the height of the price cycle, the findings were different: investors were actively seeking the commodity price exposure. Changes in investor base are not sufficient to fully explain this discrepancy: it would simply appear that investors have changed their investment rationale.

Resulting typology. Figure 2.7 summarises the firm's choices:

Figure 2.7 Which mix of levers should be used?

Investor's appetite for specific risk			
High	Highly conservative capital structure / portfolio composition / no risk transer Commodities (oil, metal)	Moderately conservative balance sheet / no risk transfer Technology companies (technology risk)
Low	Significant risk transfer / moderately conservative capital structure Pharmaceutical, manufacturing (exchange rates) Airlines (fuel)	Limited risk transfer
	Highly negative	Highly positive

Correlations cash flows vs. investment opportunities

In a recent *Harvard Business Review* article, Robert Merton[28] provides an example of a successful risk management strategy. He mentions how commercial banks reduced their equity requirement by using interest-rate swaps to transfer the interest rate risk between the rate they pay on their deposit and the rate at which they lend to their customers. In that case, Merton concludes that the optimal strategy involved more risk transfer, and less equity. Merton then suggests that other such hedging opportunities are available for firms.

The situation may be different for commodity companies. Oil companies for example are massively long oil (ie, as was observed in 2005, their profits grow as the oil price rises). They are also exposed to a series of other risks: currencies, operations, counterparty (eg, country risk), business (eg, state intervention as in Venezuela in 2006, etc). It is often the case that selling a large share of their production of oil forward would significantly reduce their cash flow volatility, hence allow them, as the commercial banks in Merton's example, to either reduce their equity level, or to grow more aggressively with the same equity level.

However, a massive forward sale program would likely conflict with investors' objectives, who buy their stock – at least in part – to benefit from a surge in oil prices. Furthermore, the value of hedging to increase financial flexibility would probably be the highest at the bottom of the cycle, when commodity prices – hence cash flow – are the lowest. However, this is precisely the worst time to sell a significant share of the production forward, and lock-in the bottom-of-the-cycle price. For these reasons, the optimal risk management strategy for oil companies – and most other commodities companies – involves more equity and less hedging. This is consistent with currently observed practice.

The gold industry provides a fascinating example of different risk management strategies, and their impact on shareholders and managers. Throughout the 1990s, two leading Canadian gold companies pursued opposite risk management strategies: Barrick gold fully hedged its production forward, while Newmont did not hedge, hence remained exposed to the gold price. Throughout that period, the gold price kept falling, hence Barrick's forward sales fetched a higher price than the relevant spot price (a situation known as contango), and Barrick's hedging program – marketed as premium hedging program – was highly regarded. However, as the gold market turned, Barrick's forward sales suddenly became massively value destroying. The CEO (who was the architect of the hedging program) was fired.

In summary, I believe than risk transfer is more limited than one might think as a risk management tool. Most risks that truly impact on a firm's cash flows are valued by investors (eg, the oil price for oil companies). To achieve their desired flexibility level, most companies need to rely on capital structure, portfolio composition and operations management.

2.5.3 Updating the risk management strategy
Most companies have an annual planning or budgeting process where: (1) each business presents its key operational and financial targets; (2) these projections are aggregated into an integrated

"plan"; and (3) choices regarding capital allocation and allowed budgets are being made. This process constitutes the natural entry point for updating the risk management strategy, and allocating capital on a risk-adjusted basis.

The first task of the risk measurement group is to develop *distributions for cash flows* for the years in the planning horizon (usually 5–10). Chapter 4 describes this analysis in more detail. I believe cash flow distributions are obtainable for all large companies, and that very few risks are beyond the creativity and the modelling capabilities of a good risk measurement team. Of course, some risks are harder to estimate than others, but the ever-growing computing power available to risk measurement teams makes it possible to simulate profitability over a wide range of scenarios for a large number of variables, hence to capture key risks to cash flows.

Once that distribution is obtained, the team then develops a *distribution of investment opportunities*. Experience suggests it is easier to produce a distribution of investment opportunities than point estimates. The future is uncertain. Managers do not know today which out of the 15 projects currently under development will come to fruition over the next three to five years or if one particular company will become fragile in three to five years hence a candidate for acquisition, or how many out of the hundreds of new drugs currently tested in the labs will justify the investment required to produce and bring to market. However, based on history and business judgement, managers can estimate probability distributions. Furthermore, the team can test different probability distributions, and see how effective the risk management strategy is for each of these different distributions.

The team then develops a *distribution of cost of capital*, ie, for a given set of financial metrics (eg, debt to capital, interest coverage, etc) a distribution of possible debt ratings, then the resulting cost of capital.

Once these inputs are integrated in a financial model, the team determines the value of the company as is, and for multiple combinations of the risk management levers (portfolio composition, target capital structure, and risk transfer).[29] The combination of levers that maximises value is then the risk management strategy.

When conducted in conjunction with the plan/budget process, this exercise is not as arduous as it would seem, as most of the issues required for the risk analysis are addressed during a "normal" plan/

budget process. For example at Alcan, we found the risk analysis adds about 20% to the analysis time. The only extra requirement is a fact-based discussion of risks and opportunities facing the businesses, which is obviously highly valuable in and of itself.

The findings from the analysis are usually robust. That does not imply that a company should set its debt to capital target to the second decimal based on the model's output. Rather, the process can quantitatively inform whether 35–40% or 50–60% is the right band for debt to capital ratio, or what are the full (ie, taking growth aspirations into account) costs and benefits of moving from a double-A to a single-A debt rating.

2.5.4 Allocating capital on a risk-adjusted basis

Capital allocation is often a critical part of the planning process. As discussed in Section 2.3, firms need to (1) change the discount rate applied to each project to reflect the true incremental risk created by the project, and (2) select the highest value-creating projects (appropriately valued).

It is critical to evaluate incremental and not stand-alone risks. For example, an investment in a power retail business, while being highly risky standalone, actually reduces the overall risk of a power producer. It creates incremental value through two channels: (1) standalone value of the business, ie, the retail margin, and (2) the volatility reduction (eg, lower cost of capital) for the entire business.

Finally, risk management strategy and capital allocation are linked: as new capital is deployed, the corporation's risk profile evolves, and the risk management strategy needs to be updated.

2.6 CONCLUDING REMARKS

The risk management approach presented in this chapter is proactive, and focused on *capturing value* created by volatility, not *avoiding* volatility.

The role of the risk management team is essential to value creation: working with business leaders, it identifies situations where proactive volatility management can add value to existing business cases, and designs strategies to capture that value. Best practice risk management can add up to 20–35% to the firm's value creation potential.

APPENDIX

2.A MODIGLIANI-MILLER IRRELEVANCE RESULTS

In two hugely influential papers, Franco Modigliani and Merton Miller (1958, 1963), who each went on to earn Nobel prizes, in no small part for their work on corporate finance, established three important and counter-intuitive results: firms cannot increase their value by altering either their (1) capital structure, (2) cash flow volatility, or (3) dividend policy. This appendix provides some intuition for the first two results, and discuss their limitations. The exposition borrows heavily from the very clear texts of Grinblatt and Titman (1998) pages 490–492 for the irrelevance of capital structure, and Doherty (2000), pages 195–199 for the irrelevance of volatility management.

2.A.1 Irrelevance of capital structure

We present here two "proofs" of the irrelevance of capital structure. Of course, they proceed from the same intuition (the value of a firm is solely determined by the value of the cash flows generated by its assets), but they offer slightly different perspectives on the issue.

The first "proof" uses the logic of arbitrage. Consider two firms that exist for one year, produce identical real assets cash flows denoted X at the end of the year, and then liquidate. Firm U is unleveraged, it is financed solely by equity, while firm L is financed by debt denoted D and equity.

Since only equity holders have a claim on firm U cash flows, the value of firm U denoted V_U is the value of its equity.

Debt holders in firm L receive $(1 + r_D) \cdot D$ at year end, and equity holders in firm L receive $X - (1 + r_D) \cdot D$. For simplicity, we assume the debt is riskless. The value of firm L is the sum of the value of its debt D and its equity E_L: $V_L = D + E_L$.

Suppose that firm U is more valuable than firm L: $V_U > D + E_L$. An arbitrageur would then buy firm L (ie, the debt and the equity) and sell short firm U. Assuming the investor pays for her purchases and receives the proceeds of the short sale immediately, its cash flow today, denoted Ω_0 is:

$$\Omega_0 = V_U - (D + E_L)$$

which is strictly positive by assumption.

Its cash flow at year end, denoted Ω_1 is:
$$\Omega_1 = -X + \left((1 + r_D) \cdot D + (X - (1 + r_D) \cdot D)\right) = 0$$

The investor would then capture a risk-free arbitrage opportunity.

The second "proof" shows how an investor can "undo" a firm's capital structure. Consider an equity holder in firm L, who finds the current leverage is too high, and wants to achieve a lower leverage. This investor can sell a portion of its stocks and buy bonds to achieve its target leverage. Precisely, denote α the current ownership fraction of the investor, and D' its target leverage, and $\pi(\alpha)$ the year-end cash flow to an investor who owns α of firm L. We can solve for $\Delta\alpha$ the fraction of ownership he must sell to achieve its target leverage. We first have:

$$\pi(\alpha) = \alpha \cdot \left(X - (1 + r_D) \cdot D\right)$$

By selling $\Delta\alpha$ shares, the investors can purchase $\pi(\Delta\alpha)$ bonds. Her year-end cash flows are then π':

$$\pi' = \pi(\alpha - \Delta\alpha) + \pi(\Delta\alpha) \cdot (1 + r_D)$$
$$= (\alpha - \Delta\alpha) \cdot \left[X - (1 + r_D) \cdot \left(D - \frac{\Delta\alpha}{\alpha - \Delta\alpha}(X - (1 + r_D) \cdot D)\right)\right]$$

To achieve leverage D', we must have:

$$D' = D - \frac{\Delta\alpha}{\alpha - \Delta\alpha}(X - (1 + r_D) \cdot D)$$

which yields:

$$\Delta\alpha = \frac{1}{1 + \frac{X - (1 + r_D) \cdot D}{D - D'}} \alpha$$

Suppose for example, $X - (1 + r_D) \cdot D' = D$ and $D' = 0$. We immediately find that $\Delta\alpha = \alpha/2$: by selling half of its share in the firm, the investors can completely unlever their investment.

The approach can be extended to risky cash flow and risky debt in the absence of bankruptcy costs.[30]

2.A.2 Irrelevance of risk transfer practices

Intuitively, risk transfers reduces a firm's cash flow volatility, hence it reduces the volatility of its value, hence it should reduce its cost of capital. In fact, that logic does not hold. To see why, we partition the risks in two classes: non-correlated with the market (called firm specific, unsystematic, or non-market risk), and correlated with the market (systematic or market risk). We then partition the second class in two sub-classes: hedgeable by outside investors (outsider-hedgeable), and not hedgeable by outside investors (non-outsider-hedgeable). We examine each of these three classes in turn.

Risk non-correlated with the market

Let us first examine the "mathematical" argument. Denote $\tilde{r}_n$ the returns of stock n, $\tilde{r}_M$ the return of the market, β_n the covariance between the returns of stock n and the market return, and ε_n the firm-specific risk. Since the firm-specific risk is uncorrelated with the market, we have:

$$var(\tilde{r}_n) = \beta_n \cdot var(\tilde{r}_M) + var(\epsilon_n)$$

The Capital Asset Pricing Model (CAPM) indicates that only market risk is priced by investors, ie, only β_n matters. Since reducing firm-specific risk $var(\varepsilon_n)$ has no impact on β_n, it has no impact on the cost of capital.

A simple example clearly demonstrates why firm-specific risk is not priced by investors. Suppose an investor holds a portfolio $\mathcal{P}$ of 25 stocks, each with expected return $\lambda = 10\%$, and standard deviations of returns $\sigma = 10\%$. Suppose these risks are firm-specific, hence perfectly uncorrelated with the market and with each other. Each stock represents 1/25 of the portfolio. From Appendix 1.A, we know that the expected return on the portfolio is $\Lambda(\mathcal{P}) = 10\%$, and the standard deviation of the portfolio $\Sigma(\mathcal{P})$ is:

$$\Sigma(\mathcal{P}) = \sqrt{\sum_{n=1}^{25} \frac{\sigma^2}{(25)^2}} = \sqrt{\frac{\sigma^2}{25}} = 0.2\sigma$$

Suppose now firm 1 increases its risk-profile, so that the standard deviation of returns is $\sigma_1 = 2\sigma$. Risks are still uncorrelated. The expected return on firm 1 remains at $\lambda = 10\%$. The expected return on the portfolio $\mathcal{P}'$ is $\Lambda(\mathcal{P}') = \Lambda(\mathcal{P}) = 10\%$. The standard deviation of the portfolio $\Sigma(\mathcal{P}')$ has increased to:

VALUE CREATION FROM RISK MANAGEMENT

$$\Sigma(\mathcal{P}') = \sqrt{\frac{4\sigma^2 + 24\sigma^2}{(25)^2}} = \sqrt{\frac{28}{(25)^2}\sigma^2} = 0.21\sigma$$

The investor can reduce the volatility of its portfolio through diversification. If the investor holds equal shares in 28 stocks, the resulting portfolio volatility is:

$$\Sigma(\mathcal{P}'') = \sqrt{\frac{4\sigma^2 + 27\sigma^2}{(28)^2}} = \sqrt{\frac{31}{(28)^2}\sigma^2} = 0.199\sigma$$

Risk correlated with the market: outsider-hedgeable
This is the case of a price risk, such as oil price, EUR/USD exchange rate, or interest rate. The investors can hedge this risk themselves in the market. For example, if an investor in an airline company does not like the exposure to oil prices, she can hedge it away by purchasing the oil forward contracts. In practice, defining the exact exposure is not completely straightforward, as one needs to know the impact of oil prices on the airlines profits.

Risk correlated with the market: non-outsider-hedgeable
This would be the case of an operational risk that can be insured. One can see two reasons why an operational risk would be correlated with the market. First, in general, the financial market is positively correlated to the overall economic activity. The plant's production is often also positively correlated with the overall economic activity. Then, if the plant has a higher production level, accidents/incidents may be more likely. Second, for a commodity business, commodity prices are often positively correlated with the market. A production failure is more costly at high prices than at low prices.

The plant can subscribe an insurance policy, while the investor cannot subscribe an insurance policy on the asset owned by a company in which she holds stock. However, the firm subscribing the insurance policy does not create value. The argument is quite subtle, but very powerful.

Suppose a firm transfers a risk that is negatively correlated with the market, ie, the loss associated with that risk is high when the market is low, and low when the market is high. Holding that risk increases the β of the firm. Then, transferring it reduces the β of the firm. If the counterparty accepts the risk at its "fair" value, ie, at the expected value of losses, then the expected cash flows of the firm have not changed, its β has decreased, hence it cost of capital has decreased, hence value has been created. If, however, the counterparty correctly prices the increase in its β resulting from the transaction, the firm expected cash flows will be reduced just so to compensate for its β reduction, hence no value is created.

Doherty (2000), page 199 provides a very clear summary of the situation:

> [D]oes hedging benefit shareholders? The answer is no, if the party assuming the hedge prices it correctly. Of course, shareholders can benefit if the insurer underprices the insurance policy. But this is hardly a justification for risk management; it is a justification for buying underpriced assets. It is really no different from the firm's buying a building, or a machine, or a license, for less than its market value.

2.A.3 Limitations to Modigliani-Miller results

Three key assumptions underpin Modigliani-Miller irrelevance results: the absence of taxes, the absence of transaction costs, and the assumptions that operating cash flows are independent of the capital structure. Each of these assumptions can be relaxed.

Including *taxes* is equivalent to introducing a third claimant on the cash flows generated by the firm: the government. Since interest payments are tax-deductible, while dividends to equity holders are not, increasing the leverage transfers value from the government to equity holders. This effect has been captured in Modigliani-Miller (1963).

We divide *transaction costs* into two categories: trading costs and bankruptcy costs. Trading costs are by now small enough to be neglected. Bankruptcy costs are too large to be ignored. As previously discussed, they give rise to the convex cost of capital.

Finally, we have seen that asymmetry of information and incentives issues imply that *operating cash flows depend on the leverage ratio*.

U-shaped cost of capital is therefore fully consistent with the Modigliani-Miller propositions (on the left of the minimum), and their limitations (on the right of the minimum).

Table 2.1 Comparison of risk typologies

This text	Basel II	Marrison	Jorion	Shimpi	Doherty	
Industry	Banks	Banks	Banks	Telecom	Insurance	Manufacture
Price	market	market	market	market	systematic	finance
Counter-party	credit	credit	credit		credit	
Business	legal		legal liquidity	business	legal actuarial liquidity	economic or market
Operations	operational	operating	operational	operational	operational	operational pure or insurable

2.B RISK TYPOLOGIES

Various authors and organisations (eg, financial regulators) have proposed typologies of risk. Table 2.1 maps the risk categories discussed in this text to five leading sources: the Basel Committee on Banking Supervision's Revised International Capital Framework[31] (2004), referred to as Basel II, Marrison (2002), Jorion (2001), Shimpi (2001), and Doherty (2000).

As can be seen from Table 2.1, the typology proposed in this text includes all risks identified by other authors. It includes a broader set of risks than the classifications developed for the banking industry (Basel II, Marrison, Jorion), as it includes business risk over and beyond legal risk. Similarly, the definition of operations risk proposed in this text includes process-related risk, which is a major concern for financial institutions, but also asset-related risk, which concerns non-financial institutions.

2.C MAPPING TO "STANDARD" VALUE CREATION CHANNELS

"Standard" risk management and corporate finance books (eg, Doherty (2000), Grinblatt and Titman (1998)) identify five main value channels from risk management, taken here in the narrow sense of reducing volatility:

(1) Reducing the expected tax burden.
(2) Reducing the direct cost of financial distress.

(3) Alleviating the incentives for dysfunctional investments when a corporation is close to financial distress.
(4) Reducing under-investment caused by costly access to external capital.
(5) Increasing the efficiency of management compensation and the accuracy of management performance evaluation.

Let us examine each value channel in turn.

While conceptually reducing volatility in the presence of a convex tax schedule does create value, the academic empirical evidence is inconclusive.[32] Furthermore, since taxes are calculated on accounting earnings (in fact tax-accounting earnings, which differ from standard accounting earnings), the link between a hedging program and convexity of the tax schedule is hard to establish empirically. Most tax departments are focused on reducing the tax burden, not so much on the volatility. For this reason, I elected not to include it in the list.

As discussed in Section 2.2 reducing the direct cost of financial distress (value channel (2)) and reducing under-investment caused by costly access to external capital (value channel (4)) are conceptually identical in the presence of U-shaped capital cost: when the firm is financially constrained it has to sell valuable businesses, curtail some its activities (value channel (2)) or pass on profitable opportunities (value channel (4)).

Similarly, I believe all the incentives issues such as value channel (3) are priced-in the convex cost of capital: creditors know that managers and owners face different incentives than they do. In Tirole's (2006) illuminating model, they simply refuse to lend. In practice, they require a higher return to lend if the leverage gets too high. Therefore, I believe all of these impacts are accounted for in the provision of financial flexibility, when facing convex cost of capital.

Finally, while it is true that reducing the volatility of financial performance of the firm allows the firm to better gauge a manager's performance and offer higher-powered incentives, hedging is not required to achieve that goal: many corporations evaluate price-adjusted performance by replacing actual prices (eg, exchange rates, interest rates, commodity prices) by the previously agreed prices (eg, "budget" prices) in evaluating a business performance. Since this is agreed upon ex ante, the managers do not face price risks, hence, managerial performance is transparent, and high-powered incentives can be used. I therefore do not consider value channel (5) as a source of value creation from hedging. However, enhanced performance management is a value channel for risk management.

In addition to the traditional channels, I include two other channels: (1) risk-adjusted capital allocation and performance management, and (2) operational and strategic flexibility. The first-one regroups the notions of risk adjustment, and performance management. The second includes option values.

2.D VALUATION FUNDAMENTALS

This short appendix summarises the main results used to value businesses, projects, and companies. Of course, it does not do justice to such a complex subject. A rich description of the details underlying the approaches can be found in Copeland *et al* (1995) for the DCF approach, and Stewart (1991) for the Economic Profit (EP) approach, from which this summary heavily borrows. The section on cost of capital borrows heavily from Grinblatt and Titman (1998). Finally, Pettit (2007) provides a very insightful discussion of practical issues encountered in valuation.

First, we introduce the main financial metrics used for valuation. Second, we the Weighted Average Cost of Capital. Finally, we introduce the two most popular valuation methods: DCF and EP, and show that they coincide.

2.D.1 Financial metrics used for valuation

Valuation relies on three financial metrics: Net Operating Profits Less Adjusted Taxes (NOPLAT), Free Cash Flow (FCF) and Invested Capital (IC). We briefly show here how to compute them from a firm's (hypothetical) financial statements.

Net Operating Profits Less Adjusted Taxes
NOPLAT is a measure of profitability that stands at the core of the EP approach. The table below shows how to compute NOPLAT from a firm's financial statements:

USD millions	
Net sales	10,000
Cost of Goods Sold (COGS)	−5,000
Selling, General and Administrative expenses (SGA)	−1,000
EBITDA[33]	**4,000**
Depreciation expense	−1,000
EBIT[34]	**3,000**
Adjusted Taxes on EBIT	−1,000
Change in deferred taxes	0
NOPLAT	**2,000**

The only "non-standard" item is Adjusted Taxes on EBIT. Copeland *et al* (1995, pp 156–8) describe how to compute them:

> [They] "represent the income taxes attributable to EBIT. They are taxes the company would pay if it had no debt, excess marketable securities, or non-operating income or expenses. Taxes on EBIT are the total income tax provision (current and deferred) adjusted for the income taxes attributed to interest expense, interest income, and non-operating items."

It immediately follows that Adjusted Taxes are in general different from the total income tax provision (and often higher, if the company carries debt hence benefits from a tax shield). Copeland *et al* (1995) then state that:

> "The taxes related to interest expense, interest income, and non-operating items are calculated by multiplying the marginal tax rate by the item (unless more specific tax information is available)."

Assuming taxes on EBIT are simply the tax rate (denoted τ) times EBIT, and using self-explaining notation, we have:

$$NOPLAT_t = (EBITDA_t - dep_t) \cdot (1 - \tau)$$

Free Cash Flow
In general, Free Cash Flow (FCF) measures the cash flow available to investors.[35] The table below shows how to compute FCF from a firm's financial statements:

USD millions	
EBIT	**3,000**
Adjusted taxes on EBIT	−1,000
Change in deferred taxes	0
NOPLAT	**2,000**
Depreciation expense	1,000
Gross cash flow	**3,000**
Increase in working capital	0
Capital expenditures	−1,000
Increase in other assets (excluding goodwill), net of liabilities	0
Gross investment	**−1,000**
Free cash flow before goodwill	**2,000**
Investment in goodwill	0
Free cash flow	**2,000**

The FCF computed using that method are usually lower than the FCF reported in financial statements, since we used adjusted taxes, while financial statements report actual taxes. The tax shield arising from interest expenses is included in the cost of capital, and not in the FCF.

Denote dep_t, ΔOWC_t, $capex_t$, and $\Delta other\_assets_t$ respectively the depreciation, increase in working capital, capital expenditures and increase in other assets including goodwill, during period t. We have:

$$FCF_t = NOPLAT_t + dep_t - (\Delta OWC_t + capex_t + \Delta other\_assets_t) \quad (2)$$

FCF equals financing flow: after tax interest income plus increase in excess marketable securities, plus after-tax interest expense plus decrease in debt, plus dividends, plus share repurchase.

Invested Capital

Invested Capital (denoted I) is described in Copeland *et al* (1995, p 159):

> Invested Capital represents the amount invested in the *operations* of the business. Invested capital is the sum of operating working capital; net property, plant, and equipment; and net other assets (net of non-current, non-interest-bearing liabilities).
>
> Invested Capital, plus any non-operating investments, measures the total amount invested by the company's investors, which we call total investors funds. Total investors funds can also be calculated from the liability side of the balance sheet as the sum of all equity (plus quasi-equity items like deferred taxes) and interest-bearing debt.

Operating Working Capital (OWC), also called Working Capital Requirement is operational cash, plus Accounts Receivables, minus Accounts Payables minus accrued liabilities.

Other assets are: goodwill plus intangible assets minus long-term non-interest-bearing liabilities. Using self-explaining notation:

$$I_t = OWC_t + net\_PPE_t + other\_assets_t$$

We then have:

$$I_t - I_{t-1} = \Delta(OWC + net\_PPE + other\_assets)$$

Since the change in net PPE between dates $(t-1)$ and t is the capex (denoted $capex_t$) minus depreciation (denoted dep_t), we have:

$$I_t - I_{t-1} = capex_t - dep_t + \Delta(OWC + other\_assets) \quad (3)$$

Link between NOPLAT, Free Cash Flow and Invested Capital

Combining Equations (2) and (3), we have:

$$FCF_t = NOPLAT_t - (I_t - I_{t-1}) \quad (4)$$

Equation (4) is used to establish the equivalence between the DCF and EP valuation approaches.

2.D.2 Cost of capital

Consider a firm with assets market value V_A. Denote r_f the risk free rate, r_M the market return, $E[r_A^*]$ the expected return on the asset, $\beta_A = cov(r_A, r_M)/var(r_M)$ the beta of the assets, and MRP $= E[r_M^*] - r_f$ the market risk premium. The CAPM suggests that $E[r_A^*]$ is given by the following:

$$E[r_A^*] = r_f + \beta_A \cdot (E[r_M] - r_f) \quad (5)$$

We now turn to the cost of capital. Denote E the market value of the equity, D the market value of debt, k_E the cost of equity, r_D the cost of debt, and τ the tax rate. For simplicity, we assume here that the debt is risk-free: $r_D = r_f \cdot (1 + \tau)$, and the market value of debt is equal to its face value. The Weighted Average Cost of Capital (WACC), denoted w^A, is equal to:

VALUE CREATION FROM RISK MANAGEMENT

$$w^A = \frac{D}{D+E} \cdot r_f \cdot (1-\tau) + \frac{E}{D+E} k_E$$

In the CAPM, we can apply Equation (5) to the cost of equity:

$$k_E = r_f + \beta_E^L \cdot (E[r_M] - r_f)$$

Then, since by construction $A = E + D$, portfolio mathematics yield:

$$\beta_A^L = \frac{D}{D+E} \cdot \beta_D + \frac{E}{D+E} \cdot \beta_E^L$$

where β_A^L and β_E^L are the "levered" βs for the assets and the equity respectively, ie, the β that take into account the impact of leverage. Since the debt is assumed risk-free, $\beta_D = 0$, and we have:

$$\beta_A^L = \frac{E}{D+E} \cdot \beta_E^L$$

and the cost of capital simplifies to:

$$w^A = \frac{D}{D+E} \cdot r_f \cdot (1-\tau) + \frac{E}{D+E} \cdot \left(r_f + \beta_E^L \cdot (E[r_M] - r_f)\right)$$

$$= r_f \cdot \left(\frac{D \cdot (1-\tau) + E}{D+E}\right) + \frac{E}{D+E} \cdot \beta_E^L \cdot (E[r_M] - r_f)$$

$$= r_f \cdot \left(1 - \tau \cdot \frac{D}{D+E}\right) + \beta_A^L \cdot (E[r_M] - r_f)$$

We now need to determine β_A^L. To do this, we consider a firm composed of two assets: a tax shield asset, denoted TXA, and an operating asset, denoted OA. The value of the asset is the value of the operating asset plus the tax shield. By construction, we immediately have:

$$\beta_A^L = \frac{TXA}{TXA + OA} \cdot \beta_{TXA} + \frac{OA}{TXA + OA} \cdot \beta_{OA}$$

The issue is then to estimate β_{TXA}. Multiple models exist. We present two in this text. The Hamada (1969) model assumes that debt is constant and risk-free, and that the tax shield is also risk free. This is appropriate for firms that maintain a constant debt level. Then:

$$TXA = \tau \cdot D \quad \text{and} \quad \beta_{TXA} = 0$$

and:

$$\beta_A^L = \frac{E + D - \tau \cdot D}{E + D} \cdot \beta_{OA}$$

$$= \left(1 - \tau \cdot \frac{D}{D + E}\right) \cdot \beta_A^U$$

since $\beta_{OA} = \beta_A^U$. We then have:

$$w^A = \left(r_f + \beta_A^U \cdot (E[r_M] - r_f)\right) \cdot \left(1 - \tau \cdot \frac{D}{D + E}\right)$$

$$= E[r_A^*] \cdot \left(1 - \tau \cdot \frac{D}{D + E}\right)$$

where $E[r_A^*]$ is the expected return on the asset in the absence of leverage.

This is exactly Modigliani-Miller (1963) adjusted cost of capital formula. In the absence of taxes, the cost of capital is constant (ie, independent of leverage) and equal to the expected returns on the asset. When taxes are taken into account, cost of capital decreases as leverage increases, as tax-advantaged debt is substituted for equity.

The Miles and Ezzel model (1980, 1985) assumes that the value of the debt is perfectly correlated with the value of the operating assets. This is appropriate if the firm maintains a constant leverage ratio. Thus, the tax savings from debt are perfectly correlated with the prior period's value of the operating assets. Then, we have, at least approximately:

$$\beta_{TXA} = \beta_{OA}$$

which then yields:

$$\tilde{\beta}_A^L = \beta_A^U$$

where the ~ refers to the Miles and Ezzel model. This suggests that β is independent of leverage. Then:

$$\tilde{w}^A = r_f \cdot \left(1 - \tau \cdot \frac{D}{D+E}\right) + \beta_A^U \cdot (E[r_M] - r_f)$$

$$= E[r_A^*] - r_f \cdot \tau \cdot \frac{D}{D+E}$$

As with the Hamada model, in the absence of taxes, the cost of capital is equal to the expected returns on the assets.

For assets with positive β_A^U, $E[r_A^*] > r_f$ and $\tilde{w}^A > w^A$: the Miles and Ezzell model generates higher cost of capital than the Hamada model. As one would expect, empirical studies suggest truth lies somewhere in between these two models.

Copeland *et al* (2003, pp 581–88) show that these results can be extended to include risky debt, by combining the CAPM with the Black-Scholes-Merton option pricing model. The cost of capital in the Hamada model can be written as:

$$w^A = E[r_A^*] \cdot \left(1 - \tau \cdot \frac{B}{B+E}\right)$$

where B is the market value of debt and E is the market value of equity. This relation is used in Chapter 5 to determine the cost of capital taking risk capital into account.

2.D.3 Free Cash Flow (FCF) and Economic Profit (EP) valuation approaches

The FCF approach states that the value of the firm is the discounted present value of its FCFs. Denote FCF_t the free cash flow during period t, ie, between dates $(t-1)$ and t, and assume the discount rate w is constant. The value of the firm – denoted V – is then:

$$V = \sum_{t=1}^{\infty} \frac{FCF_t}{(1+w)^t}$$

An alternative valuation approach uses the concept of EP. For every period, the EP is the profits generated by the

Invested Capital, net of the profits required to remunerate this Invested Capital. Specifically, if we denote I_t the invested capital at date t, and EP_t the EP during period t, we have:

$$EP_t = NOPLAT_t - w \cdot I_{t-1}$$

Denote $r_t = (NOPLAT_t/I_{t-1})$ the ROIC realised during period t. The EP can be expressed as:

$$EP_t = (r_t - w) \cdot I_{t-1}$$

The EP has an intuitively appealing interpretation: a firm creates value (ie, generates positive EP) if and only if its ROIC is larger than its cost of capital. The economic profit is the excess return over and above the cost of capital, applied to all invested capital.

Using Equation (4), one can then express the value of the firm as a function of the discounted sum of EPs:

$$\begin{aligned} V &= \sum_{t=1}^{\infty} \frac{FCF_t}{(1+w)^t} = \sum_{t=1}^{\infty} \frac{NOPLAT_t - (I_t - I_{t-1})}{(1+w)^t} \\ &= \sum_{t=1}^{\infty} \frac{NOPLAT_t - w \cdot I_{t-1} + w \cdot I_{t-1} - (I_t - I_{t-1})}{(1+w)^t} \\ &= \sum_{t=1}^{\infty} \frac{EP_t}{(1+w)^t} + \sum_{t=1}^{\infty} \frac{(1+w) \cdot I_{t-1}}{(1+w)^t} - \sum_{t=1}^{\infty} \frac{I_t}{(1+w)^t} \end{aligned}$$

Then, since

$$\sum_{t=1}^{\infty} \frac{(1+w) \cdot I_{t-1}}{(1+w)^t} = \sum_{t=1}^{\infty} \frac{I_{t-1}}{(1+w)^{t-1}} = \sum_{t=0}^{\infty} \frac{I_t}{(1+w)^t}$$

we have:

$$V = \sum_{t=1}^{\infty} \frac{EP_t}{(1+w)^t} + I_0$$

The EP approach has an intuitive interpretation: the value of a firm is the (book) value of its invested capital, plus the economic profit created by the operation of the assets, over and above the adequate return to these assets.

Alternatively, the NPV of a project is the discounted sums of the EPs generated by the project:

$$NPV = V - I_0 = \sum_{t=1}^{\infty} \frac{EP_t}{(1+w)^t}$$

Note that, if the EP flows are constant over time, then:

$$V = I + EVA \cdot \sum_{t=1}^{\infty} \frac{1}{(1+w)^t} = I + \frac{EP}{w}$$

2.E CALCULATIONS FOR EXAMPLES 2.1 AND 2.5: THE PHARMACEUTICAL COMPANY

2.E.1 No purchase case

We immediately observe that the current business creates $VC_C =$ US$800m (= US$8,000m · (11% − 10%)/10% = US$80m/0.1).

2.E.2 Purchase case

First, the core business generates value created $VC_C^P = -$US$373m:

(a) if no downgrade, the core business generates a 1% spread on US$8,000 *million*, or $EP = $ US$80 *millon* per year, which, discounted in perpetuity at 10%, yields a value creation $VC = $ US$800 *millon*;

(b) if downgrade, the core business generates a −1% spread on US$8,000 *million*, or $EP = -$US$80 *million* per year, which, discounted in perpetuity at 12%, yields a value creation of $VC = -$US$667m;

(c) since downgrade has an 80% probability, the expected value created by the core business is $VC_C^P = 80\% \times$ (−US$667m) + 20% × US$800m = −US$373m.

Second, a similar analysis shows that the growth business has an expected value creation $VC_G^P = -$US$253m:

(a) if no downgrade, the growth business generates a 3% spread over US$2,000 million invested capital, or $EP = US\$60$ *milion* per year, which, discounted in perpetuity at 10%, yields a value creation $VC = US\$600m$;
(b) if downgrade, the growth business generates a 1% spread on US$2,000 million, or $EP = US\$20$ *million* per year, which, discounted in perpetuity at 12%, yields a value creation of $VC = US\$167m$;
(c) since downgrade has an 80% probability, the expected value created by the growth business is $VC_G^P = 80\% \times US\$167m + 20\% \times US\$600m = US\$253$.

Finally, the value created by the firm is the sum of the value created by the core and the growth businesses (assuming no synergies): $VC^P = -US\$373m + US\$253m = -US\$120m$.

Since the investment is value destroying, the firm will not undertake it.

2.E.3. Volatility management technology

The value created and enterprise value for the businesses and the firm with a volatility management technology are summarised in the Table 2.2.

Table 2.2 Valuation with volatility management technology

	Downgrade	No downgrade	Expected
US$ millions			
Prob (%)	20%	80%	n/a
Core VC VC_C^{VM}	−667	+800	+507
Growth VC VC_G^{VM}	+167	+600	+513
Total VC VC^{VM}	−500	+1,400	+1,020

Since the value created is positive and larger than in the no purchase case, the firm undertakes the investment. The expected value created by the volatility management technology is the difference between the expected value created with the volatility management technology (and the investment) and the expected value created without the volatility management technology (no investment): $\Delta V^{VM} = VC^{VM} - VC^C = US\$1,202m - US\$800m$ US$220m.

2.E.4 Uncertain investment opportunity

If the firm does not acquire the volatility management technology, it never invests in the growth opportunity, and its value created is VC_C. If the firm acquires the volatility management technology, it invests in the growth opportunity when it occurs (with probability p), and creates VC^{VM}. With probability $(1-p)$, the growth opportunity does not occur, the firm does not invest, and creates VC_C. The incremental value created attributable to the volatility management technology is then:

$$\Delta V^{VM}(p) = p \cdot VC^{VM} + (1-p) \cdot VC_C - VC_C$$
$$= p \cdot \left(VC^{VM} - VC_C\right)$$

2.F CALCULATIONS FOR EXAMPLE 2.2: THE OIL COMPANY

In this example, we ignore growth considerations, as this would not change the underlying story.

2.F.1 The no-sale case

First, the downstream business has an expected value $V_D^{NS} =$ US\$7,627m:

(a) if no downgrade, the downstream business generates a 1% spread on US\$8,000 million, or $EP =$ US\$80 *million* per year, which, discounted in perpetuity at 10%, yields a value creation $VC =$ US\$800m;

(b) if downgrade, the downstream business generates a −1% spread on US\$8,000 million, or $EP = -$US\$80 *million* per year, which, discounted in perpetuity at 12%, yields a value creation of $VC = -$US\$667m;

(c) since downgrade has an 80% probability, the expected value created by the downstream business is $VC_D^{NS} = 80\% \times (-$US\$667m$) + 20\% \times $ US\$800m $= -$US\$373m;

(d) the value of the downstream business is the capital invested plus the value created $V_D^{NS} = $ US\$8,000m $-$ US\$373m $=$ US\$7,627m.

Second, a similar analysis shows that the upstream business has an expected value creation $VC_U^{NS} =$ US\$426m, hence an expected value of $V_U^{NS} =$ US\$2,000m $+$ US\$426m $=$ US\$2,426m:

(a) if no downgrade, the upstream business generates a 4% spread over US$2,000 million invested capital, or $EP = -US\$80\ million$ per year, which, discounted in perpetuity at 10%, yields a value creation $VC = US\$800m$;
(b) if downgrade, the upstream business generates a 2% spread on US$2,000 million, or $EP = US\$40\ million$ per year, which, discounted in perpetuity at 12%, yields a value creation of $VC = US\$333m$;
(c) since downgrade has an 80% probability, the expected value created by the upstream business is $VC_U^{NS} = 80\% \times US\$333m + 20\% \times US\$800m = US\$426$;

Finally, the value of the firm is the sum of the value of the upstream and the upstream businesses (assuming no synergies):
$V^{NS} = US\$7,627m + US\$2,426m = US\$10,053m.$

2.F.2 The sale case

The expected value created by the downstream business is now $VC_D^S = US\$171m$, which implies that the expected value of the downstream business is $V_D^S = US\$8,171m$.

The breakeven sale price is therefore $P = US\$1,882m = US\$10,053m - US\$8,171m$.

2.F.3 Risk management technology

The value created and enterprise value for the businesses and the firm with a risk management technology are summarised in the Table 2.3:

Table 2.3 Valuation with risk management technology

	VC	V
US$ millions		
Downstream	507	8,507
Upstream	707	2,707
Total	1,213	11,213

If the firm sells the downstream business, the value of the downstream business is $V_D^S = 8,171m$, which leads to a breakeven price $P' = US\$3,042m = US\$11,213m - US\$8,171m$.

2.G RISK ADJUSTMENT

The profit is the product of two random variables: profitability margin (m) and sales (Q). Probability theory shows that:

$$E[m \cdot Q] = E[m] \cdot E[Q] + cov(m, Q)$$

where $cov(m, Q)$ is the covariance between profitability margin and sales volume.

The assumption about sales volume can be described mathematically as:

$$Q = 5 + 10 \cdot z$$

where z is a binary random variable, taking the values $z = 1$ with probability 50% and $z = 0$ with probability 50%. We immediately verify that $E[Q] = 5 + 10 \cdot E[z] = 5 + 10 \cdot 0.5 = 5 + 5 = 10$.

Similarly, the assumption about profitability margin can be described mathematically as:

$$m = 5 + 10 \cdot y$$

where y is a binary random variable, taking the values $y = 1$ with probability 50% and $y = 0$ with probability 50%. We immediately verify that $E[m] = 10$.

We now need to evaluate the covariance term. By definition:

$$cov(m, Q) = \rho \cdot \sigma_m \cdot \sigma_Q$$

where ρ is the correlation coefficient between sales and profitability, σ_m is the standard deviation of the profitability, and σ_Q the standard deviation of sales. We immediately find that $\sigma_m = 10 \cdot \sigma_y$ and $\sigma_Q = 10 \cdot \sigma_z$ where σ_y and σ_z are the standard deviations of y and z respectively. A well-known property of binary variables is that $\sigma_y = \sigma_z = 0.25$. Hence, with $\rho = -1$ by assumption, we have:

$$cov(m, Q) = \rho \cdot \sigma_m \cdot \sigma_Q = -100 \cdot 0.25 = -25$$

Hence:

$$E[m \cdot Q] = 100 - 25 = 75$$

CORPORATE RISK MANAGEMENT FOR VALUE CREATION

2.H CALCULATION FOR EXAMPLE 2.4: THE OPTION VALUE

The expected value created by the project is:

$$V = \frac{(10\% - 8\%)}{8\%} \cdot 1,000 \text{ US\$ million}$$

$$= \frac{2\%}{8\%} \cdot 1,000 = \frac{1,000}{4} = 250 \text{ US\$ million}$$

Denote r the return of the project. If the firm has the option to invest in phases, it does not invest the second phase if $r \leq 6\%$. The value created by the project is:

$$V' = \frac{(10\% - 8\%)}{8\%} \cdot 500 \text{ US\$ million} +$$

$$\Pr(r \geq 6\%) \cdot \frac{E\{r/r \geq 6\%\} - 8\%}{8\%} \cdot 500 \text{ US\$ million}$$

$$= 125 \text{ \$ million}$$

$$+ \Pr(r \geq 6\%) \cdot \frac{E\{r/r \geq 6\%\} - 8\%}{8\%} \cdot 500 \text{ US\$ million}$$

Numerical simulations then show that: $V' = \text{US\$290 million}$.

---

1 Precisely, the standard deviation of pre-tax cash flows attributable to a price risk is the exposure times the standard deviation of this price.
   In a few instances, price risk is not linear. For example, gas stations pass to their customers the increase in wholesale oil price. Therefore, under normal conditions, they have only a small exposure to wholesale oil price, due to lags and other imperfections in the passthrough. If oil price exceeds a certain level, however, demand decreases, and gas stations lose margins. Gas stations are then short wholesale oil prices. This effect is discussed in detail in Chapter 4.
2 See Merton and Culp (1999) for an insightful discussion of the Metallgesellshaft case.
3 Minton and Schrand (1999).
4 Quoted in Doherty (2000), p 213.
5 Tirole (2006) provide a very thoughtful and clear overview of the issues (Chapters 1 and 2), and describes a very simple yet powerful model that provides microfoundations for the convexity of the cost of capital (Chapter 3).
6 Appendix 2.D discusses the impact of leverage and taxes on the WACC, that borrows heavily from Grinblatt and Titman (1998).
7 Leland (1994) and Leland and Toft (1996) develop the mathematical formulation describing this phenomenon.

VALUE CREATION FROM RISK MANAGEMENT

8 The "pecking order" theory was first developed by Donaldson (1961). It has since been enriched by numerous theoretical and empirical analyses (eg, Myers and Majluf (1984) provide a theoretical justification based on signalling). Grinblatt and Titman (1998), pp 592–4 provide a clear and insightful discussion.
9 Mayer (1990).
10 Rajan and Zingales (2003).
11 Lee *et al* (1996) report on the average costs of raising capital for US corporations from 1990 to 1994. They find the direct costs of seasoned equity offerings vary from 3.1% to 13% of the proceeds, with a 7.1% average.
12 See Tirole (2006), pp 101–2 and the references included.
13 Reported in Grinblatt and Titman (1998).
14 Culp (2002), and Shimpi (2001) provide a thorough exposition of the convergence of the four levers discussed in this section, including the description of many innovative financial solutions.
15 Pettit (2007).
16 Minton and Schrand (1997).
17 In the previously mentioned linear regression of credit ratings against multiple variables, Pettit (2007) reports that size is a positive and statistically significant coefficient.
18 Of course, there are examples of long-term risk transfer products, such as long-dated forward contracts.
19 The choice depends largely on the currency of determination of the costs.
20 See for example the *International Herald Tribune* online at http://www.iht.com/articles/2007/01/16/business/bp.php.
21 Chapter 3 provides a longer discussion of Value at Risk and its limitations. For an in-depth discussion of Value at Risk, see for example Jorion (2001). For a rich discussion of Economic Capital and their implementation to financial institutions, see Marrison (2002), and Dev (2004).
22 Merton and Perold (1993). In this section, we discuss the concept at a high level, the mechanics of calculation of risk capital and the link with Economic Capital used by banks are discussed in detail in Chapter 5.
23 Taleb (2001).
24 Bertrand and Mullainathan (2001) quoted in the Economist special report on executive pay, January 20th 2007.
25 If the firm has secured hedge-accounting treatment for its hedging program, hedging results are included in its operational EBIT. If the firm has not secured hedge accounting, the adjustment will be booked "below the EBIT line", which will require management to make some "*ex post*" adjustement to explain the results.
26 See for example the theoretical treatment in Dixit and Pindyck (1994), and the more practitioners' oriented presentation in Copeland and Antikarov (2003).
27 Real Options Group (http://www.rogroup.com/) in a private communication with the author.
28 Merton (2005).
29 Specifically, for each combination of levers, and for each scenario of cash flows and investment opportunities, the team estimates the value of the firm (1) if the investment opportunity is fully captured (with the cost of capital adjusted to reflect the impact of the investment), and (2) if the investment opportunity is not captured. The value of the firm for this scenario is the higher of the two (or the highest of many, if many investment choices are possible). The value of the firm for this combination of levers is the average value accross all scenarios.

While theoretically there could be an infinity of viable combinations, in practice only a few are worth modelling. Each lever is bounded: not all risks can be transferred, not all capital

structure are attainable nor realistic, not all portfolio composition are congruent with the firm's strategic vision.
30 See Copeland *et al* (2003), pp 579–81.
31 http://www.bis.org/publ/bcbsca.htm.
32 For example Graham and Rogers (2002) find "no evidence that firms hedge in response to tax convexity".
33 Earnings Before Interest, Taxes, Depreciation and Amortisation.
34 Operating Earnings Before Interest and Taxes.
35 In some instances, one needs to add non-operating cash flows and balance sheet translation effects to reach cash flow available to investors.

3
A Review of Risk Management Practices

As discussed in Chapter 1, the last decade has seen numerous advances in firms' risk management practices. Providing an exhaustive description of the new risk management universe lies therefore beyond the scope of this book. Instead, this chapter highlights three critical risk management topics and offers perspectives and opinions on these. Multiple books and articles are referenced throughout the chapter for readers interested in furthering their understanding of each topic.

Section 3.1 discusses *managing with volatility*. It presents briefly ERM, an integrated risk management process being progressively adopted by corporations. Section 3.2 then focuses on *measuring volatility*. It reviews the different risk metrics used by corporations, from VaR to Economic Capital. Finally, Section 3.3 discusses *managing volatility*. It reviews academic and practitioners' evidence on derivative usage, which is one highly visible element of risk management.

One common thread runs through this survey – and indeed, this book: corporate risk management practices are still work in progress, as theoretical advances are passed on to practitioners, and as practitioners' experience is used to enhance theory. This theme is briefly discussed in Section 3.4.

3.1 MANAGING WITH VOLATILITY: ENTERPRISE RISK MANAGEMENT

Over the last few years, many financial and non-financial firms have adopted an integrated risk management process generally referred to as ERM. One definition is as follows:[1]

> A process, affected by an entity's board of directors, management, and other personnel, applied in strategy setting and across the enterprise, designed to identify potential events that may affect the entity, and manage risks to be within its risk appetite, to provide reasonable assurance regarding the achievement of entity objectives.

This thoughtful definition includes the main features of ERM: (1) ERM is a comprehensive process involving all layers of the corporation ("board of directors, management, and other personnel"), (2) all risks must be measured and aggregated, ("across the enterprise"), (3) the risk management strategy is linked to the overall corporate strategy ("applied in strategy setting", "reasonable assurance regarding the achievement of entity objectives").

In practice, most firms implementing ERM set up a risk management organisation, often reporting to the CFO, sometimes to the CEO. This organisation manages a risk identification process in conjunction with the businesses, reports regularly on risks, and proposes risk management strategies to senior management and the board of directors.

ERM programs have a broad reach, and constitute a significant advance in firms' risk management practices. By identifying and aggregating all risks across the firm, they reduce (optimists would say eliminate) risk management silos that were previously found in most firms.

ERM has profound implications for a firm in terms of governance (eg, segregation of duties), organisation (eg, creation of risk measurement groups/capabilities), and processes (eg, risk monitoring). Therefore implementing a fully-fledged ERM program is a significant (and costly) undertaking.

ERM's main objective is to *systematically include risk management considerations in corporate decision-making*. For example, a recent survey[2] listed the highest priority ERM objectives as: ensure risk issues are explicitly considered in decision-making (44%), avoid surprises and "predictable failures" (40%), align risk exposures and risk mitigation programs (24%), institute more rigorous risk measurement (19%), and integrate ERM into corporate practices like strategic planning (17%).

However, few ERM programs today *clearly articulate value creation mechanisms*, in particular for non-financial firms. As mentioned in Chapter 1, this arises mostly because many ERM programs are defensive, and were initiated primarily for compliance reasons.

In the same survey, when asked how ERM creates value, firms mention a variety of reasons that fall under two categories:

(1) *Hard drivers, consistent with the "theory" presented in Chapter 2*: better-informed decisions (86%), increased management accountability (79%), ability to meet strategic goals (76%), increased profitability (59%), use risk as a competitive tool (46%), and accurate risk-adjusted pricing (41%).
(2) *Soft drivers and enablers*: greater management consensus (83%), smoother governance practices (79%), better communication to Board (69%), and reduced earnings volatility (62%).

While these are valid value-creation channels (with the possible exception of reduced earnings volatility), they are also too generic to be quantifiable, hence cannot easily be tracked. As a result, firms in the midst of an ERM implementation are not always able to prioritise initiatives and projects to deliver most value. In some instances, ERM runs the risk of being perceived as – yet another – corporate process that adds to the cost and complexity of doing business, with few clear benefits.

I anticipate that firms that have not demonstrated how their ERM initiatives create value will progressively scale them down. On the other hand, some firms will enhance their ERM program by focusing them more on value creation mechanisms. ERM programs and initiatives in such firms will be designed and prioritised according to the value-creation channels discussed in Chapter 2. The resulting, next generation ERM programs will be less costly to administer, and will deliver greater value to shareholders.

3.2 MEASURING VOLATILITY: VALUE AT RISK, CASH FLOW AT RISK, ECONOMIC CAPITAL

Over recent decades, significant technical advances have been achieved in measuring volatility. As mentioned in Chapter 1, ever growing computing power allows managers to actually measure and compute risks throughout the corporation. In parallel, "theoretical" work by finance scholars has yielded many advances in defining and estimating stochastic processes (eg, pricing complex options). Therefore, multiple volatility metrics have been developed and adopted. This section reviews the main ones.

This review adopts an historical perspective: it starts with VaR, the first volatility metric. It then moves to Cash Flow at Risk (CFaR). Finally it discusses Economic Capital, an important extension of VaR.[3]

3.2.1 Value at Risk

We first briefly summarise the history of VaR, then define it formally, then show how it is computed. Finally, we discuss some of its limitations.

A brief history of VaR
Historians of risk management are tempted to state:

> At the beginning was VaR.

VaR is – if not the first – at least the most successful attempt by risk managers to quantify the risks embedded in a portfolio of assets.

VaR can be traced to Harry Markowitz's seminal 1952 article[4] on portfolio selection where he introduces the mean-variance framework.

In the early 1980s, two American investment banks, Bankers Trust and JP Morgan, led the early development and usage of VaR to manage their trading portfolios. Bankers Trust developed its Risk Adjusted Return on Capital (RARoC) system used to formally take trading risk into account in the computation of (risk adjusted) profits and in the development of trading limits. RARoC is the profit generated by a trader divided by the capital at risk, defined as the amount of capital needed to cover 99% of the maximum expected loss over a year. As will be seen below, this is very similar to the notion of Economic Capital. A few years later, Till Guldimann, head of global research at JP Morgan in the late 1980s is credited with coining the term "VaR".[5]

In July 1993, the Group of 30,[6] a non-profit organisation assembling senior executives, regulators, and academics, seeking to deepen understanding of economic and financial issues, published a very influential report, discussing best practices for risk management. It appears to be the first publication to use the phrase "VaR".

In 1994, JP Morgan launched its free RiskMetrics service, intended to promote the use of VaR among the firm's institutional clients. The service comprised a technical document describing how to implement a VaR measure and a covariance matrix for several hundred key factors updated daily on the internet.

VaR has proven to be a highly successful intellectual innovation. It has become the standard for financial reporting of trading portfolios. It now stands as the analytical cornerstone of banking capital regulations, such as the Basel Committee on Banking Supervision International Capital Framework (more on this in the discussion of Economic Capital below). Non-financial institutions also use VaR, in particular to manage their trading operation.

VaR theory and practice have evolved over the last 20 years, as many institutions have adopted it. Presented below are practices and open issues as they are defined at the time of writing.

Definition of VaR
In the introduction of his reference textbook on VaR, Philippe Jorion[7] provides the following formal definition:

> VaR measures the worst expected loss over a given horizon under normal market conditions at a given confidence level.

A simple example helps understand the definition, and its limits. Stating that a portfolio has a US$10 million one-day VaR at the 5% confidence level is equivalent to the statement:

> Under normal market conditions, the most the portfolio can lose at the 5% confidence level over one trading day is US$10 million.

A direct implication of this statement is that there is a 5% chance that the portfolio loses at least US$10 million over the next trading day. Or if the portfolio is held for at least an entire month (22 trading days on average), we expect that one day it will lose at least US$10 million in value.

Every term in Jorion's definition matters.

The horizon – often called the holding period – is often chosen to be the orderly liquidation period, ie, the period it would take a trader to unwind the position under normal market conditions should the market move against him. Then, saying that a portfolio has a US$10 million one-day VaR at the 5% confidence level means that, under normal market conditions, the most the portfolio can lose at the 5% confidence level (while we liquidate it) is US$10 million. Many firms use one to five days as an orderly liquidation period. Everything else being equal, the longer the liquidation period, the higher the VaR. For example, the 5-day VaR for the portfolio discussed above is approximately US$22.4 million.[8]

Of course, there is no formal definition of "normal" market conditions. One practical definition: market volatility and liquidity comparable to historical averages. As we will see below, this is a critical assumption.

There is no rule to select the appropriate confidence level. Bankers Trust initially used 1%. Other firms use 5%, which corresponds to one trading day per month on average. One approach, recommended for example by Chris Marrisson,[9] is to select the confidence level corresponding to the probability of default implied by the firm's credit rating. Table 3.1 provides the 1-year historical probabilities of default per credit rating, and the corresponding number of standard deviations for the normal distribution.[10]

For example, Baa1-rated bonds have historically a 0.13% annual probability of default, hence Baa1-rated firms should estimate and report VaR at 99.87% confidence level, while A1-rated firms have a 0.05% annual probability of default, hence should estimate and report VaR at 99.95% confidence level. Again, increasing the confidence level increases the VaR significantly. For example, the 1-day VaR on our portfolio is US$18.2 million at the 99.87% confidence level, and US$21.4 million at the 99.95% confidence level.

From the above example, the VaR on the same portfolio can vary from US$10 million (1-day, 95% confidence level) to US$48 million (5-day, 99.95% confidence level) depending on the confidence level and the holding period. It is critical to define these parameters to compare VaR across companies.

Computation of VaR

Multiple approaches exist to compute VaR. We present here the simplest and most intuitive, the parametric VaR, to illustrate the approach and some key elements.

A REVIEW OF RISK MANAGEMENT PRACTICES

Table 3.1 Historical probabilities of default per credit rating

Credit rating (Moody's)	1-year historical default probability (%)	Standard deviation multiple
Aaa	0.01	3.72
Aa1	0.02	3.54
Aa2	0.02	3.54
Aa3	0.03	3.43
A1	0.05	3.29
A2	0.06	3.24
A3	0.07	3.19
Baa1	0.13	3.01
Baa2	0.16	2.95
Baa3	0.70	2.46
Ba1	1.25	2.24
Ba2	1.79	2.10
Ba3	3.96	1.76
B1	6.14	1.54
B2	8.31	1.38
B3	15.08	1.03

As of date $t = 0$, we create a portfolio composed of a single asset, a contract to sell 10,000 ton of aluminium one year from now, at price $p = \text{US\$}2{,}500/ton$. As of date t, the forward price is F_t and the value of the asset is V_t. We have:

$$V_t = 10{,}000 \cdot (2{,}500 - F_t)$$

Since the asset is fairly priced, $F_0 = p = \text{US\$}2{,}500/ton$ and the initial value of the asset, denoted V_0, is equal to zero.

Suppose that the quantitative analysis group estimates that the orderly liquidation period is one day, hence one-day VaR is computed and reported, and that F is normally distributed with mean $F_0 = \text{US\$}2{,}500/ton$ and (daily) standard deviation $\sigma_{F_0} = \text{US\$}50/ton$.

The standard deviation of the value of the asset, denoted σ_{V_0} is then:

$$\sigma_{V_0} = 10{,}000 \cdot \sigma_{F_0} = \text{US\$}500{,}000$$

We are interested in estimating and reporting VaR at the 99.9% confidence level. The table of the standard normal distribution indicates that the 0.1% worst loss corresponds to three times the standard deviation. Then:

$$VaR_{99.9\%} = US\$1.5\ million$$

A few weeks later, the market has moved, and the forward price is normally distributed with mean $F_1 = US\$3,000/ton$ and (daily) standard deviation $\sigma_{F_1} = US\$50/ton$. The value of the asset is then:

$$V_1 = 10,000 \cdot (2,500 - 3,000) = -US\$5\ million$$

The loss on the asset is much larger than the VaR. This is not inconsistent, since the actual holding period is a few weeks, much longer than the 1-day holding period assumed in computing the VaR. In fact, the value loss is consistent with the VaR if the portfolio is held for approximately five months. Additionally, the VaR indicates the expected loss at the 1% confidence level, but does not say anything about the loss beyond the 1% confidence level.

If the volatility of the forward price has not changed, and if the distribution is still assumed to be normal, the VaR is unchanged. The realised loss is incorporated in the value of the asset, and is no longer a risk.

The choice of the distribution is obviously critical. Suppose instead a Student-t distribution is used. The number of standard deviations corresponding to 0.1% worst loss is now 5.67. The VaR, denoted $\widetilde{VaR}$ is then:

$$\widetilde{VaR}_{99.9\%} = US\$2.8\ million$$

Limitations of VaR

The first practical limitation is that *VaR is not priceable*. While the meaning of VaR is easy to communicate, its economic implications are less immediately clear. Recent advances in psychology confirm significant cognitive biases in our understanding of probabilities. For example, I am not sure how many people truly understand that a loss greater or equal to the 5% VaR will happen on average once every month.

Practically, how much is a firm willing to pay for a US$5 million reduction in 0.1% daily VaR? One possible answer could be

0.1% × US$5 *million* = US$5,000 per day, or assuming 252 trading days per year, US$1.26 million per year. However, this turns out to be wrong. This limitation is addressed by introducing Economic Capital, as will be discussed below.

A second – and harder to resolve – limitation concerns the *accuracy of VaR estimation,* in particular under extreme market conditions, which is precisely when potential losses can be the most severe. Two examples illustrate that point: first, the Long Term Capital Management (LTCM) debacle in 1998, where a firm founded by Wall Street legend John Meriwether (of *Liar's Poker* fame), staffed by the best and brightest bond traders, on whose board sat two Nobel Prize recipients, almost engulfed the US banking system in its collapse.[11] LTCM's demise has multiple causes, most notably a failure of the VaR models – arguably the most sophisticated of the day – to evaluate the impact of the lack of liquidity in the Russian bond market.

A second example: during the summers of 1998 and 1999, several electric power traders in the US lost hundreds of millions of dollar, while their VaR models were predicting worst-loss between US$5 and 10 million. The causes were not only unprecedented price levels, but also a flaw in the unwinding assumption. The VaR models assumed implicitly that the positions could be unwound on the forward markets, while in fact, since electric power cannot be stored, the positions had to be unwound hour by hour on the spot markets, where prices were, for a few critical hours, 500 times higher than their historical average. Had the trading companies used the correct unwinding rule, they would have had a starker picture of the risks created by their position, and – in some instances – reduced their exposure earlier (thereby lowering volatility in the market).

Two lessons can been drawn from these failures: first, the unwinding assumptions must be carefully selected, and continuously validated. For example, power traders now often use the spot price as an unwinding mechanism (which is equivalent to using Cash Flow at Risk, see below). Second, worst case scenarios must be carefully stress-tested, as future events may lie outside of the range defined by previous events. This point is revisited in Chapter 4.

A third limitation is that VaR does not provide any indication on *losses beyond the confidence interval selected*. One can easily construct portfolios that have the same 1% worst-loss, but for which the 0.1%

worst-loss varies significantly. This means that decisions made using the 1% worst loss can potentially be misleading.

A final limitation of VaR is that it does not always capture *portfolio diversification*: one can construct portfolios for which the VaR is higher than the sum of the VaR of the parts.[12] This may sound a bit technical and esoteric, but, it can create problems in some instances.

The last three limitations to VaR are more serious than it seems. Even if these limitations have a limited range of relevance (how many times do we meet "pathological" distributions where the 0.1% worst loss is very, very different from the 1% worst-loss?), these are precisely the instances where accurate risk measurement is critical. Ex ante, the likelihood of LTCM's trades all turning against them was too small to compute, yet it did happen, and cost the firm its existence. As the discussion above illustrated, the "term worst possible loss", when used without the accompanying qualifications (eg, confidence level, normal market conditions, orderly liquidation period) is misleading, and could lead senior management teams to underestimate the true extent of risks being taken.

This does not mean that VaR should be discarded as a risk metric. For once, it is widely used, and a change would be impractical. Besides, it does convey valuable information on the risk of a (portfolio of) asset(s). The practical recommendation would be for risk management teams to alert senior managers on the limitations of VaR when reporting and using it.

3.2.2 Cash Flow at Risk

VaR measures the risk of holding a portfolio of (fairly) liquid instruments where orderly liquidation within one to five days is possible. Many corporate exposures do not fall in that category, for example: (a) a corporate portfolio of physical assets (eg, buildings and factories) and businesses requires months to sell, or (b) illiquid trading instruments such as some power forward contracts must be unwound in the spot market of the delivery hour. For these exposures, practitioners use CFaR. A formal definition could be:

> Cash Flow at Risk measures the worst expected cash flow loss over a given horizon under normal market conditions at a given confidence level.

The horizon can be the orderly liquidation period, or a given period (a quarter, a year, etc). As in the case of VaR, there is no specific guidance on the selection of the confidence level, although the default probability implied in a firm's credit rating appears like a natural choice.

CFaR is usually a little more challenging to compute than VaR. First, as illustrated in Example 3.1, CFaR requires a distribution of prices for all periods covered in the evaluation horizon. Furthermore, CFaR often applies to commodities spot prices, that often exhibit spikes caused by tight physical supply and demand conditions, and require sophisticated modelling.

Example 3.1 *Consider a simple representation of an aluminium smelter as a long position on aluminium spot price. We estimate the CFaR over one year for a smelter that produces one million tons of aluminium, and is a Baa1 company. Aluminium produced at this smelter is sold at the monthly average of the spot price, denoted p_t for months $t = 1, \ldots, 12$. We assume that the production costs are constant, denoted c. Finally, we assume that production is constant across months equal to $\frac{Q}{12}$ where Q is the annual aluminium production. Denote π the Free Cash Flows, τ the corporate tax rate, assumed constant for simplicity, and ΔI the gross investment. We have:*

$$\pi = (1 - \tau) \cdot \sum_{t=1}^{12} \frac{Q}{12} \cdot (p_t - c) - \Delta I$$

Then:

$$var(\pi) = (1 - \tau)^2 \cdot Q^2 \cdot var\left(\sum_{t=1}^{12} \frac{p_t}{12}\right)$$

$$\Leftrightarrow$$

$$\sigma_\pi = (1 - \tau) \cdot Q \cdot \sigma_{\bar{p}}$$

where $\bar{p}$ is the yearly average price. Analysis presented in Chapter 4 indicates that monthly aluminium prices are mean reverting. We therefore cannot apply a parametric VaR method, and instead must resort to Monte Carlo simulations. The yearly average aluminium price is presented in Figure 3.1. We find that:

$$E[\bar{p}] = US\$2,650 \text{ / ton} \quad \text{and} \quad \sigma_{\bar{p}} = US\$437 \text{ / ton}$$

Figure 3.1 Average annual aluminium price

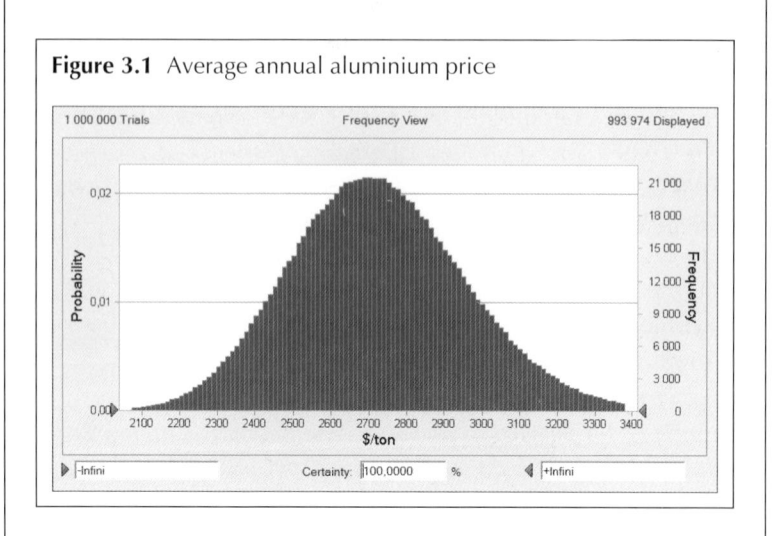

Denote $\bar{p}_{0.13}$ the 0.13% lowest yearly average price. Monte Carlo simulations show that:

$$\bar{p}_{0.13} = \text{US\$1,624 / ton}$$

then the worst possible loss per ton, at the 99.87% confidence level is:

$$E[\bar{p}] - \bar{p}_{0.13} = \text{US\$1,027 / ton}$$

We observe that

$$\frac{E[\bar{p}] - \bar{p}_{0.13}}{\sigma_{\bar{p}}} = 2.35 < 3.01$$

The distribution of yearly average price has "slimmer" left tail than the normal distribution. Then, assuming $\tau = 40\%$ and $Q = 1$ million tons, we have:

$$CFaR = \text{US\$616 million}$$

Due to the tremendous increase in computing power and stochastic modelling over the last few years, it is now possible to compute CFaR for most companies on a laptop. Consequently, the measure has grown more popular. A few industrial firms, for example mining giant BHP-Billiton and chemical leader Dupont, report externally on their computation of CFaR. Professional services firms have developed and are marketing CFaR models. For example National Economics Research Associates (NERA), an economic and management consulting firm, reports having applied this model to various industries, from computer manufacturers to electric power utilities.[13]

CFaR is a very helpful metric. First, it provides a band in which cash flows (or earnings) are likely to fall. Second, the process to estimate CFaR is in itself extremely valuable for firms, as it generates a fact-based discussion of risks. Finally, CFaR is a prerequisite of any corporate risk management strategy discussion and decision-making.

However, CFaR suffers from the same limitations as VaR: cash flow volatility is not directly priceable, and worst case scenarios need to be stress-tested.

3.2.3 Economic Capital

Economic Capital[14] is a powerful extension of the VaR and CFaR concepts, extensively used by financial firms.[15] Various definitions have been proposed. For example, Chris Marrison defines Economic Capital as:

> the net value the firm must have at the beginning of the year to ensure that there is only a small probability of default within that year. *The net value* is the value of assets minus liabilities. The *small probability* is the probability that corresponds to the bank's target credit rating.

Economic Capital estimation incorporates all types of risk: price, operations, counterparty and business.

The simplest example is that of a trading firm. Suppose that the firm is rated A1. Its debt holders therefore expect a 0.05% probability of default. Suppose that the trading portfolio has a US$10 million one-day, 99.95% VaR, ie, that there is a 0.05% chance that the worst loss during a day exceeds US$10 million. As seen in Appendix 1.A, under certain – strong – assumptions, the 0.05% cumulative annual worst loss can be inferred from the daily worst loss by applying the "square root of time" rule, ie, by multiplying the daily loss by the square root of the numbers of trading days. Since there are about 252 trading days per year, and $\sqrt{252} = 15.875$, the 0.05% annual worst loss – hence the cash reserve the trading firm should hold – is about US$160 million.[16] If the trading firm aspires to a double-A1 credit rating, it needs to increase its cash reserve to US$170 million to meet its obligations 99.98% of the time.

Economic Capital is consistent with the practice of issuing margin calls, common in the trading business: if a trading party holds a negatively valued position, ie, owes (future) money to its counterparty, the latter is entitled to ask for (part or totality of) the value to be posted as collateral.

Economic Capital is a measure of net assets. It often translates into equity (on the liabilities side of the balance sheet) required to purchase risk-free assets.

Economic Capital transforms VaR into a price-able quantity, hence it allows firms to evaluate the gains from volatility reduction: in our example above, reducing daily VaR by US$5 million reduces the cash reserve requirement by US$80 million. If the firm pays on average 8% on its capital, this reduction is worth US$6.4 million a year.

Economic Capital is an extremely useful concept: it combines the volatility of the assets and the firm's financial structure, it is reasonably simple to compute (subject to stress-testing as discussed before), and it has an intuitive and clear interpretation. For these reasons, its usage among financial firms has grown steadily over the last decade, in particular for capital allocation and performance management. In addition, Economic Capital is the framework used by the Basel Committee on Banking Supervision to set regulatory capital for financial institutions (ie, the minimum capital required).

3.3 MANAGING VOLATILITY: HEDGING AND DERIVATIVES

As mentioned in the introduction, managers and investors are increasingly aware of the importance of risk management. As a result, volatility management through the use of derivatives has grown substantially over the last 20 years.[17] Today, most large multinational corporations are engaged in some form of volatility management through derivatives, most likely interest rates and foreign exchange rates swaps (92% according to a survey by the International Swap Dealers Association (ISDA)). Other derivatives commonly used include commodities futures and forward. As one of the academic surveys reviewed in this section observes, this is a significant change compared with the 1980s, where derivatives were considered dangerous instruments in most boardrooms.

This dramatic increase in hedging activity raises two questions: (1) why do firms use hedge? Or equivalently, which firms hedge more? and (2) does hedging create value for these firms?

A series of academic surveys[18] published in the late 1990s and early 2000s has attempted to answer these questions. As discussed in Section 3.3.1, they found that actual derivative usage is broadly consistent with the financial flexibility argument presented in Chapter 2, namely that firms with higher growth expectations and tighter financial constraints hedge more. However, the evidence on value creation, reviewed in Section 3.3.2, is mixed, which suggests additional research is needed.

3.3.1 Which firms hedge using derivatives?

Consistent with the financial flexibility argument presented in Chapter 2, firms appear to *use hedging to protect their financial flexibility when financially constrained*.

For example, Christopher Geczy and his colleagues[19] examine the use of currency derivatives for 372 of the Fortune 500 US non-financial firms in 1990, and find that:

> "firms with greater growth opportunities and tighter financial constraints are more likely to use currency derivatives. This result suggests that firms might use derivatives to reduce cash flow variation that might otherwise preclude them from investing in valuable growth opportunities."

In particular, Geczy *et al* found that firms with higher R&D expenditures were more likely to use currency derivatives, and that higher financial liquidity implies a significantly lower probability of using financial instruments.

A similar conclusion is reached by David Haushalter,[20] who examines the risk management activities of 100 oil and gas producers from 1992 to 1994, and finds that:

> "the fraction of the production hedged is positively related to the differences in financial leverage, measured as the ratio of total debt to total assets."

Additionally, the surveys find *economies of scale in hedging*. Haushalter provides a particularly illuminating summary:

> "I also conduct tests in which the determinants of a company's decision to hedge are estimated separately from the determinants of the extent of hedging by companies that do hedge. These tests find substantial differences between the determinants of these decisions. The likelihood of hedging is greater for firms with more total assets... In contrast, among oil and gas producers that hedge, the extent of hedging is related to proxies for financing costs".

Geczy *et al* also find evidence of economies of scale:

> "larger firms and firms that use other types of derivatives instruments, including interest-rate based and commodity-based derivatives, are more likely to use currency derivatives instruments."

This finding is somehow inconsistent with theoretical predictions: one expects smaller firms to have a less robust capital structure, hence to place greater value on volatility reduction as a risk management tool. However, there are practical reasons why smaller firms may hedge less. As will be discussed below, hedging is a costly activity. Larger firms, or firms with higher exposures are more likely to invest in setting up a hedging group than others. Furthermore, derivatives traders (eg, investment banks) are more likely to call on larger firms to convince them of the virtues of hedging.

Finally, in a fascinating study, Peter Tufano[21] shows that the structure of managerial compensation is also a driver of hedging decisions. Tufano examines hedging decisions by gold mining firms. He starts from an intriguing observation: while all gold producers face the same risk (a fall in gold price), and hedging in the forward market is readily available to all of them, significant differences in hedging strategies can be observed. He finds that variables that proxy for financial distress have no explanatory power in explaining the differences in hedging strategies. On the other hand, he finds that firms whose management holds more *stock* engage in more risk management, but firms whose managers hold more *stock options* manage less risk.

These findings are consistent with the hypothesis that hedging decisions are made to suit managers' and not shareholders' interests. Since managers are risk-averse as individuals, when a significant share of their personal wealth is tied in a firm's stock, their personal preference is for lower volatility.[22] On the other hand, since the value of stock-options increases with the volatility of the underlying cash flows, holders of stock options prefer higher volatility.

3.3.2 Hedging and value creation

How much value is created by hedging programs?

A few surveys suggest that *the use of currency derivatives increases the firm's value*. For example, the cross-sectional survey by George Allayannis and James Weston[23] which is probably the most widely quoted, considers a sample of 720 large US non-financial firms between 1990 and 1995, and finds that firms that use currency derivatives have a higher market valuation relative to the book value of their assets[24] than firms that do not hedge. Specifically, the hedging premium is estimated to be on average 5.7% of a firm's value creation.

Subsequent academic studies[25] found that the use of currency derivatives is associated with higher firm value for industrial firms. Graham and Rogers[26] document a positive relation between derivative usage and debt capacity in a broad sample of firms, and argue that derivatives-induced debt capacity increases firm value by 1.1% on average.

Academic surveys findings on the impact of *commodity hedging* are mixed: Carter and his colleagues[27] examine 26 airlines between 1994 and 2000, and find a positive relation between the use of fuel price derivatives and firm's value. On the other hand, Y. Jin and Phillipe Jorion[28] examine 119 US oil and gas producers over 1995–2001 and find hedging is not related to firm's values.

How is value not created?

That currency hedging significantly increases firm's value has puzzled academics and practitioners, who question how often the cash flow volatility reduction enabled by currency hedging is sufficient to (a) truly increase financial flexibility, or (b) decrease the cost of capital (ie, justify an increase in leverage at constant debt rating).

As discussed in Chapter 2, academics and practitioners agree that lower volatility increases the firm's ability to pursue investment opportunities, and to a certain extent also reduces the cost of capital. All also agree that in some cases, hedging does have an impact on cash flow volatility. For example, hedging the interest rate exposure can significantly reduce cash flow volatility for a commercial bank. The question is whether currency hedging programs have a sufficient impact to alter the cash flow volatility of non-financial firms.

The incremental volatility reduction from currency hedging programs is unclear, for two reasons: (1) global firms have a diversified portfolio of currency exposures, so while the volatility created by one particular exposure may be large, it is often diversified away in the portfolio, and (2) currency-driven volatility is often much smaller than volatility driven by core business: the price of crude oil or the market penetration of its new generation of cell phones are much more important profitability and volatility drivers than exchange rates fluctuations respectively for oil companies and Motorola. In some instances hedging currencies may in fact increase cash flow volatility. Many commodity companies, that incur costs in currencies that are positively correlated with commodity prices (eg, AUD, CAD, ZAR) constitute a clear example. For this reason, many large metals and mining companies (such as Anglo-American, and BHP-Billiton) have no currency hedging program.

Pursuing that line of questioning, Wayne Guay and S. Kothari[29] set out to estimate the magnitude the incremental cash flows from a firm's derivative portfolio under very severe market conditions. They found that, even if one considers perfectly correlated three sigma adverse movements in exchange rates and interest rates, the median cash flow impact is only US$15 million, or 10% of the three-year average Cash Flow from Operation, and 9% of the three-year average investing cash flow. They also estimate that, even under this extreme shock, the median change in value of the portfolio of derivatives is US$31 million, around 1% of the market value of equity. Clearly, the impact on cash flows and value is too small to account for the incremental value observed by Allayannis and Weston. Similarly, a detailed case study of a large multinational company (named HDG to protect its confidentiality) conducted by Gregory Brown[30] reaches the conclusion that hedging reduces the year-over-year standard deviation of HDG's cash flows by only 13%.

In addition, contrary to what is portrayed in some textbooks, running a hedging program is extremely costly. The hedging team must identify and gather the exposure to be hedged (otherwise the hedging program could increase volatility instead of reducing it). The hedging team executes the transactions with banks and/or brokers, which creates direct transaction fees. These derivatives must be entered into a "trading system", that needs to be operated, maintained and regularly upgraded. Another team, independent from the first one, must control execution, and evaluate and report to senior management derivatives position, Mark-to-Market and VaR. Proper accounting entries must be generated and reconciled, which has become extremely onerous since the implementation of a new accounting standard known as FAS 133. This activity will be audited, probably once a year. Finally, for US traded companies, this process must be documented to comply with the requirements of the Sarbanes–Oxley Act. Brown provides an estimate of US$3.8 million for HDG in the spring of 1998. I believe that, in today's more demanding accounting and compliance environment, these costs can raise up to US$10 million per year for a large multinational company, excluding any options premium.[31]

This suggests that currency hedging appears to have too small an average positive impact to enhance financial flexibility to the point of explaining 6% of incremental value created.

Similarly, the volatility reduction from interest rate swaps, entered into by 92% of firms according to a survey by the ISDA, is unclear. It has been observed that interest rates are positively correlated to commodity prices, which are positively correlated to profits for commodity companies. Hedging interest rates could therefore increase cash flow volatility for these firms.

How is value created then?
How does one reconcile the value creation from hedging measured by Allayannis and Weston and the magnitude measured by Guay and Kothari?

I believe two effects are simultaneously present: first, I suspect there is a wide dispersion of returns on hedging programs, yielding the 5.7% average premium estimated by Allayannis and Weston: "well-designed" hedging programs for firms with real liquidity constraints create significant value, while other, "poorly designed" programs for firms with ample liquidity simply reduce volatility and create no or negative value. This is confirmed by the wide variation measured by Guay and Kothari: while the median cash flow sensitivity to the extreme price movement is only US$15 million, the average sensitivity is US$108 million, driven by a few large companies (the maximum sensitivity is US$3,239, which suggests a US$1 billion impact for a one-sigma event), and the standard deviation of the sensitivities is US$295 million, clearly indicating a large variation. This is also confirmed by the model presented in Chapter 6, where the incremental value from hedging ranges from 1% to 18% depending on the firm's circumstances.

Second, to the chagrin of finance theorists, firms appear to get rewarded by investors for earnings stability, ie, firms that "take the noise out" and "meet their numbers" through a hedging program are sometimes perceived as more tightly managed, hence could receive a valuation premium. Earnings stability is certainly the driver of numerous hedging programs I have been exposed to. Similarly, Brown reports it was the main driver behind HDG's.

We enter here the debate between positive and normative sciences: what companies and investors do versus what they ought to do. Corporate finance argues that free cash flows (or EP) and not earnings drive value. Furthermore, volatility reduction alone should not create value, as discussed in the Appendix 2.A. In fact, since equity holders hold a call on the value of the firm, higher volatility increases the value of equity. Therefore, why should reducing earnings volatility increase the value of firms to investors? I do not have a satisfactory answer here. The fact is, firms get rewarded for "meeting their numbers". A quarterly earnings call with analysts and investors that starts with "we met our numbers, this is how we did it, and this is how are going to continue doing it" is obviously easier than one that starts with "we missed our target, but really it is not our fault, it is driven by exchange rate fluctuations". I believe shedding light on this issue should prove a fertile avenue for further research.

Finally, academics have questioned whether the association reported in Allayannis and Weston and others arises from causality (hedging increases the value of the firm) or correlation (better managed firms have higher value, and also use derivatives). Allayannis and Weston argue that their statistical approach allows them to separate both effects, hence to correctly measure the incremental impact of hedging on firm value. I tend to agree with them, hence do not retain that as a potential explanation.

3.4 WHAT COMES NEXT?

One common thread runs through this survey – and indeed, this book: risk management practices are still work in progress. Over the last decade, tremendous activity has taken place, as many corporations have established the infrastructure, either ERM process and/or hedging programs. Next will come focusing on truly value-creating risk management activities. The shift will probably take 10 to 15 years, as best practices are disseminated, and knowledge circulates between researchers and practitioners through research projects, training programs, books, seminars, etc.

One comparison comes to mind: the adoption of the NPV rule as a management tool. It took almost one hundred years for the DCFs rule to be widely adopted as the analytical framework of business decision making.[32] It can be traced back to Arthur Mellen Wellington, a railway engineer, who applied the present value concept to validate railways investments in 1887. In the 1920s, AT&T used the present value rule to systematically analyse all capital budgeting decisions. However, it was not before the 1950s that other industries, in particular oil and chemical firms, used the present value rule to appraise their own capital expenditure decisions. In 1988, only 65% of Fortune 500 companies reported using the DCF rule routinely for business decision-making. Hopefully, the adoption time for risk management will be shorter.

This survey has also highlighted avenues for further research, in particular concerning the effectiveness of risk management programs. This analysis will likely involve academics and practioners, and detailed case studies of specific companies' risk management activities.

---

1 This definition is provided by the Committee of Sponsoring Organisations (COSO) in their 2004 report (COSO (2004)), which also offers a clear introduction to Enterprise Risk Management.
2 Slywotzky and Drzik (2005).
3 This section borrows heavily from Jorion (2001) and Marrison (2002). Jorion (2001) provides an extensive treatment of VaR, covering VaR estimation and usage, and applying VaR to numerous well publicised trading failures. Marrison (2002) offers a more synthetic treatment of VaR, with a good discussion of the different types of risk and their estimation approach.
4 Markowitz (1952).

5 Both Bankers Trust and J.P. were later purchased by other financial institutions.
  Interestingly, trading scandals hastened the demise of Bankers Trust: in 1994, the bank suffered significant reputational damage when major corporate clients suffered heavy losses on complex derivative products sold by the bank. Two of these – Gibson Greetings and Procter & Gamble (P&G) – successfully sued Bankers Trust, asserting that they had not been informed of or [in the latter case] had been unable to understand the risks involved. The bank's row with P&G made the front page of major US magazines. This was worsened when several Bankers Trust bankers were caught on tape remarking that their client [Gibson Greetings] would not be able to understand what they were doing. Additionally, the bank suffered major losses in the summer of 1998, as Russia defaulted on its debt. A few weeks later, in November 1998, Deutsche Bank agreed to purchase Bankers Trust for US$9.8 billion.
6 The Group of 30 has been influential in several domains. See http://www.group30.org/home.php or http://en.wikipedia.org/wiki/Group_of_Thirty.
7 Jorion (2001), p. xxii.
8 Applying the "square root of time" rule discussed in Appendix 1.A, ie, assuming that the portfolio returns are independently and normally distributed.
9 Marrisson (2002).
10 Source: Jorion (2001), p. 386.
11 *When Genius Failed*, by Roger Lowenstein provides a fascinating account of the Long-Term Capital Management debacle (Lowestein, 2000). The rise of John Meriwether on Wall Street and of Salomon Brothers as a bond trading house is told by Roger Lewis in *Liar's Poker* (Lewis, 1989).
12 Dowd and Blake (2006) provide a very thoughtful, although quite technical, discussion of various risk metrics, that includes the limitations of VaR.
13 LaGattuta *et al* (2000).
14 Economic Capital is called "risk capital" by some authors. Since another definition of risk capital is introduced in Chapter 5, "Economic Capital" is used in this section.
15 For example see Marrison, 2002 and Dev, 2004.
16 In fact, since the reserves earn interest, the cash reserve should be slightly lower.
17 For-profit derivatives trading has also dramatically increased, however this is not discussed in this section.
18 See Smithson and Simkins (2005) for a survey of surveys.
19 Geczy *et al.* (1997).
20 Haushalter (2000).
21 Tufano (1996).
22 As reviewed in Appendix 2.A, the argument does not hold for diversified investors.
23 Allayannis and Weston (2001).
24 A metric known as the Tobin's Q.
25 Bartram *et al* (2006), Nain (2004), Kim *et al* (2005) and Allayannis *et al* (2004)
26 Graham and Rogers (2002).
27 Carter *et al.* (2004).
28 Jin and Jorian (2006).
29 Guay and Kothari (2003). From an epistemologic perspective, it is interesting to observe that both Guay and Kothari are professors of accounting and not finance.
30 Brown (2001).
31 Theoretically, options premia are not a cost, since, if the option is fairly priced, the premium is exactly equal to the expected payoff. In practice, however, management teams view option premia as a cost (or an investment), and often agree on an "options budget".
32 I am grateful to Eric Lamarre, who recounted that story to me.

Part 2

The "How" of Risk Management

4
Enterprise Risk Analysis

A robust distribution of cash flows is required to develop a risk management strategy. This is the objective of enterprise risk analysis. The challenge for the analyst is to combine rigourous mathematical modelling with thorough understanding of business conditions and processes.

This chapter presents a two-step approach to identifying and quantifying risks to a firm (or a project), hence developing a cash flow distribution. In the process, it introduces and discusses key concepts in risk analysis.

In the first step, the risk analyst proposes a distribution of future cash flows based on past variations in cash flows. This is the outside-in approach, described in Section 4.1. It constitutes only a first step, that provides an indication of the magnitude of the risks to cash flows of a firm (eg, cash flow volatility as a percentage of average). It also indicates whether there is a skew in the cash flow distribution (eg, negative surprises have greater impact than positive surprises), or whether there is a temporal pattern in the cash flows (eg, mean reversion).

In the second step, the risk analyst disaggregates then re-aggregates the risks to estimate a distribution of future cash flows. Specifically, she: (1) identifies the main risks to cash flows, (2) evaluates their individual volatility, and (3) combines them to evaluate the aggregate volatility of the firm (or project) cash flows. This is the inside out approach, described in Section 4.2. Inside-out risk analysis is required to truly understand the risks to the company, and to develop an effective risk management strategy.

The risk analysis can be used to examine dynamic issues, such as the distributions of cash flows over time, or the distribution of value of the firm. These are briefly illustrated in Section 4.3.

Finally, the specificities of enterprise risk analysis compared with the well-developed financial markets risk analysis are discussed in the concluding Section 4.4.

All the notions discussed are illustrated through numerous short examples. We also introduce two "long" examples. For the outside analysis, we examine Overseas Shipholding Group (OSG), a leading bulk shipping company, chosen by a group of students as a case study for the risk management class I teach at the University of Toulouse. For the inside-out analysis, we examine an aluminium smelter. While this aluminium smelter is located in Canada it does not represent the economics of any (or the average of) Alcan's smelters in Canada. I use publicly available data for the aluminium price, the operating costs and investment cost. I use the smelter as an example because it has proven a very effective pedagogical tool.

Consistent with this book's overall objective, this chapter focuses on the approach, and does not discuss the details of the "technical" aspects of the mathematical models introduced here, nor of their estimation. The interested reader can find multiple excellent text books. Marrison (2002) is a good introductory text on the techniques of risk measurement: while it has some mathematics, it remains fairly accessible. Hull (2003) is probably the "reference of derivatives": it strikes a good balance between technical rigour and accessibility, and is very helpful for price-risk measurement. Saunders and Allen (2002) provides a rich discussion of credit risk measurement models. All of these texts have a "financial markets" flavour hence are probably more directly applicable to financial than non-financial institutions. I am not aware of a comprehensive technical text on enterprise risk measurement, that describes the appropriate stochastic models to use, and their mathematical properties.

4.1 OUTSIDE-IN RISK ANALYSIS
4.1.1 Overall approach

In the outside-in approach, the risk analyst estimates the distribution that best fits the historical data, and then extrapolates historical behaviour to future periods, ie, assumes that the future cash flows follow the distribution she has estimated. In this introductory section, we discuss three critical methodological issues: the invariance of distribution hypothesis, the selection of an appropriate volatility metric, and the impact of growth on observed volatility.

First, some notation. For $t \geq 1$, we define period t as running between dates $(t-1)$ and t. The date of last available data is denoted t_0: $t \leq t_0$ is the past, where historical data are used for estimation, and $t > t_0$ is the future, where data are projected. In practice, one can obtain quarterly data for most publicly traded firms (certainly for firms that are traded in the US, hence have to file quarterly with the Security and Exchange Commission). With around ten years of data, that gives around 40 observations, which is sufficient to run statistically robust estimations.

Invariance of distribution
The key assumption underpinning the approach is the *invariance of distribution*. This does not mean that past performance is a predictor of future performance. In fact, some statistical models discussed below explicitly contradict that notion, that rely on reversion to the mean. In these models, high financial performance today *implies* lower performance tomorrow. Rather, invariance of distribution means that the shape and key parameters of future distributions can be inferred from past data. As will be discussed in Section 4.4, there are limitations to that approach, as the future may be distinct from the past. The risk analyst must therefore complement the statistical analysis with a strategic, scenario-based analysis as part of the inside-out analysis. What discontinuities could possibly occur? What is their likelihood? What would be their impact?

Appropriate volatility metric
We denote π_t the Operating Cash Flow (OCF) at date t, both expressed in million US$. OCF is computed as EBITDA (Sales − Cost of Good Sold (COGS) − Selling, General and Administrative expenses (SGA)) − changes in Operating Working Capital (OWC) − cash income taxes paid. Cash taxes paid are included in OCF, since firms must pay their income taxes before considering any other use.

I believe OCF is the appropriate metric for risk analysis, as it measures the cash available for investment, interest and dividend payment, or debt repayment. Earnings and other accounting metrics are not appropriate, as they rely on accounting treatment. FCF is not appropriate, as it comes post-investment, hence already includes the firm's investment choice.

The main weakness of OCF is it incorporates the impact of capital structure and tax history (eg, tax loss carry forward) through the cash taxes paid: two firms with the same EBITDA and changes in OWC will have different OCFs depending on their capital structure and tax history. NOPLAT could be an alternative metric, as it corrects for the capital structure and other effects in computing taxes. On balance, I prefer using OCF as it truly represents the cash available to a firm.

Impact of growth on observed volatility
OCF changes over times for two reasons: the intrinsic profitability of the firm changes, and its perimeter changes. Consider for example two firms with constant OCF per unit of invested capital, equal to 10%. Over the ten-period of study, firm A has no growth, while firm B grows at 10% per year. Firm A has constant OCF, hence no dispersion, while firm B's OCF has a standard deviation of 29% of the average OCF. The dispersion measures the growth, not the variability in performance. This effect is also illustrated on the Air Liquide example below. For risk analysis, it is essential to disentangle both effects.

The natural question is then: what is the appropriate metric for the size of the firm? Is it sales? Is it number of employees? Is it asset base? For most firms, invested capital constitutes a good proxy for size. Therefore, we also introduce $\rho_t = \pi_t / I_{t-1}$ the cash profitability during period t expressed as a percentage of invested capital (denoted I_t). However, in some instances, alternative metrics should be used. For example, professional services firms have traditionally small invested capital. A better metric there would probably be OCF per employee.

> **Example 4.1** *Consider the case of Air Liquide, a French gas converter: Air Liquide produces and sells oxygen, nitrogen, and hydrogen. Figure 4.1 displays Air Liquide's EBIT from 1996 to 2006. The standard deviation of EBIT is €309 million, 27% of the average EBIT over the period. That would suggest very high volatility.*

Figure 4.1 Air liquide historical EBIT

Figure 4.2 Air liquide historical ROCE

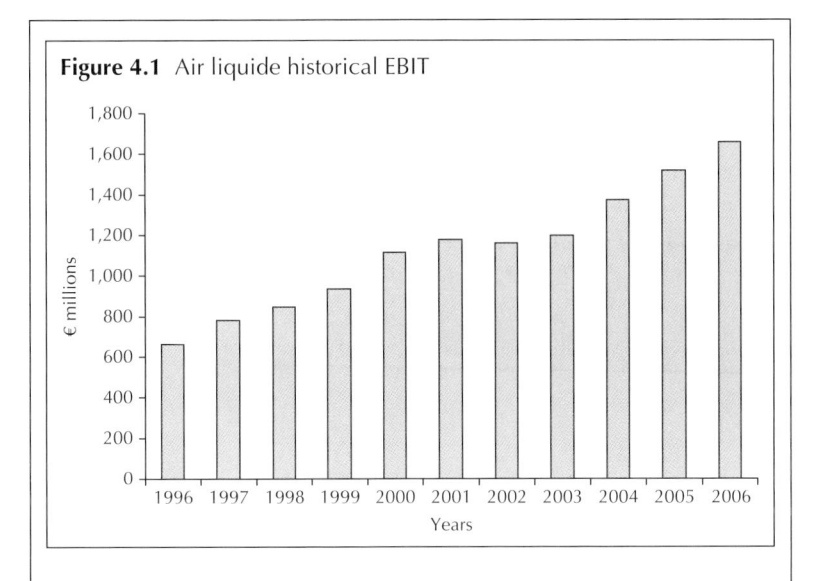

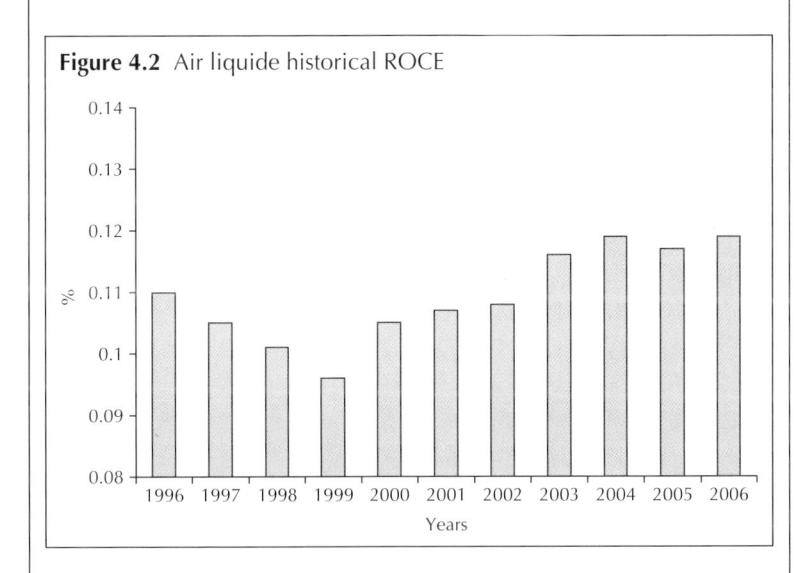

Consider now Air Liquide's ROCE, displayed in Figure 4.2. The standard deviation is now 0.8%, only 7% of the average ROCE. This is much more in line with the volatility of the Air Liquide's business model. The normalisation controls for Air Liquide's significant growth through the period, and focusses on the volatility of the underlying profitability.

CORPORATE RISK MANAGEMENT FOR VALUE CREATION

To estimate the distribution of OCF, the analyst must (1) estimate a distribution for cash profitability ρ_t, (2) estimate a distribution for invested capital I_t, and (3) simulate both variables jointly. We examine each task in turn. We first discuss two possible specifications for cash profitability, then propose one specification for invested capital. Of course, the analyst has to determine the most appropriate distribution for the firm(s) she is studying.

4.1.2 Constant volatility profitability

The first specification assumes realised profitability is equal to a constant plus a random term with constant volatility. Mathematically:

$$\rho_t = \rho + \eta_t$$

where ρ is constant, and the random terms η_t are independently and identically distributed with mean 0 and variance σ_ρ.

The parameters ρ, σ_ρ and the distribution of the random terms η_t are estimated from historical financial data. First, the risk analyst plots ρ_t for $t \leq t_0$ as a time-series, and validates the constant profitability assumption, by visual inspection, or – data permitting – statistical testing. Then, the analyst estimates the mean ρ and the standard deviation σ_ρ of the profitability. She then determines the statistical distribution that best fits the observed volatility.

Example 4.2 Overseas Shipholding Group[1] (OSG) profitability. OSG is a US-based global bulk shipping company, with about US$1 billion turnover. It is primarily engaged in the ocean transportation of crude oil and petroleum products, and owns over a 100 vessels (as of 31 December 2006). Quarterly profitability (EBITDA over Invested Capital) from March 1996 to December 2006 is represented on Figure 4.3. OSG's quarterly profitability can be best approximated by a maximum extreme value distribution[2], with expectation $E[\rho] = 4.80\%$ and standard deviation $\sigma_\rho = 2.91\%$. The distribution is presented in Figure 4.4.

Figure 4.3 OSG historical profitability

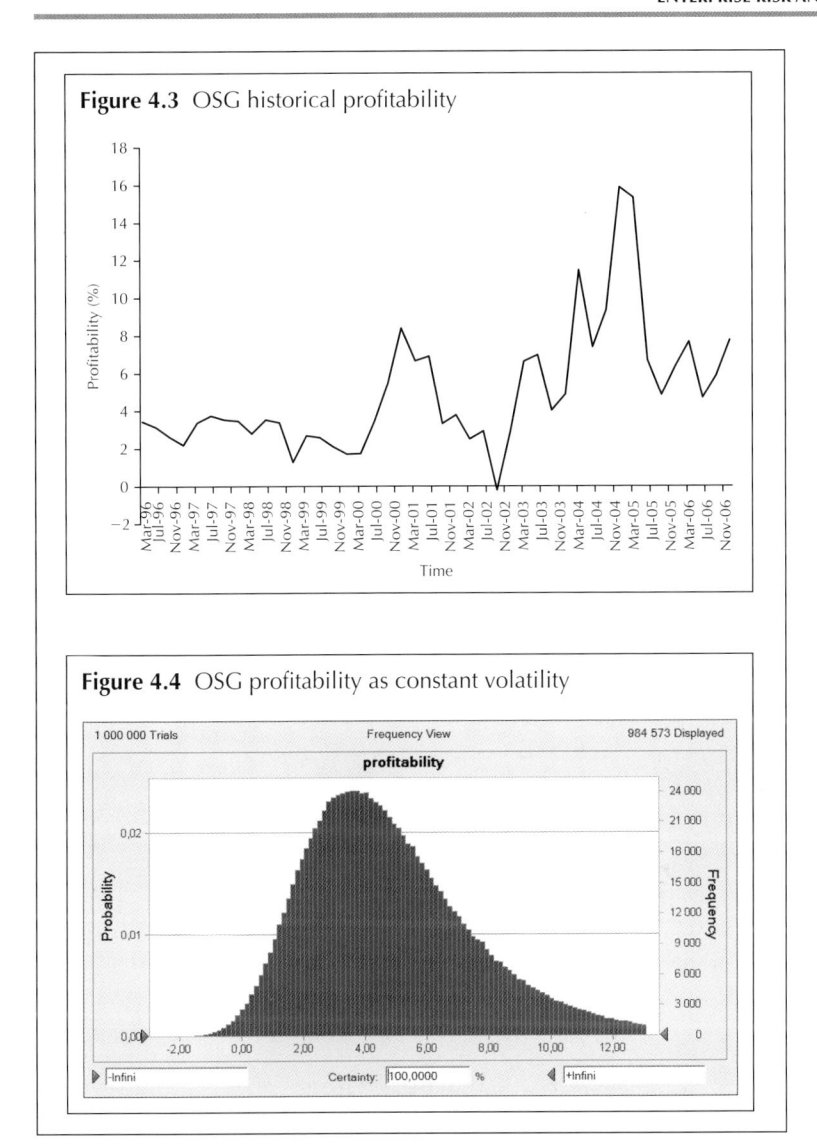

Figure 4.4 OSG profitability as constant volatility

4.1.3 Mean reverting profitability

Alternatively, we could assume that profitability is mean reverting over time, to capture the cyclicality of profits present in many industries.

Rationale for mean-reversion

Firms in commodity/natural resources industries (eg, metal, oil, pulp and paper, and recently electric power), display cyclical profitability:

Figure 4.5 Aluminium price from 1986 to 2005

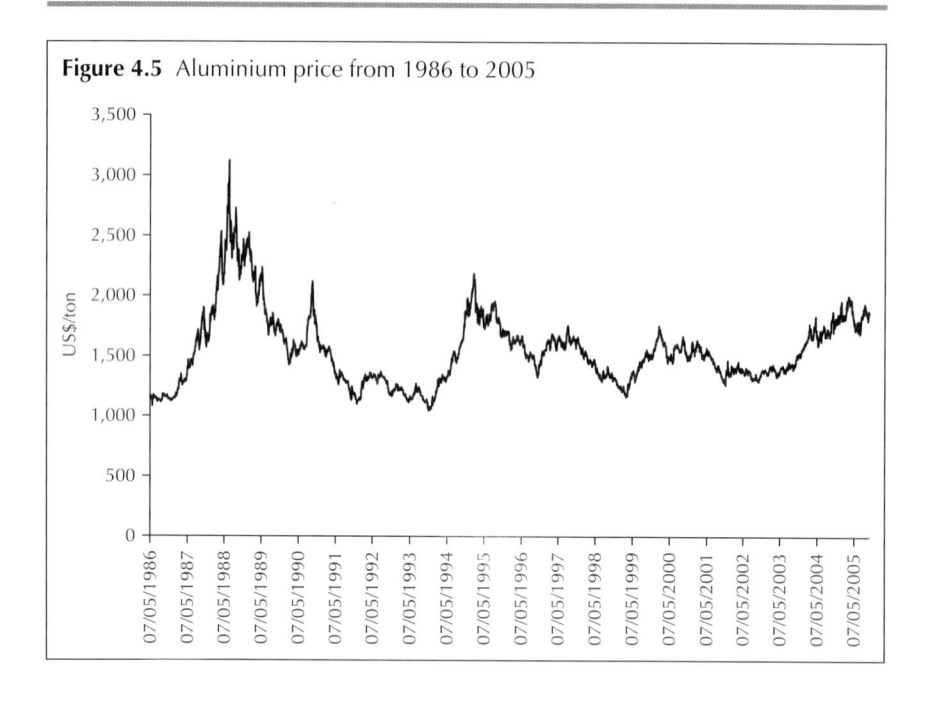

they are usually long the price of their underlying commodity, which is itself cyclical, as evidenced in Figure 4.5, which displays the daily aluminium price, as quoted on the London Metal Exchange, over a 20-year period ranging from May 1986 to September 2005.

This effect, well documented by academics and practitioners,[3] is due to the mismatch between lumpy capacity addition and continuously growing demand. As demand grows while capacity remains roughly constant, commodity prices increase. This leads to high OCFs for most incumbent firms, and at some point, lumpy capacity addition, which puts downward pressure on prices. Less efficient units then get pushed out, and capacity is reduced. As demands continues to grow, prices go up again, and the cycle resumes. This inability to coordinate capacity addition is the familiar curse of commodity companies.

Many firms in non-commodity sectors (eg, airlines industry, hotels, auto manufacturing) also follow "build-to-bust" cycles. These industries are notorious for alternating over- and under-capacity periods.

I believe mean reversion applies to all firms. As a firm innovates, it secures high profitability through its first-mover advantage. However, high profitability can be short-lived: a new technology can be developed, suppliers and/or stakeholders can claim a higher share of the value, competitors and imitators can enter to capture that same opportunity, or the former innovator might become too large and lose its edge. The first mover's profitability then reverts to the industry's average (ie, the zero economic profit in equilibrium condition). Economic mean reversion is a consequence of Shumpeterian creative destruction.

Anecdotal evidence is ubiquitous: the rise of Airbus against Boeing in the 1990s, followed by a reversal of fortunes in the 2000s, culminating with the delays launching the A380; the rise of Dell's historic founder Computers in the 1990s to become the world largest and most profitable computer-maker, leveraging its innovative direct-sales business model, followed by serious challenges from 2004 onwards, leading to HP-Compaq becoming the largest computer-maker in 2006, and the return of Dell's historic founder in February 2007.[4]

To develop statistical evidence on creative destruction, Dick Foster and Sarah Kaplan[5] have studied the historical (1962–1998) financial performance of more than 1,000 large US companies. As illustrated in Figure 4.6, reproduced from their analysis they find the decreases profitability of new entrants over time, as their first-mover advantage erodes. Furthermore, they report significant attrition: more than 80% of the companies in the sample in 1962 did not exist by 1998.

Of course, mean reversion is not mechanistic: first-mover advantages can sometimes be long-lasting (eg, Microsoft's dominant position in computers' operating systems), and growth often enables the firm to capture economies of scale. However, I believe that mean reversion sets in at some point for all firms.

In a broader context, the rise and fall of all great civilisations can be seen as an illustration of mean reversion: the ancient Egyptian empire, Athens, the Roman Empire, etc all rose to become powerful institutions before falling into (quasi) oblivion. Interestingly enough, in his classical essay, "The Rise and Fall of Great Powers", the historian Paul Kennedy[6] argues that competition among emerging nation states at the beginning of the sixteenth century provided the impetus that led Europeans to

CORPORATE RISK MANAGEMENT FOR VALUE CREATION

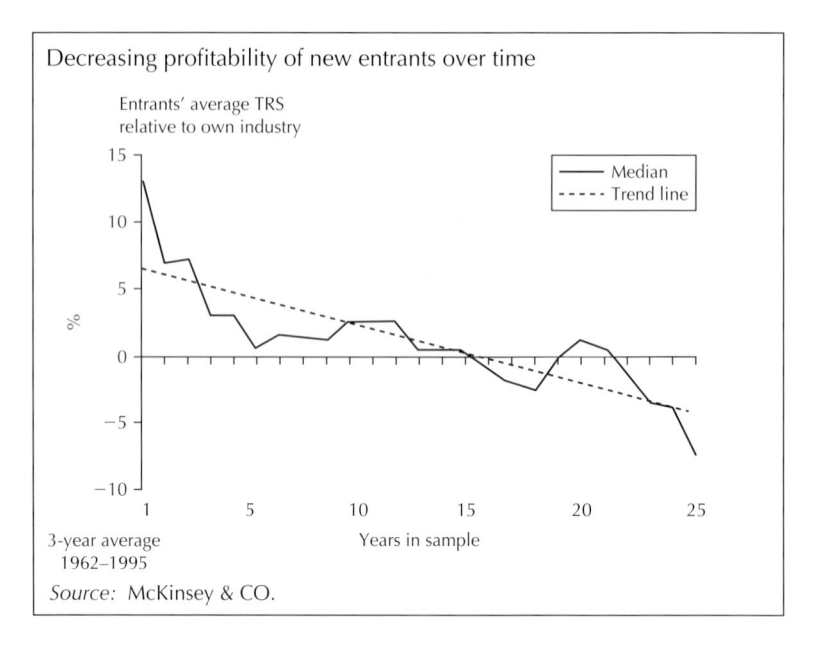

> **Decreasing profitability of new entrants over time**
>
> Entrants' average TRS relative to own industry
>
> [Chart showing median and trend line decreasing from ~15% to ~-5% over years 1 to 25]
>
> 3-year average 1962–1995
> Years in sample
>
> *Source:* McKinsey & CO.

dominate the world until the beginning of the twentieth century, while the strong Turkish and Chinese empires, facing less competition, retreated. The argument is a form of creative destruction: local powers that were more pressed at home invested in new technologies that gave them an advantage, while established powers did not.

The implications for risk analysis are clear: it should include the possibility of reverting to (industry) average profitability, as illustrated in the example of Total, an oil company, below.

> **Example 4.3** *Oil companies provide a "perfect" example of cyclical profitability. Consider the case of Total, a global oil company, that has seen its profitability increase constantly over the last ten years, as illustrated in Figure 4.6. A cursory analysis could conclude that Total is on an increasing profitability path, with random variations around the average growth rate. While many factors, such as improved productivity, may account for that improvement, the surge in oil prices over the last ten years largely explain the increased profitability, as illustrated in Figure 4.7. The risk to Total is therefore not random variations*

Figure 4.6 Total historical ROIC

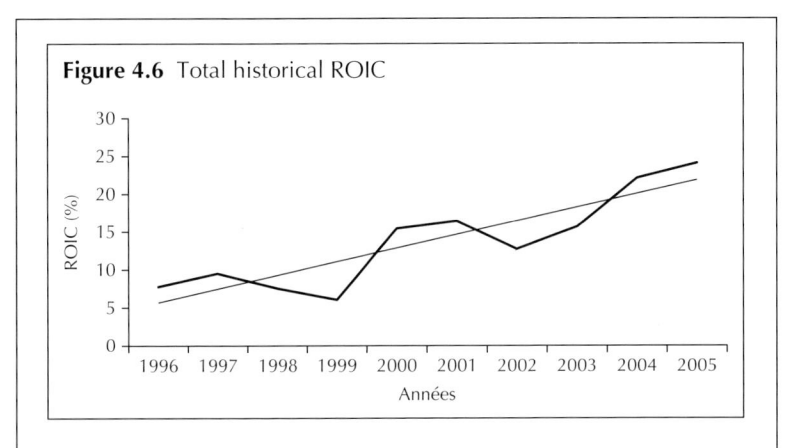

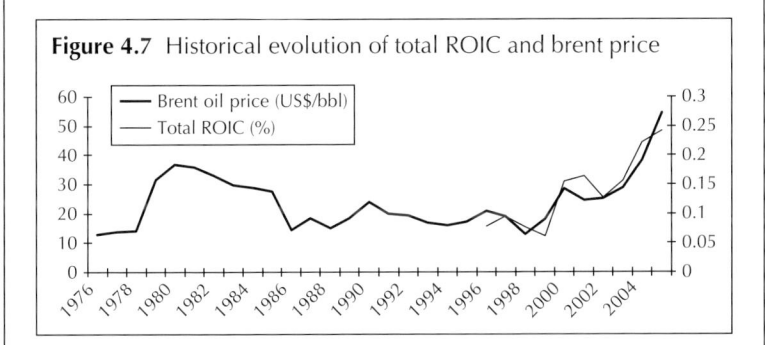

Figure 4.7 Historical evolution of total ROIC and brent price

around its growth path, but reversion to the mean for oil prices, as happened in 1980.

Mathematical formulation

Mathematically, the mean-reverting assumptions can be expressed as:[7]

$$\rho_t = \bar{\rho} + (\rho_{t-1} - \bar{\rho}) \cdot \exp(-\kappa) + \sigma_\rho \cdot \sqrt{\frac{1 - \exp(-2\kappa)}{2\kappa}} \cdot \eta_t \quad (1)$$

where $0 < \kappa < 1$ is the speed of mean reversion and $\bar{\rho}$ the long-term average profitability. In perfect markets, $\bar{\rho}$ should be equal to the cost of capital in the business. The random terms η_t are independently, identically, and normally distributed with mean 0 and variance 1.

The mean-reverting property is best seen by re-arranging Equation (1):

$$\rho_t - \rho_{t-1} = (\exp(-\kappa) - 1) \cdot (\rho_{t-1} - \bar{\rho}) + \sigma_\rho \cdot \sqrt{\frac{1 - \exp(-2\kappa)}{2\kappa}} \cdot \eta_t$$

Suppose ρ_{t-1} is higher than the long-term average $\bar{\rho}$: $\rho_{t-1} - \bar{\rho} \geq 0$. Then, since $\exp(-\kappa) < 1$, on average, $\rho_t - \rho_{t-1} \leq 0$: profitability is reduced, it reverts to the mean. Similarly, one can see that if ρ_{t-1} is lower than the long-term average $\bar{\rho}$, profitability increases on average. One can think of profitability as a spring: when it deviates from its "normal" length, it gets pulled – or pushed – back to it. The strength of the pull is proportional to the deviation and to the constant κ.

A very appealing feature of Equation (1) is that parameters $\bar{\rho}$, κ, and σ_ρ can be estimated through a simple linear regression. Equation (1) can be written as: $\rho_t = \alpha + \beta \rho_{t-1} + u_t$ where the random terms u_t are independently, identically, and normally distributed. Ordinary Least Square is then the Best Linear Unbiased Estimator. The coefficients $\bar{\rho}$, κ, and σ_ρ can be derived from α, β, and σ_u the standard deviation of u_t as follows:

$$\bar{\rho} = \frac{\alpha}{1 - \beta}$$

$$\kappa = -\ln \beta$$

$$\sigma_\rho^2 = \frac{1 - \exp(-2\kappa)}{2\kappa} \cdot \sigma_u^2$$

Example 4.4 OSG revisited. *As it turns out, bulk shipping is a cyclical business, following the same logic as other commodity industries. One can therefore attempt to model OSG's profitability not as an extreme value random variable, but instead as a mean reverting process following Equation (1). Linear regression leads to:*

$$\rho_t = \underset{(2.36)}{1.58} + \underset{(6.19)}{0.70} \rho_{t-1} + u_t$$

where the t-statistics are reported below the estimates. The process as estimated fits the actual data, although with a lag, as illustrated in Figure 4.8. We then have:

$$\bar{\rho} = 5.25\%$$
$$\kappa = 0.36$$
$$\sigma_\rho = 1.84\%$$

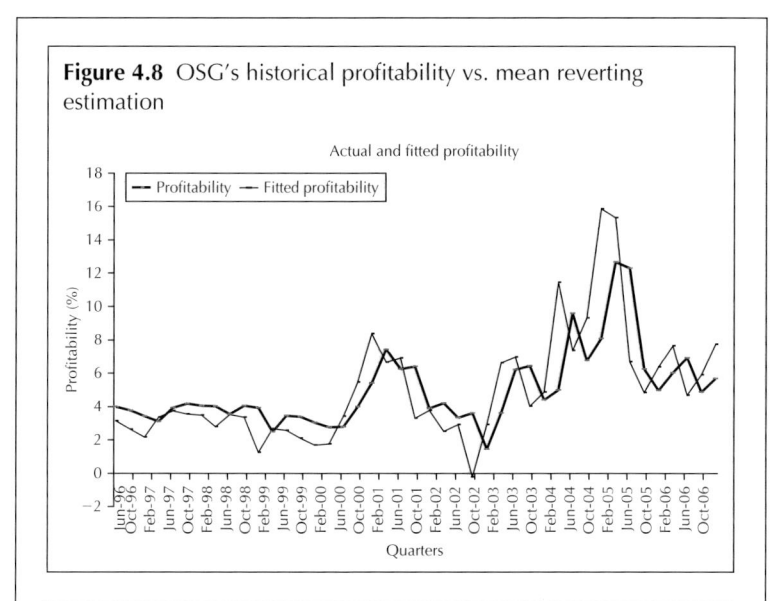

Figure 4.8 OSG's historical profitability vs. mean reverting estimation

Figure 4.9 Distributions of OSG's profitability: extreme value vs. mean reverting (starting from high)

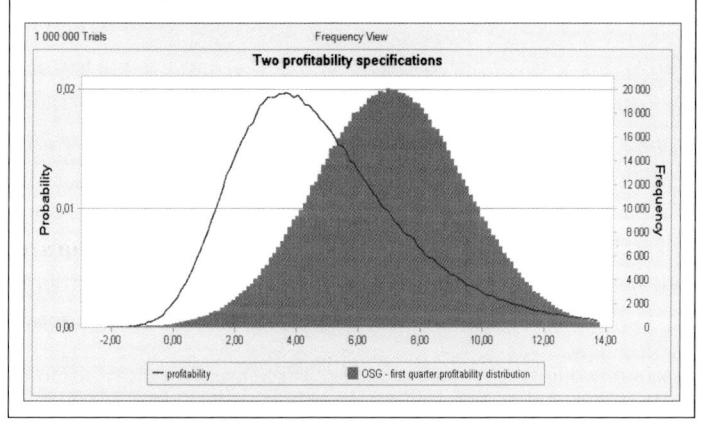

Equation (1) can then be written as:

$$\rho_t = 5.25 + (\rho_{t-1} - 5.25) \cdot 0.70 + 1.55 \cdot \eta_t \qquad (2)$$

For the first quarter of estimation, quarterly profitability estimated as a mean reverting process (labelled profitability) is represented against the "extreme value" distribution estimated previously (labelled OSG-first quarter profitability distribution) (Figure 4.9).

Figure 4.10 Cumulative distributions of OSG's profitability: extreme value vs. mean reverting (starting from high)

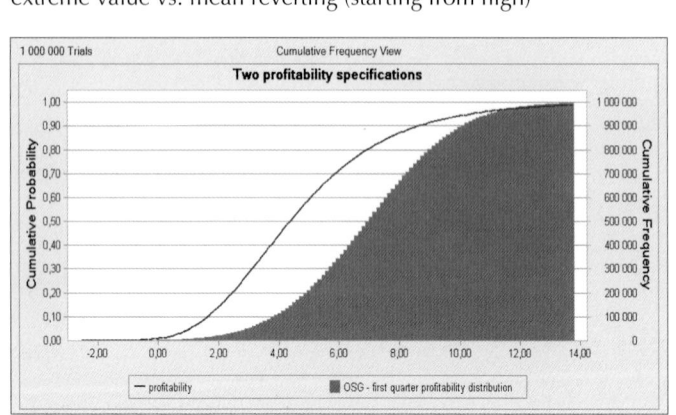

Figure 4.11 Distributions of OSG's profitability: extreme value vs. mean reverting (starting from low)

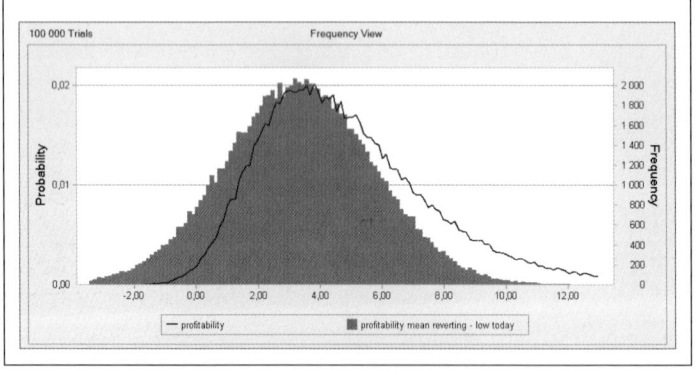

Since the last quarter of data recorded high profitability (7.76%), the expected value of the mean reverting distribution is higher than average (7%). The standard deviation is also lower (2.42% vs. 2.91%). As a consequence, the mean reverting profitability places much lower probability on low profitability. This may best be illustrated by comparing the two cumulative distributions (Figure 4.10).

Of course, the situation is reversed if the starting point is a low profitability point, as illustrated in Figure 4.11.

Statistical testing as well as business knowledge suggest that the mean reverting profitability constitutes a better fit.

4.1.4 Diffusion-like profitability

Brownian diffusion constitutes the workhorse of financial modelling for derivatives. For example, in the Black–Scholes model, the stock price S_t follows a geometric Brownian motion:

$$dS_t = \mu S_t + \sigma S_t dW_t$$

where μ is the drift, σ the standard deviation, and W a standard Brownian motion. Translation to our context would be:

$$\rho_{t+1} = (1 + \mu)\rho_t + \sigma \rho_t \eta_t \qquad (3)$$

where the random terms η_t are independently, identically, and normally distributed with mean 0 and variance 1.

Equation (3) implies that profitability grows indefinitely:

$$E[\rho_t / t = 0] = (1 + \mu)^t \cdot \rho_0$$

While this may be valid for the short-term behaviour of stock prices, I do not believe this applies to firms' long-term profitability. A more realistic specification would then assume no drift:

$$\rho_{t+1} = \rho_t + \sigma \rho_t \eta_t$$

This process is known as a random walk: profitability tomorrow is profitability today plus a random shock. Such a specification leads to virtuous and vicious circles, where high profitability today raises expected profitability tomorrow.[8] I believe more in mean reversion than in virtuous circles over the long-term, but that remains to be validated empirically.

4.1.5 Invested capital growth distribution

Invested capital growth is often about constant, with small variations around that average growth rate, and a few "spikes" of "jumps" when a significant investment or an acquisition is undertaken. This pattern is observed for example for Chevron, and OSG (see examples below). Of course, a particular firm may exhibit a different pattern, and alternate periods of high – but constant – growth, with periods of lower growth.

Mathematically, we define $g_t = (I_t - I_{t-1})/I_{t-1}$, and assume that:

$$g_t = g + \varepsilon_t + \zeta_t \qquad (4)$$

where g is constant, the random terms ε_t are independently, and identically distributed with mean 0 and variance σ_ε, and ζ_t is a variable size shock. For example, one could have:

$$\zeta_t = \begin{cases} 0 & \text{with probability } p \\ m_t & \text{with probability } (1-p) \end{cases}$$

where m_t is the random (conditional) size of the shock. This family of stochastic processes resembles jump diffusion processes, that are increasingly used in stochastic modelling, for example to represent on-peak spot power prices, where sudden spikes arise.

Estimation proceeds in two stages. First, the analyst excludes the shocks. She then estimates the mean g of the growth rate of invested capital for $t \leq t_0$, and determines the distribution of ε_t.

Second, the analyst must estimate the distribution of the shock parameters. While statistically robust estimation is possible for series of power prices, this is unlikely to be the case in this situation. The analyst has to make a best guess, based on her knowledge of the company and of the industry, of the likelihood of a significant investment. For example, when Chevron merged with Texaco in 2001, Chevron's invested capital almost doubled. If the analyst believes such a large merger is highly unlikely in the future, she would use a low estimate for the probability of a merger. In another situation, (possibly large) acquisitions might be more likely. For example, between 1993 and 2000, Cisco systems made more than 70 acquisitions. In that case, the analyst would estimate a higher likelihood of other acquisitions.

> **Example 4.5** Chevron invested capital growth. *Figure 4.12 displays quarterly growth rate of invested capital of Chevron, a major oil company, from March 1994 to September 2006. For most quarters, invested capital is slightly positive: investment slightly exceeds depreciation. The first "spike" in 2001 corresponds to the purchase of Texaco, while the second spike in 2005 corresponds to the purchase of Unocal.*

Figure 4.12 Chevron: invested capital growth

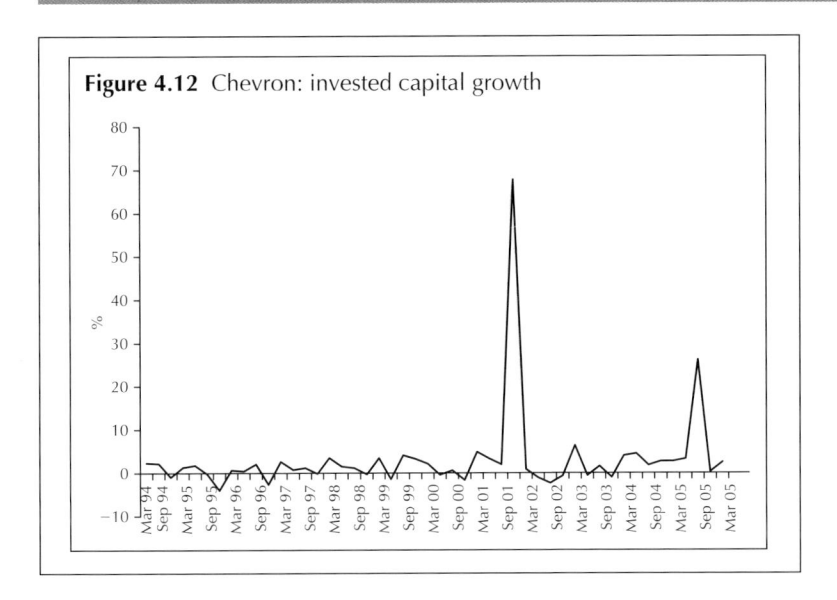

Example 4.6 OSG invested capital. *As illustrated in Figure 4.13, OSG's Invested capital is roughly constant most of the times, with a spike in the second quarter of 2005, where Invested Capital grew 80% roughly doubling the size of the firm. This corresponds to a large acquisition. Excluding the spike, the average growth of invested capital is barely positive (g = 0.36%), but highly variable (σ_g = 4.94%). Including the spike, the average growth is much higher: 2.20%, and also more volatile (standard deviation equal to 13.13%). The best fit for the growth of*

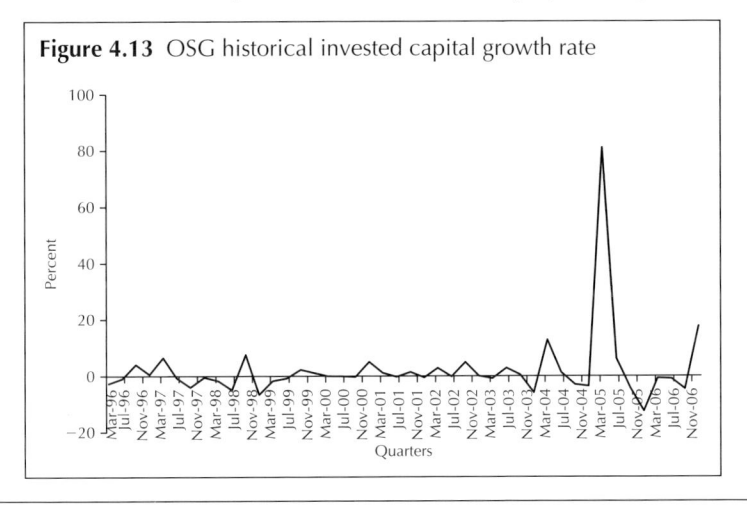

Figure 4.13 OSG historical invested capital growth rate

123

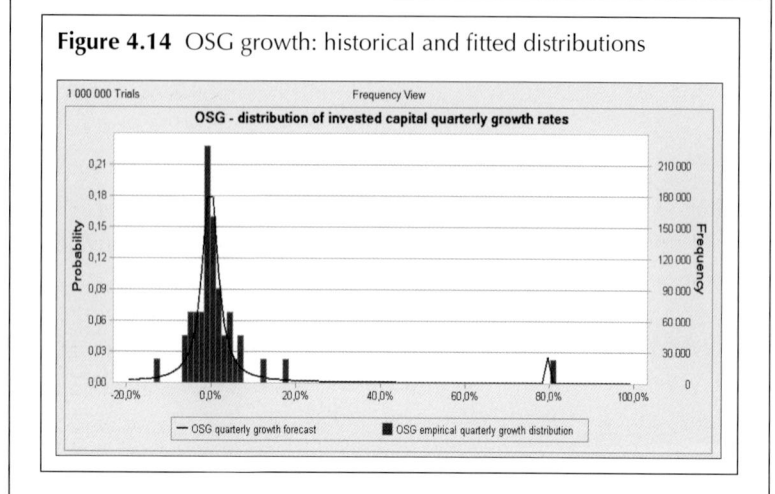

Figure 4.14 OSG growth: historical and fitted distributions

invested capital excluding the spike is not a normal distribution, but a Student-t distribution with one degree of freedom.[9]

Estimation of the distribution of spikes requires a rich understanding of the industry dynamics. Is that extremely spiky growth representative of the industry? is it likely to re-occur? or will we observe less spiky growth (eg, a 50% tonnage increase spike on average every five years)? In the absence of any other information, we assume here that spikes are distributed as a Bernoulli trial: every quarter, there is a 2.5% chance of a 80% increase in invested capital. Thus, we expect one spike every 40 quarters, which matches historical observations.

The resulting distribution of invested capital growth combines the Student-t distribution and the spike. As shown in Figure 4.14, it provides a close description of the actual distribution of growth rates.

Joint estimation
Finally, a more accurate approach is to jointly estimate profitability and investment, to take into account correlations between these two variables, as one expects high profitability today to lead to higher investment. This requires a bit more data, to justify the heavier statistics.

4.1.6 Distribution of future OCF
Once the distributions ρ_t and I_t are determined, the analyst simulates $\pi_t = I_{t-1} \cdot \rho_t$ for $t > t_0$ according to the distributions selected.

Example 4.7 OSG future EBITDA. *As discussed above, we assume (1) OSG's quarterly profitability is mean reverting, and follows Equation (2), and (2) OSG's quarterly growth rate follows Equation (4), where ε_t follows a student-t distribution, and ζ_t is a Bernoulli trial with probability 2.5% and amplitude 80%.*

For the first quarter of estimation ($t = t_0 + 1$) the invested capital I_{t_0} is known. Profitability is the only random variable. The distribution of first-quarter EBITDA forecast is represented in Figure 4.15.

The expected EBITDA is $E[\pi_{t_0+1}] = US\$181$ million, and the standard deviation is $\sigma_{\pi t_0+1} = US\$63$ million.

For the second quarter of estimation ($t = t_0 + 2$), both invested capital and profitability are random variables. One therefore expects the standard deviation to increase. Indeed, the simulation shows that $\sigma_{\pi t_0+2} = US\$91$ million. The expected EBITDA, on the other hand, is reduced to $E[\pi_{t_0+2}] = US\$170$ million (Figure 4.16).

This 6% reduction in expected EBITDA is mostly attributable to mean-reversion in the profitability. Expected profitability in the first quarter is $E[\rho_{t_0+1}] = 6.99\%$. Equation (2) leads to $E[\rho_{t_0+2}] = 6.41\%$, which is of course confirmed by the simulations. The expected profitability is reduced by 8% $((E[\rho_{t_0+2}] - E[\rho_{t_0+1}])/E[\rho_{t_0+1}] = -8\%)$. Then, since $\pi_t = I_{t-1} \cdot \rho_t$, we have approximately:

$$\frac{E[\pi_{t+2} - \pi_{t+1}]}{E(\pi_{t+1})} \approx E[g_{t+1}] + \frac{E[\rho_{t+2} - \rho_{t+1}]}{E[\rho_{t+1}]}$$

Since the expected growth rate is $E[g_{t_0+2}] = 2\%$, we find that the reduction in expected EBITDA is 6%.

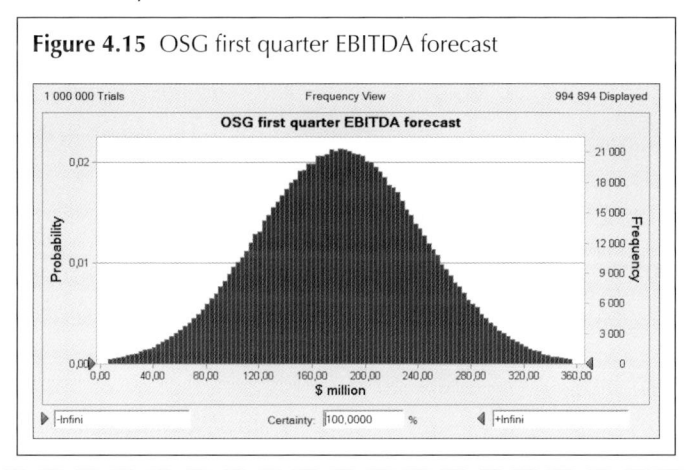

Figure 4.15 OSG first quarter EBITDA forecast

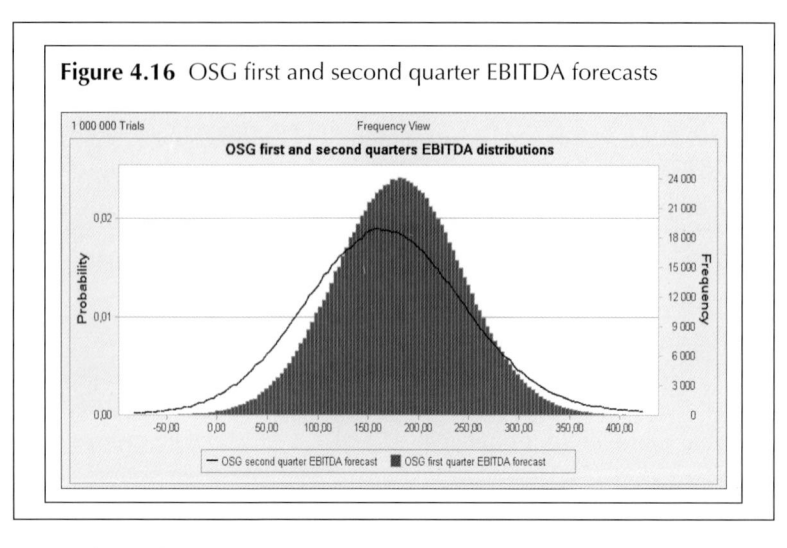

Figure 4.16 OSG first and second quarter EBITDA forecasts

4.2 INSIDE-OUT RISK ANALYSIS

Following the previous approach, inside-out risk identification and measurement aim at understanding and modelling separately each driver of cash flow volatility. Risk disaggregation is the key concept. It is helpful to think of risk disaggregation in terms of a matrix. The rows of the matrix are the lines of the cash flow statement: revenues, costs, etc. The columns of the matrix are the various risk drivers. The risk analyst disaggregates each line of the cash flow statement in terms of its risks, then adds up the risks along each column. Figure 4.17 represents an "empty" exposure map. We will fill it in the next examples.

Figure 4.17 Exposure map

	Risk categories			
	Price	Counterparty	Operations	Business
Net sales				
Costs of good sold				
SG&A				
EBITDA				
Changes in OWC				
Cash income taxes paid				
OCF				
Capital expenditures				
FCF				
Net exposure				

In this section we review first the disaggregation process: how to identify and quantify each type of risk. We then discuss how to aggregate risks using correlations.

The relevant cash flows are usually OCFs, although sometimes FCFs (post-capital expenditures) are also analysed. Firms sometimes elect to analyse "earnings exposure", that include non-cash items.

4.2.1 Price risk

This is often the first step of any risk management initiative. We start by the following:

Definition 4.1 *The exposure to a price risk is the change in cash flows created by a unit change in that price.*

For most firms, price risk arises primarily from commodity prices, exchange rates and interest rates. Fluctuations in the price of manufactured goods and services are usually considered a business risk, not a price risk, unless there exist a "commodity-like" market where that good and/or service is traded. Of course, there is no bright line. For example "standard" container shipping appears to be commoditising, with an index being published. However, local truck rates are probably considered business risk in most geographies, although the diesel price component of the truck rate is a price risk.

In most instances, the price exposure is simply the volume subject to the variations in that price, as illustrated in the examples below.

Example 4.8 Aluminium producer. *The firm produces 1 million tons of aluminium per year. At the current market price of US$2,000/ton, its expected revenues are US$2,000 million. The revenues exposure to aluminium is 1 million ton: if the price of aluminium moves by US$100/ton, the revenues move by US$100 million. This illustrated in Table 4.1.*

Table 4.1 Aluminum producer aluminum revenue exposure

	Aluminum price exposure (tons)
Net sales	1,000
Costs of good sold	
SG&A	
EBITDA	
Changes in OWC	
Cash income taxes paid	
OCF	
Capital expenditures	
FCF	
Net exposure	1,000

Example 4.9 Gold producer. *Consider now a Canadian firm that produces and sells gold. Its expected revenues are US$1,000 million. These revenues are exposed to 2 risks: (1) the price of the gold expressed in US$/oz. on the open market, and the (2) CA$/US$ exchange rate. The risk analyst will create two columns: the gold price risk and the CA$/US$ exchange rate risk, and record US$1,000 million in each, as illustrated in Table 4.2.*

Table 4.2 Gold producer revenue exposure map

	Gold price exposure (US$ million)	CA$/US$ exchange rate exposure (US$ million)
Net sales	1,000	1,000
Costs of good sold		
SG&A		
EBITDA		
Changes in OWC		
Cash income taxes paid		
OCF		
Capital expenditures		
FCF		
Net exposure	1,000	1,000

However, in some cases, identifying the exposure can be more challenging. We first introduce a few definitions, then go through a few examples. A common theme runs though these: a deep understanding of the business is required to understand and properly quantify price risk.

Long vs. short
A key concept is whether a firm is long or short:

Definition 4.2 *A firm is long a price if it stands to gain if the price increases. A firm is short a price if it stands to lose if the price increases.*

For example, the aluminium producer is long aluminium, and the gold producer is long gold, and long the CA$/US$ exchange rate.

Net exposure
Net exposure results from the difference between the terms under which the commodity is sold and the terms under which it is purchased.

Example 4.10 *Let us first revisit the aluminium producer. Alumina is one critical input in producing aluminium: around two tons of alumina are required to produce one ton of aluminium. As it turns out, alumina is usually priced as a percentage of aluminium price. This ratio varies depending on the supply-demand situation in the alumina market. The long-term average is around 12.5%. For a company producing 1 million tons aluminium, the cost exposure to aluminium is therefore equivalent to 250,000 tons of aluminium (2 times 12.5% times 1 million tons of aluminium). The net exposure to aluminium price is then only 750,000 tons, as highlighted in Table 4.3.*

Table 4.3 Aluminum producer aluminum exposure map

	Aluminum price exposure (tons)
Net sales	1,000
Costs of good sold	−250
SG&A	
EBITDA	
Changes in OWC	
Cash income taxes paid	
OCF	
Capital expenditures	
FCF	
Net exposure	750

CORPORATE RISK MANAGEMENT FOR VALUE CREATION

Figure 4.18 Net exposure determination matrix

	Fixed-price	Perfectly indexed
Indexed to raw materials prices (Selling terms)	Long price risk	No price risk (Long-term position?)
Fixed-price (Selling terms)	No price risk	Short price risk

Purchasing terms

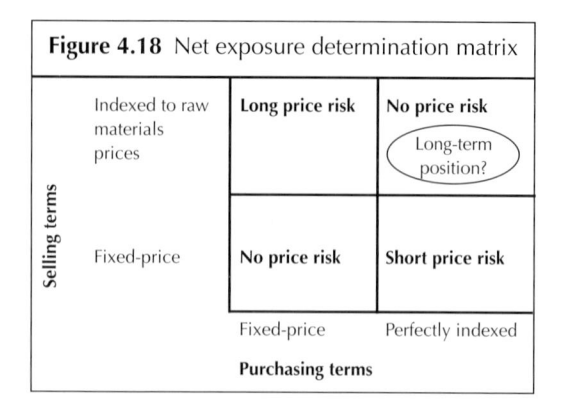

Netting can be more complex. For example, a company agrees with its oil supplier to purchase a fixed volume for the next 12 months, at the price of an published index. Is it long or short oil? This question cannot be answered. It all depends if and how this company passes the price of oil in the products and services it sells. If the company uses the oil for heating its buildings and factories, it is unlikely to systematically pass on the price of oil in its pricing structure. At best, it may increase the price with a lag. The company is short oil, and its exposure to oil prices is probably the full volume purchased.

If the company converts the oil in its production process (eg, to make plastics), it is highly likely to explicitly link the price of its goods to the cost of oil. The company could have no direct exposure to oil prices: it is neither long nor short.

More generally, it is helpful to introduce the two-by-two matrix on Figure 4.18. The purchasing terms of the raw material are represented on the x-axis: fixed-price on the left, perfectly indexed on the right. The selling terms of the finished product are represented on the y-axis: fixed price at the bottom, indexed to raw material price at the top.

Raw materials in the bottom-left and top-right quadrants do not generate price risk. The bottom-right quadrant generates a short price risk (buy at index, sell at a fixed price). The top-left quadrant generates a long price risk (buy at fixed price, sell at index).

In practice, contractual agreements often fall "in the middle" of both axes, due to lags, imperfect index adjustment, renegotiations, etc. Furthermore, in the long-term, one expects all exposures to be in the top quadrant, as sustained price changes are passed on to customers. However, significant mismatch sometimes exist in the short-run. The key driver of exposure is the elasticity of demand to prices, both in the short-run and in the long-run.

Price exposures may be embedded in contract clauses. A common example: some freight and transportation contracts include a fuel adjustment clause, that stipulates that, should the relevant fuel price exceed a given level, the transportation price will be adjusted accordingly.

"Hidden" price exposures may be embedded in purchasing costs. For example, a pharmaceutical firm buys packaging for a specific medicine. As the price of raw materials (including energy) used to manufacture the package grows, the supplier will seek a price increase, even though no explicit pass-through clause may have been negotiated.

More subtly, embedded price risk may be caused by demand reduction at high prices. Consider the transportation example. Under a perfect pass-through contract, the transportation company is not exposed to oil prices. However, as oil prices – hence the freight cost – increases, users will reduce their demand whenever feasible, either by reducing shipping, or by seeking alternatives. The transportation company is therefore short oil price, for prices above a certain level.

Similarly, aluminium can making companies have an embedded long exposure to the steel-aluminium spread (Example 4.11).

Example 4.11 *Aluminium and steel compete directly in the can market. In North America, aluminium has virtually 100% market share, while in Europe aluminium is still substituting for steel. Using the cost of rolling cans – including the value of recycled aluminium – one can compute an economic equation, illustrated on Figure 4.19: if the steel to aluminium (wholesale) price spread exceeds a certain level, aluminium is the preferred can-making material. If the spread exceeds another – higher – level, steel can-making units will be converted to aluminium (ie, the value of the savings on the material costs from switching from steel to aluminium exceeds the conversion costs). In 2004 and the first half of 2005, as steel price was at historically high prices while aluminium remained at moderately high prices, new can*

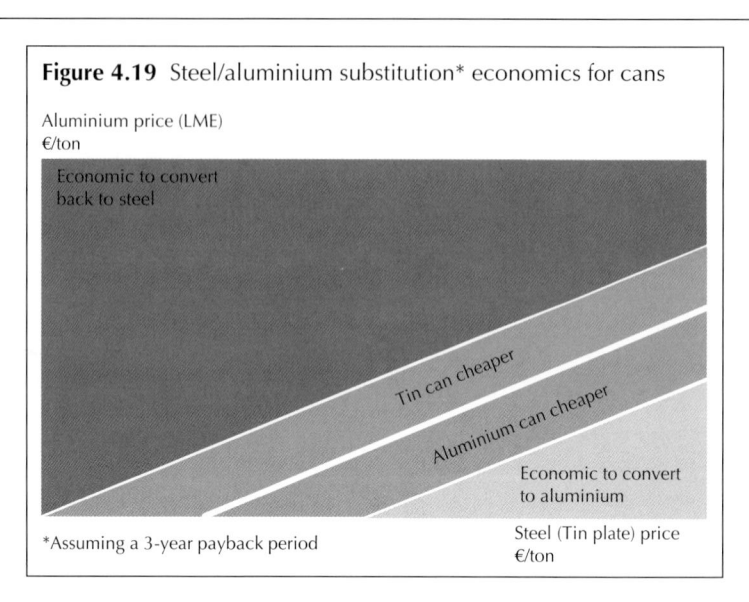

Figure 4.19 Steel/aluminium substitution* economics for cans

Aluminium price (LME) €/ton

- Economic to convert back to steel
- Tin can cheaper
- Aluminium can cheaper
- Economic to convert to aluminium

*Assuming a 3-year payback period

Steel (Tin plate) price €/ton

factories setup mostly to serve growing Eastern European markets selected aluminium. In 2006, with aluminium at record-high prices, while steel has returned to moderately high prices, aluminium has stopped its penetration.

Finally, it must be noted that systematic analysis of the position can lead to counter-intuitive results. Consider for example Total, a vertically integrated oil company, that produces in its upstream business 2.5 million barrels per day, and sells through its downstream business 4 million barrels per day. The firm has to purchase 1.5 million barrels per day. It is short physical oil. However, Total's profitability increases with the oil price, as illustrated in Figure 4.7. What is the explanation of this apparent paradox? Since the oil is purchased and sold at market prices, the 1.5 million barrels per day creates no price risk. The firm is therefore long the oil price on its own production of 2.5 million barrels per day.

Spread risk
Most industrial companies are long the spread between commodities. For example, a coal-fired power plant is long power, short coal, or equivalently, long the spread electricity-coal. However, the true

underlying spread risk depends on the market where the plant is located, as discussed in the example below.

> **Example 4.12** Coal-fired plant in different markets. *Consider first a coal-fired plant located in the Midwest in the US. The power price in the Midwest is set by gas-fired plants on-peak (usually corresponding to office hours on weekdays), and coal-fired plants off-peak (the rest of the time). We assume price is close to the marginal cost of the marginal plant: price of fuel used times the thermal efficiency of the marginal plant (the conversation factor from fuel to electric power). For simplicity, we ignore variable O&M costs.*
>
> *Denote p_{coal} and p_{gas} the marginal cost of coal and gas respectively, measured in US$/MWh of fuel, α_{coal} and α_{gas} the conversion factor for the marginal coal plant and gas plant respectively, and α the conversion factor for our coal plant. Gas is more expensive than coal per MWh, so we have: $p_{gas} > p_{coal}$. A higher conversion factor means a less efficient plant, so we have: $\alpha_{coal} \geq \alpha \geq \alpha_{gas}$. Finally, denote p the price of electric power, and π the profit of our plant.*
>
> *From the above discussion, we have: $p^{off\text{-}peak} = \alpha_{coal} \cdot p_{coal}$ and $p^{on\text{-}peak} = \alpha_{gas} \cdot p_{gas}$. Therefore, $\pi^{off\text{-}peak} = (\alpha_{coal} - \alpha) \cdot p_{coal}$ and $\pi^{on\text{-}peak} = \alpha_{gas} \cdot p_{gas} - \alpha \cdot p_{coal}$. Off-peak, the coal-fired plant has a small coal price risk exposure. Somehow counter-intuitively, it is long the coal price.[10] On-peak, the coal-fired plant is long the gas-coal spread: it is long the gas price, and short the coal price.*
>
> *Consider now the same plant in continental Europe, where the Emission Trading Scheme (ETS) is implemented. It has been observed that power producers have passed the emission permit costs in the wholesale power prices, even though most of them were allocated the permits "for free" by their government. Therefore, the price of power is equal to the marginal fuel cost of the marginal plant, plus the price of the emission permit. Furthermore, it has been hypothesised that the emission price will be set to allow for switching between coal and gas at the margin, both on-peak and off-peak. Following Green (2006), Appendix 4.A shows that, under these conditions the expected profit for our plant is:*
>
> $$\pi = \frac{\alpha_{coal} - \alpha}{2\frac{\alpha_{coal}}{\alpha_{gas}} - 1} \cdot (2p_{gas} - p_{coal})$$

> *Of course, the plant is still long gas and short coal. However, the exposure has changed. In particular, a marginal coal plant $\alpha = \alpha_{coal}$ realises no expected profit, as the permit price is such that it is always at the margin.*
>
> *Finally, suppose our coal-fired power plant is selling its power in the Nordpool through the interconnection between Germany and Norway. Nordpool is a primarily hydro-based power system. The price of power is the opportunity cost of water in the reservoirs. Our plant would then be long water in Norway, short coal price.*

This example illustrates how a detailed understanding of the business conditions is required to determine the true price exposure.

Currency risk exposure
In general terms, a currency exposure arises when there is a currency mismatch between a firm's revenues and its costs. It is convenient to distinguish three types of exposure:

- Direct exposures arise from purchase or sales of goods *determined* in a currency other than a firm functional currency
- Transaction exposures arise from purchase or sales of goods *committed* in a currency other than a firm functional currency
- Translation exposures arise when cash flows generated in a foreign subsidiary are *exchanged* to be used in another country.

Direct exposure. It is critical to distinguish the *currency of determination*: the currency in which the price of the goods sold (or purchased) is determined, from the *currency of invoicing*: the currency in which the goods sold (or purchased) are paid. As the examples below illustrate, they need not coincide. For locally produced and traded goods and services, the local currency is the currency of determination (and often the currency of invoicing). For globally produced and traded goods (eg, commodities, raw materials, some manufactured equipment), the US$ is often the currency of determination, even though invoicing may take place in other currencies.

ENTERPRISE RISK ANALYSIS

> **Example 4.13** *Suppose that our aluminium producer sells aluminium to European customers in euros. In most instances, she multiplies the price in US$/ton by the prevailing EUR/US$ exchange rate to quote a price in EUR/ton. For example, suppose that the price of aluminium on the wholesale market remains constant, but that the EUR appreciates against the dollar. The producer will reduce the price it charges in EUR, and receive the same amount of US$ per ton of aluminium. Even though the aluminium producer "physically" receives euros, it really receives US$.*

In the previous examples, gold and aluminium prices are determined in US$, on global open markets, which creates the direct exposure.

> **Example 4.14** *Since the gold price is determined in US$, on global open market, the Canadian gold producer is long US$/short CA$ on its sales. Let us now consider the cost structure of the gold producer. Suppose that a portion of the firm's operating costs are determined in US$, for example US$ 100 million linked to fuel purchases. The risk analyst will record −US$ 100 million in the CA$/US$ column. The resulting net exposure to the CA$/US$ exchange rate is therefore US$900 million, as illustrated in Table 4.4.*

Table 4.4 Gold producer currency exposure map

	Gold price exposure (US$ million)	CA$/US$ exchange rate exposure (US$ million)
Net sales	1,000	1,000
Costs of good sold		−100
SG&A		
EBITDA		
Changes in OWC		
Cash income taxes paid		
OCF		
Capital expenditures		
FCF		
Net exposure	1,000	900

Example 4.15 *Besides alumina, other cash costs in aluminium production include electric power, labour, raw materials, additional energy. Assume they amount to CA$1,000 per ton of aluminium produced, and that they are all determined in the currency where the production plant is located. A Canadian aluminium company will then be short CA$/long US$. The exposure is −CA$1,000 million.*

Table 4.5 Aluminum producer price exposure map

	Aluminum price exposure (tons)	CA$/US$ exchange rate exposure (CA$ million)
Net sales	1,000	
Costs of good sold	−250	−1,000
SG&A		
EBITDA		
Changes in OWC		
Cash income taxes paid		
OCF		
Capital expenditures		
FCF		
Net exposure	750	−1,000

Direct currency exposure can be very subtle, in which case it is sometimes called "economic exposure". Consider a US-based domestic luxury car manufacturer in the early 1990s. The manufacturer's costs and revenues are all in US$. At that time, the particular market in which this manufacturer competes was dominated by German manufacturers, who set the price. German auto-makers manufacture cars in Europe, hence set the sales price to achieve their margin in Deutsche Mark (DM), which is their functional currency (ie, their "main" currency). If the DM strengthens compared with the US$, they quote higher prices in US$ to meet their margin target. If the DM weakens, they quote lower prices. As long the German auto-makers are market leaders, they are able to pass their costs through. Therefore, they have almost no exposure to the exchange rate, even though a – possibly significant – portion of their revenues is received in US$.[11] The US-based auto-manufacturer, on the other hand, is long DM/short US$: if the euro strengthens compared with the US$, higher revenues will be achieved. This is counter-intuitive, as DMs never appear on any financial statements.

Transaction exposure. Transaction exposure arises when a timing and a currency mismatch interact. Suppose for example that our German car manufacturer fixes its price for every quarter. For example, in March it sets the price in USD at which its cars will be sold in the US for April–May–June. Cars sold in June will be produced in April, possibly May. So, if the DM appreciates against the USD, the German car manufacturer will not be able to increase its price, hence will be exposed. Even though the sale price and the production costs are determined in DM, an exposure is created.

Many firms systematically hedge transaction exposure. While it may be appropriate for long-term commitments (eg, multi-year), I am not sure it is worth the cost for short-term commitments (eg, less than a quarter) as these are often a small contributor to cash flow volatility.

Translation exposure. The most common example of translation exposure is a foreign subsidiary, producing and selling in its own local currency. As an independent entity, it probably has very little exchange rate risk. However, the parent company faces exchange rate risk when it wants to repatriate the cash flow to the parent company, ie, translate them into the domestic currency. In this situation, the parent company is long the foreign currency, short the domestic currency.[12]

Migration of exposures. While the distinction between the types of exposure is helpful conceptually, in practice the boundaries are less clear, as the Airbus example below illustrates:

> **Example 4.16** Airbus currency exposures. *Airbus, a large European aircraft manufacturer, offers an intriguing example of currency exposure. At the current EUR/US$ exchange rate, Airbus is a price taker: the price for aircrafts is largely set by Boeing. Since Boeing's manufacturing and R&D costs are largely determined in US$, aircraft prices are determined in US$. This of course has implications for Airbus and its*

CORPORATE RISK MANAGEMENT FOR VALUE CREATION

> suppliers that are primarily located in Europe. To reduce its exchange rate exposure, Airbus increasingly requires its suppliers to quote a price in US$ (even though invoicing may take place in EUR). Since suppliers are competing globally, at the current exchange rate, US-based suppliers are likely to be price setters, and European suppliers face a significant exchange rate risk. Structural solutions, such as moving production outside of the Euro-zone are considered. This would create translation exposure, as the cash flows from these subsidiaries would have to be translated into euro, which is likely to remain the functional currency of Airbus and its European suppliers.
>
> Suppose now that the EUR/US$ exchange rate goes back to where it was around year 2000, and furthermore, that Airbus reduces its cost base enough to become the price-setter. Even though planes will be invoiced in US$, in practice their price will be set based on Airbus' cost, ie, determined in Euros. Airbus would then have no direct exposure. However, if Airbus sets a price in US$ for delivery over multiple years, it will create a transaction exposure.

Fixed price commitments in the trading business

In the trading business, only fixed price commitments create an exposure. This can first appear counter-intuitive, as one would expect fixed price to reduce the volatility of cash flows, hence to reduce the risk. The explanation of this apparent paradox is that, in the trading world, contracts are evaluated against an index, ie, the underlying "thought experiment" is that commitments are unwound in the market, at the then-prevailing price. This is captured in the concept, critical in trading, of mark-to-market. If a trader buys 10 million barrels of oil for June next year at the price of an index for June (eg, Brent), by definition there is no profit realised: he will buy at the June price and sell at the June price. If a trader buys 10 million barrels for June next year at US$40/bbl, he will make money if the June price is above US$40/bbl, and lose otherwise. A risk is thus created.

Resulting price risk

Once all price exposures have been identified, the cash flow can be expressed as a function of the price exposures. Denote π the operating cash flow for the period considered, and for $n = 1, ..., N$, p_n

the price n, and q_n the exposure to price n. For simplicity assume that the exposures are constant at all prices. We also denote π_0 the component of cash flow independent of prices. It is helpful to introduce $\mathbf{q} \in \mathbb{R}^N$ and $\mathbf{p} \in \mathbb{R}^N$ the vectors of exposure and prices. We immediately have:

$$\pi = \pi_0 + \sum_{n=1}^{N} q_n \cdot p_n$$

which, using standard matrix notation, can be rewritten as:

$$\pi = \pi_0 + \mathbf{q}^T \cdot \mathbf{p}$$

The distribution of prices can then be estimated using statistical techniques discussed in Appendix 4.B. Since long data sets are available for most liquidly traded commodities, sophisticated estimation is often possible.

Denote Σ_p the variance-covariance matrix of the prices. Since the exposures are independent of price, basic statistics give:

$$E[\pi] = \pi_0 + \mathbf{q}^T \cdot E[\mathbf{p}]$$

and:

$$Var[\pi] = \mathbf{q}^T \cdot \Sigma_p \cdot \mathbf{q} \tag{5}$$

Equation (5) is central in risk measurement. Even though cash flow volatility may be determined using sophisticated Monte-Carlo simulations, it is recommended to compare the resulting variance with that predicted by Equation (5). Furthermore, risk analysts use Equation (5) decompose the variance in its main components, ie, to determine how the various risk drivers impact the total risk profile of the firm.

Example 4.17 Aluminium producer price risk. *Our aluminium producer as a smelting capacity of one million tons of aluminium per* year. As previously discussed, since alumina, a critical input to aluminium, is priced off aluminium, the resulting net exposure to aluminium price is 750,000 tons per year. Other operating costs are determined in CA$, and amount to CA$1,000 per ton of aluminium produced. The EBITDA per ton is:

$$EBITDA = 0.75 \cdot p_{Al} - 1,000 \cdot p_{\frac{US\$}{CA\$}}$$

where p_{Al} is the price of aluminium, expressed in US$/ton, and $p_{US\$/CA\$}$ is the value in US$ of one CA$. Statistical analysis presented in Appendix 4.B indicates that the average aluminium price is $\bar{p}_{Al} = 2,598$ US$/ton, the average annual exchange rate is $\bar{p}_{US\$/CA\$} = 0.8429$ US$/CA$, the annual standard deviation of aluminium price is $\sigma_{Al} = 214$ US$/ton, the annual standard deviation of exchange rate is $\sigma_{US\$/CA\$} = 0.0194$ US$/CA$, and the correlation between aluminium price and exchange rate is $\rho = 0.28$. The expected EBITDA for the year is:

$$EBITDA = 0.75 \cdot 2,598 - 1,000 \cdot 0.8429 = 1,105 \text{ US\$/ton}$$

Equation (5) then yields:

$$\begin{aligned}Var[EBITDA] &= (0.75 \cdot \sigma_{Al})^2 + \left(1,000 \cdot \sigma_{\frac{US\$}{CA\$}}\right)^2 \\ &\quad - 2 \cdot \rho \cdot (0.75 \cdot \sigma_{Al}) \cdot \left(1,000 \cdot \sigma_{\frac{US\$}{CA\$}}\right) \\ &= (161)^2 + (19)^2 - 2 \cdot 0.28 \cdot 161 \cdot 19 \\ &= (156)^2\end{aligned}$$

This then leads to $\sigma_{EBITDA} = 156$ US$/ton. The standard deviation of EBITDA is lower than that of the aluminium exposure alone, since the cost in CA$ acts as a natural hedge. The distribution of EBITDA, obtained through Monte Carlo simulation, is presented in Figure 4.20.

To derive OCF, one needs to subtract cash taxes from EBITDA. To simplify the example, we assume no tax carry forward: the cash tax paid is simply the tax rate applied to Earnings Before Taxes. Denote dep_t the depreciation charge, D_t the (face value of) debt, i_t the effective

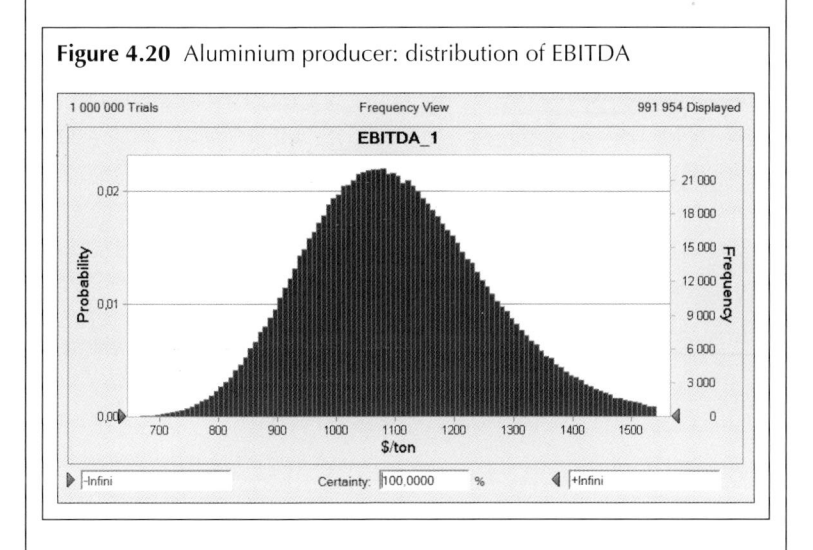

Figure 4.20 Aluminium producer: distribution of EBITDA

interest rate, and τ the effective tax rate during period t. Interest payments are $D_t \cdot i_t$ and OCF_t can be expressed as:

$$OCF_t = EBITDA_t - \tau \cdot (EBITDA_t - dep_t - D_t \cdot i_t)$$
$$= (1 - \tau) \cdot EBITDA_t + \tau \cdot (dep_t + D_t \cdot i_t) \quad (6)$$

Assuming fixed rate debt, we immediately see from Equation (6) that:

$$\sigma_{OCF} = (1 - \tau) \cdot \sigma_{EBITDA}$$

With the tax rate $\tau = 40\%$, we have $\sigma_{OCF} = 94$ US\$/ton.

We further assume straight line depreciation over 30 years (ie, 3.33% per year). The initial investment is US\$3,500 per ton of annual production.[13] The annual depreciation charge is therefore $dep_t = 117$ US\$/ton. The debt to asset ratio is 55%, and the pre tax cost of debt 5%, assumed fixed. The annual interest payment is $D_t \cdot i_t = 3,500 \cdot 0.55 \cdot 0.05 = 96$ US\$/ton. From Equation (6), the expected OCF is then:

$$E[OCF_t] = 0.6 \cdot 1,105 + 0.4 \cdot (117 + 96) = 747 \text{ US\$/ton}$$

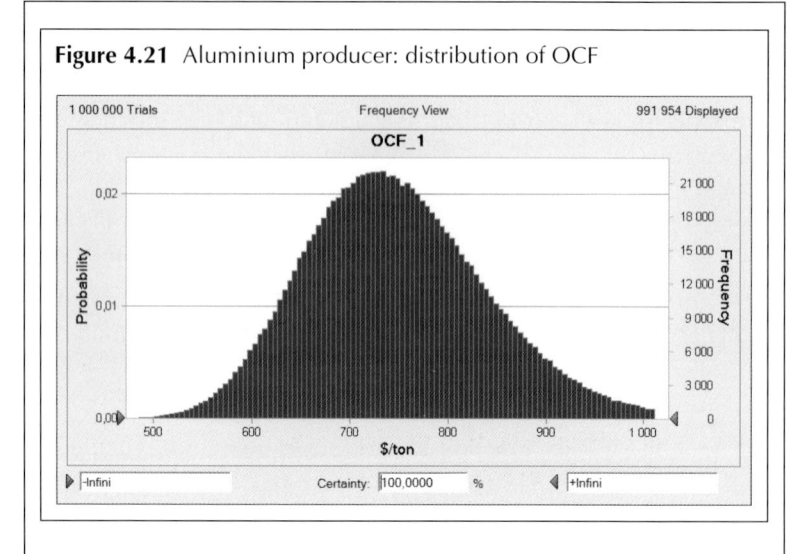

Figure 4.21 Aluminium producer: distribution of OCF

The distribution of OCF, obtained through Monte Carlo simulation is presented in Figure 4.21.

Finally, we can also compute the distribution of Economic Profit. Assume the beta of the asset is $\beta = 1$. Applying the Miles–Ezzel model discussed in Chapter 2, the cost of equity is $k_e = 16.1\%$. We can compute the Weighted Average Cost of Capital $w = 8.9\%$. Then:

$$EP_t = NOPLAT_t - w \cdot I_{t-1}$$
$$= (1 - \tau) \cdot (EBITDA_t - dep_t) - w \cdot I_{t-1} \quad (7)$$

From Equation (7), we immediately observe that $\sigma_{EP_t} = (1 - \tau) \cdot \sigma_{EBITDA_t} = \sigma_{OCF}$. We also observe that:

$$E[EP_t] = 0.6 \cdot (1,105 - 117) - 0.089 \cdot 3,500 = 281 \text{ US\$/ton}$$

4.2.2 Counterparty risk

Counterparty risk arises when a customer or supplier could default on its obligations, hereby reducing the firm's cash flows. Counterparty risk management is *the* core competency in the banking industry. Non-financial firms need to manage counterparty risk as well, as they all have customers and suppliers.

For each customer or supplier, the counterparty risk is the Probability of Default (PD) times the value lost in the event of default, called the Loss Given Default (LGD) in the credit risk measurement literature, which we call "exposure" to a customer or supplier.

Exposure determination
The first practical challenge is to determine the exposure. Most firms track account receivables (ie, amounts invoiced to customers, but not yet paid). Many firms use account receivables as a measure of counterparty exposure. This often severely underestimates the true exposure to a counterparty, which is the market value of the commitment between the two parties, including – but not limited to – receivables and payables.

Consider the following example: a manufacturing plant has a fixed price gas contract with a local energy marketer. The contract is set at US$3/MMBtu for 1,000,000 MMBtus. The current market price for gas is US$10/MMBtu. The market value of the contract is US$7 million (US$7/MMBtu for 1,000,000 MMBtus). If the supplier defaults (which is likely if all of its contracts are so unfavourable!), the plant will have to purchase the gas on the market. The resulting cost increase would be US$7 million, the market value of the contract. Since the plant has no receivables from the energy marketer, it may not include that contract in its counterparty risk analysis. That could prove to be a US$7 million mistake.

This example is not theoretical. Electric power suppliers in the Midwest of the United States during the summer of 1998 faced that exact situation: some had purchased electric power from marketers that simply went bankrupt as prices rose during the summer, forcing these suppliers to source from the wholesale markets at extremely high prices (up to US$10,000 per MWh compared to an average price of US$20 per MWh). Since they had no receivable with these suppliers, they had not identified these contracts as a potential source of counterparty risk.

Market value of commitments may be difficult to determine, as it involves identifying and pricing the next best alternative to the current contract. In the previous gas example, a liquid market provides that next best alternative. Suppose that our manufacturing plant has a 12-month, 10,000 widgets per month contract with a customer. If the customer defaults, where will these widgets be sold? At which price? Will the plant continue to manufacture widgets, or switch to another product?

A final word on counterparty exposure: netting. Large corporations often have multiple commitments with entities belonging to another corporation. For example, an industrial firm will have multiple credit facilities, currency and interest rates derivatives with a financial institution. It could owe money on loans, and be owed money on derivatives. Netting of exposures is not always possible, in particular in the case of bankruptcy (which is the only case when it truly matters).

These examples illustrate the point that counterparty exposure quantification goes well beyond accounting. It must involve the business leaders as well as the legal advisers.

Probability of default
Academics and practitioners have developed a rich literature on approaches to estimate a counterparty's PD. This constitutes a very dynamic field of research, with obvious economic impact. We summarise below four main families of approaches:

Expert systems. These are often the judgement of a credit professional. A well-known evaluation grid relies the 5Cs of credit: *Character*, a measure of the reputation of the firm; *Capital*, a measure of debt to capital; *Capacity*, which reflects the volatility of borrowers' earnings; *Collateral*, and *Cycle (or economic) conditions*. In practice, credit officers rely on the 5Cs as well as on other quantitative metrics provided by specialised firms such as D&B (formerly Dun and Bradstreet). A variation on expert judgement involves artificial neural networks: these sophisticated computer programs, designed to mirror the brain's learning process, learn by trial and errors, and adapt. In some instances, they have been shown to outperform human experts and credit scoring systems.

Quantitative scores. The most famous may be Altman (1968) Z-score model, initially developed to assess bank loans. The Z-score takes the form:

$$Z = 1.2 \cdot X_1 + 1.4 \cdot X_2 + 3.3 \cdot X_3 + 0.6 \cdot X_4 + 1.0 \cdot X_5$$

where X_1 is the working capital to total assets ratio, X_2 is the retained earnings to total assets ratio, X_3 is the EBIT to total assets ratio; X_4 is the market value of equity to book value of total liabilities ratio, and X_5 is the sales to total assets ratio. If the Z-score for a potential lender falls below a critical value (1.81 in the initial study) the loan is rejected.

A more recent example of credit scoring model is Moody's rating methodology for the global mining industry.[14] Moody's identifies five rating factors for mining debt issuers:

(1) Reserves, expressed in years.
(2) Cost efficiency and profitability, measured by EBIT margin, return on (five-year) average tangible assets, and "other" liabilities to book equity.
(3) Financial policies, measured by debt to capitalisation and debt to EBITDA.
(4) Financial strength, measured by interest coverage, cash from operations less dividends to debt, and free cash flow to debt.
(5) Business diversity and size, measured by a score of five elements: operational diversity (single vs. multiple mines/plants), commodity diversity (single vs. multiple metals) regional diversity (single vs. multiple regions), nature of product (commodity vs. value added), and market share (inconsequential vs. significant market share).

The methodology then proceeds to define a precise factor for each metric, and a band corresponding to each credit rating for each metric. For example, reserves of more than 20 years correspond to an A rating, between 15 and 20 years to a Baa rating, between 10 and 15 years, to a B rating, and less than 10 years, to a B rating. The ratings on each metric are then weighted (the exact weights are not communicated) to obtain a composite rating.

Information contained in equity prices. This method builds on a seminal insight by Robert Merton, who observed that purchasing risky debt is equivalent to purchasing risk-free debt and selling a put option to the equity holders: if the firm's value falls below the face value of the debt, the equity holders can file for bankruptcy, in effect putting the assets to the creditors. That put option can be valued using the "standard" Black–Scholes–Merton option pricing formula. However, the value of the firm as well as its volatility are unobservable, which poses technical problems.

A company called KMV built on that insight, and observed that equity holders' own a call on the value of the assets, at strike price the face value of debt. The (observable) value of equity can then be priced using the Black–Merton–Scholes formula. This leads to an estimation technique for the PD. KMV added another layer of sophistication by comparing "theoretical" probabilities of default from their model to actual observed probabilities of default, using their proprietary databases of bankruptcies. The KMV metric has been shown to perform extremely well.

Information contained in bond prices. The main insight is to observe that bond yield is the sum of a risk-free rate and a risk premium, that compensates for the expected cost of default. The problem of course is that the expected cost of default includes not only the PD, but also the expected LGD. Various authors have proposed models to tease out these two effects.

Which approach to use? The first two approaches are more static, and rely on accounting data. They are slower to adjust to changes in the economic reality of a firm. The last two approaches can be constantly updated to reflect latest information available on the firm. Unsurprisingly, a combination of all approaches appears to outperform each individually.

Correlations

One counterparty's default may not be independent of other risks to the corporation. For example, it is sometimes triggered by factors that affect other counterparties. If our manufacturer sells to the US electric power industry, and that this industry goes through a massive crisis as was the case in 2001/2002, defaults among counterparties will likely be correlated. Banks, which have the most experience with counterparty risks, have developed sophisticated methods, and measure their exposure to a sector as well as to a particular counterparty.

4.2.3 Operations risk

The disaggregation logic discussed for price and counterparty risk also applies to operations risk. The risk analyst must identify all aspects of the operation that could "go wrong", then estimate for each the probability of failure, and the cost of failure, conditional on failure (eg, 2-hour plant shutdown, 12-hour plant shutdown, 24-hour plant shutdown). This combines analysis of historical data (eg, historical availability of this particular plant or process as well as similar plants/processes in other companies/industries), and scenarios development (eg, what if this component were to fail?).

Operational risk analysis has progressed significantly over the last decade, driven mostly by the increases in data storage and processing capabilities. Specialised firms have built datasets of plant and processes failures, analysed them, and developed appropriate statistical models. Robust theoretical models are available, for example that predict time to failure. Yet, applying the models to many business processes remains an area for further work.

Example 4.18 *Production interruption risk. All facilities are exposed to mechanical, electrical, or other technical failures that reduce their production. Based on historical production data, one can estimate the probability of an interruption, and the (conditional) duration of an interruption.*

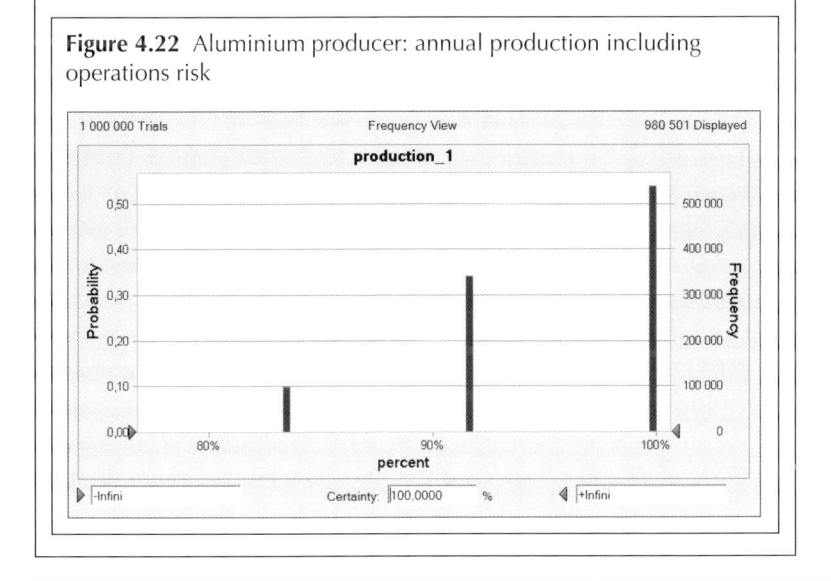

Figure 4.22 Aluminium producer: annual production including operations risk

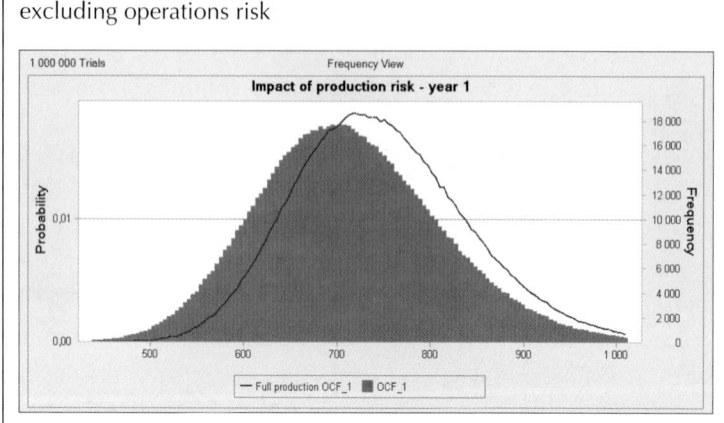

Figure 4.23 Aluminium producer: distribution of OCF including vs. excluding operations risk

Let us consider the impact of a simplified model on our aluminium smelter. Let us assume that each month, there is a 5% chance of a one-month interruption,[15] and that each month is independent from the others. First, the annual production is represented in Figure 4.22.

The expected production is only 95% of the full production. The expected EBITDA and OCF are therefore lower than their full production counterpart (shifted to the left), as shown in Figure 4.23.

Production risk has a small impact on the standard deviation of OCF. However, its impact on the left-tail is not negligible. One approach to quantify the left-tail impact is risk capital, as will be discussed in Chapter 5.

Example 4.19 Construction cost overrun. Anyone who has dealt with contractors knows that every capital investment is subject to numerous contingencies. A few years ago, most corporations would simply select a few sensitivities (cost overrun by 15%, underrun by 10%) and estimate the value created in these circumstances. Today, corporations are more sophisticated, and conduct rigourous risk analyses of their investment projects: the risks associated with each step are identified, and a distribution is developed. Adding these risks together, taking into account the dependencies, creates a distribution of costs for the project. The exact shape and parameters of the distribution depend on each project. In general, the right-tail of the cost distribution (cost overruns) is much longer than the left-tail (underrun).

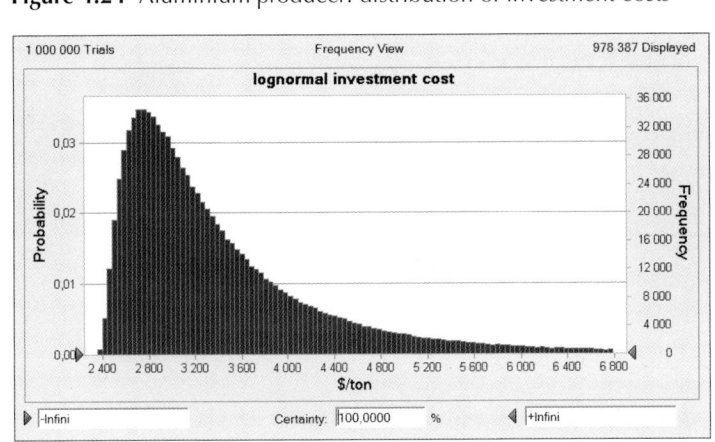

Figure 4.24 Aluminium producer: distribution of investment costs

In our example, we assume the distribution of construction costs overrun is log-normal, which satisfies our long right-tail property. Specifically, we introduce a log-normal variable z and assume that the initial investment $I_0 = 3{,}500 \cdot (1+z)/(1+E[z])$ US\$/ton. We immediately verify that $E[I_0] = 3{,}500$ US\$/ton, and $\sigma_{I_0} = 3{,}500 \cdot (\sigma_z)/(1+E[z])$ US\$/ton. For example, assume that $E[z] = \sigma_z = 0.5$. We have $\sigma_{I_0} = 1{,}167$ US\$/ton, and I_0 is distributed as shown in Figure 4.24.

By construction, the investment cost has a long right tail, corresponding to very high (but very unlikely) cost increases. Assuming that cost overruns are uncorrelated to other variables, using the distribution of costs instead of a point estimate has no impact on the expected EBITDA or OCF since the expected cost is unchanged.

4.2.4 Business risk

Science, in particular microeconomics, probabilities and statistics are almost sufficient to estimate price, counterparty, and operations risk. Business risk requires this science, but sound business judgement ("art") as well. What is the distribution of outcomes of a massive produce liability suit for a pharmaceutical company? What is the probability that carbon dioxide regulation be imposed on a coal-based electric power producer in the Midwest of the US in the next three years? Five years, Ten years? What form would the regulation take? What is the likelihood of mobile phone users purchasing mobile television services? These are the issues at the core of business risk analysis.

Risk analysis is the best analytical mindset to examine these questions. Risk analysis is not concerned about precisely predicting the future. Rather it aims at developing a quantitative perspective on possible future states of the world. While risk analysts cannot predict exactly the outcome of a product liability lawsuit, they can estimate a worst case, base case, and expected case.

Business risk analysis relies on facts. For the examples mentioned above, there have been multiple comparable medical liability trials in the US. For the carbon regulation, political parties and candidates have stated position, and have a track record. At its best, business risk analysis can foster a fact-based dialogue around a business plan or proposition.

The analytical tools are identical: disaggregation of risks, estimation of individual risks, and re-aggregation. The statistical specifications discussed for the outside-in approach also apply to the business risk. The analyst will strip out of the risk profile the commodity, operations and counterparty risks, then determine the best representation for the residual business risk. Two examples are presented below.

> **Example 4.20** Emission regulation risk for the aluminium producer. *One critical risk for many industries is the timing and the form of emissions regulations, in particular carbon regulations. As seen on Example 4.12, these can impact the plant directly, or indirectly through electric power price. In Europe, the regulatory framework has been established – at least until 2012. The main question for most plants is the impact of carbon trading on electric power price, that can be viewed as mostly price risk. In the US, the regulatory framework is highly uncertain. While the US has not ratified the Kyoto protocol, multiple states are preparing – or imposing – some form of carbon control. Similarly in Canada, the details of the regulation (and its economic impact) are still being negotiated. For an investor estimating the value of an asset, the economic impact of carbon regulation is truly a random variable.*
>
> *As we have seen before, it is helpful to separate (1) the probability of some form of carbon regulation being enacted from (2) the impact if enacted. The probability of regulation being enacted in any given year is a*

simple binary random variable. Usually, the probability of a yes increases with time. For our smelter example, we assume the probability to be very low for the first ten years (1% for every year), then much higher for years 11 to 20 (30%), and again higher for years 21 to 30 (60%). As discussed above, there is a fair part of business judgement involved in selecting these probabilities. However, many facts are also available to inform the discussion: governments and political parties have stated opinions, global negotiations are under way, etc.

The impact if enacted depends mostly on the details of implementation. Usually assets installed before the regulation comes into effect receive "grand-fathered" carbon rights. The impact is then indirect, through power prices. If these assets have long-term power supply contracts at a fixed price, they are therefore protected. However, anticipating a possible carbon regulation, hence a possible increase in power prices, power producers may be reluctant to lock-in long term contracts that forgo that potential value source. Again, a fact-based analysis can uncover a range for the impact of carbon regulations on assets. In our example, we assume that, if enacted, carbon regulation would increase operating costs by an average of US$150/ton. Furthermore, we assume the cost increase is lognormally distributed, with standard deviation 100 US$/ton. The expected impact of carbon regulation is negligible in the first year, as the probability of enactment is very low. However, it matters for later years. For example, for year 11 and 21, we can compare the distribution with and without the regulation, as shown in Figures 4.25 and 4.26.

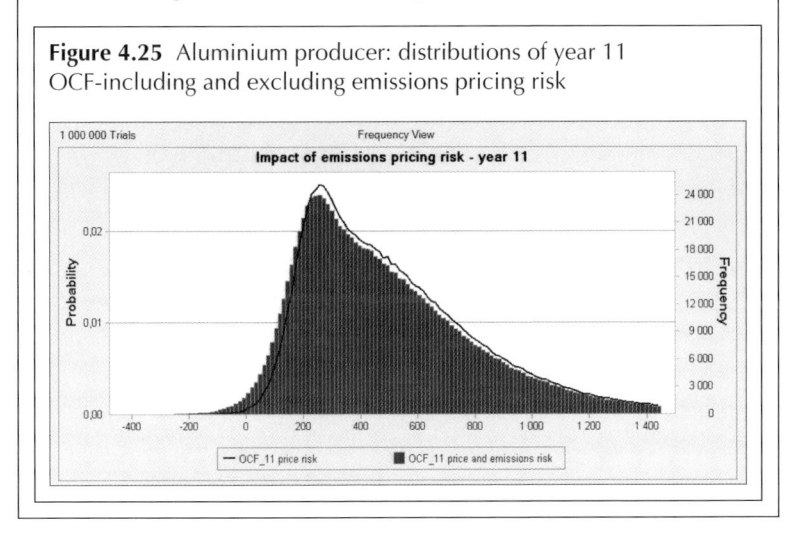

Figure 4.25 Aluminium producer: distributions of year 11 OCF-including and excluding emissions pricing risk

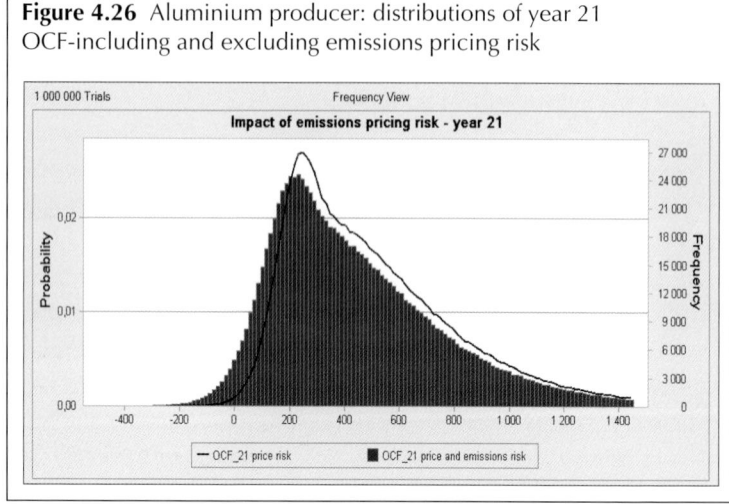

Figure 4.26 Aluminium producer: distributions of year 21 OCF-including and excluding emissions pricing risk

As would be expected, the distortion is greater for year 21, when the probability of emissions pricing being imposed is higher.

Example 4.21 Apartment occupancy. *Investors in residential real estate face a significant occupancy risk, that varies with the specific market considered, the type of property, and the overall economic conditions. Still, one expects the shape of the distribution of days without tenant to remain constant. A group of students elected to conduct a case study of the real estate market, and found data on apartment occupancy.[16] Their sample included 1,728 properties, with numbers of days without an occupants per property per month. The distribution of the number of consecutive days without an occupant is represented in Figure 4.27. It follows a Weibull distribution, with mean $\mu = 36.45$ days and standard deviation $\sigma = 58.04$ days. Slightly more than 16% of apartments are fully occupied.*

The properties can be further broken down according to their type. The three largest types account for over 96% of total properties. Their reverse cumulative distributions are represented in Figure 4.28. While the distributions are similar in shape, differences exist. We find that two-bedroom apartments (type 2), have the lowest probability of being unoccupied for all numbers of day: for example, there is around 25% chance of more

Figure 4.27 Distribution of days without occupants – all properties

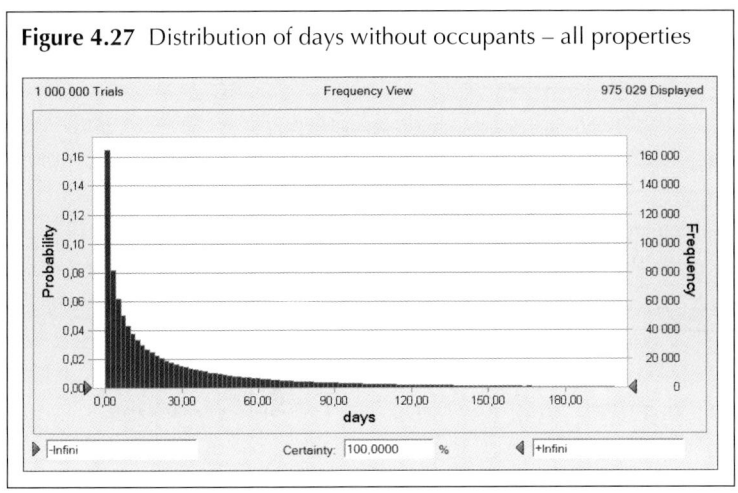

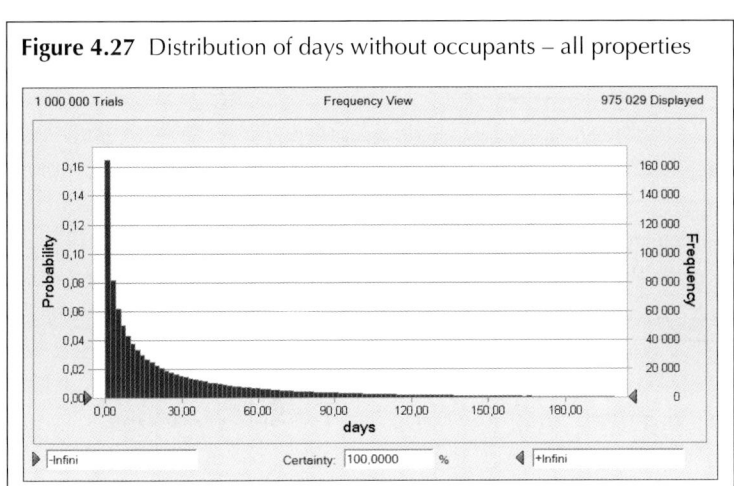

Figure 4.28 Distribution of days without occupants – per type

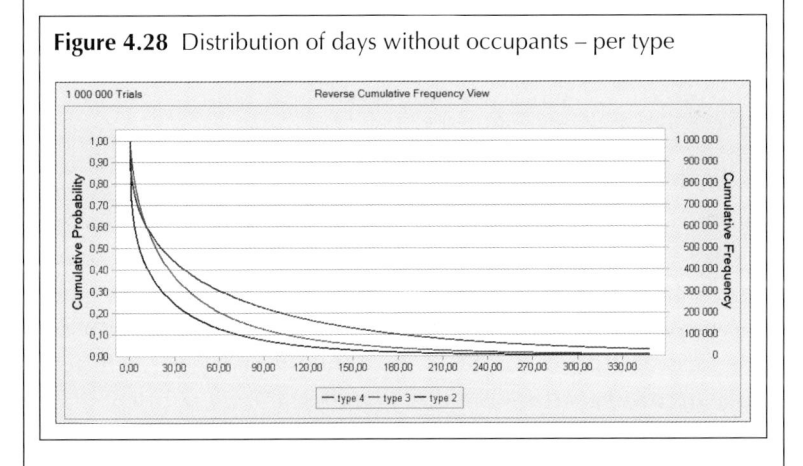

than 30 days of unoccupancy for two-bedroom apartments, compared to 40% chance for three-bedroom ones, and around 45% chance for four-bedroom apartments. Similarly, the average number of days without occupant is 24.29 for two-bedroom apartments, compared with 39.34 for three-bedroom ones, and 62.67 for four-bedroom apartments.

Once the distributions have been estimated using historical data, they can be used for prospective analysis, for example to price occupancy rental insurance.

4.2.5 Risk aggregation – hunting for correlations

Once she has developed a distribution for each risk individually, the risk analyst then aggregates all risks, taking correlations into account. This requires solid econometrics, but more importantly, strong business sense, as risks are often correlated in subtle ways across categories, creating true worst-case situations, or natural offsets.

As discussed earlier, during the 1998 and 1999 power price spikes in the Midwest of the US, some power traders found themselves simultaneously exposed to a price risk and a (positively correlated) counterparty risk. Consider a power trader who had built a portfolio of purchase and sale contracts, with a resulting net short position, anticipating low prices for the summer. As power prices rose steadily throughout the summer, the cost of covering his short position increased dramatically. Furthermore, some of his suppliers defaulted on their contract, precisely because prices were significantly higher than expected. The power trader would then panic and bid up the power price, contributing to a vicious circle of higher prices and default: counterparty and price risks were positively correlated. On the other, during off-peak hours, ample power was available, and no correlation existed between counterparty and price risks.

4.3 MULTI-PERIOD ANALYSES

The risk analysis can then be used to examine multi-period issues, for example 5% worst Operating Cash Flows over five to ten years, or the distribution of the value of a firm (or a project). In the outside-in approach, the assumption of the invariance of distributions carries forward: for all $t > t_0$, the distribution of I_t, ρ_t hence the profitability π_t are known. The inside-out approach, as usual, is more demanding, and requires the analyst to develop a dynamic perspective of risks. In Example 4.20, the probability of emissions pricing is increasing over time.

> **Example 4.22** Distribution of values of the aluminium company.
> *Two elements are required: (1) a financial valuation model, and (2) a multi-year risk model. We use the Discounted Free Cash Flow (DCF) approach as a valuation framework. To simplify the model, we assume*

(1) no incremental capital investment over the 30-year life of the asset, hence no residual value, and (2) the debt-to-asset ratio is held constant. Of course, in practice, more realistic and sophisticated financial models are used. Similarly, the aluminium production and the operating costs are assumed constant. More realistic models include yearly production increase resulting from continuous improvement initiatives ("production creep"), and inflation in the operating costs. Both rates of increase are often stochastic. The aluminium prices and exchange rate forecasts are produced using the statistical models described in Appendix 4.B. Ignoring the operations and business risk, the DCF gives a base value created by the asset as:

$$VC_0 = US\$2,256\ US\$/ton$$

In addition to the price risk, we include in the valuation the investment costs, production, and emissions pricing risks, as discussed above. The resulting value creation is presented in Figure 4.29.

The expected value created is:

$$E[VC] = 1,690\ US\$/ton$$

This is sometimes called the risk-adjusted value created. This is the true expected value created by the project, that should be used when evaluating the investment decision. It is much lower than VC_0 since

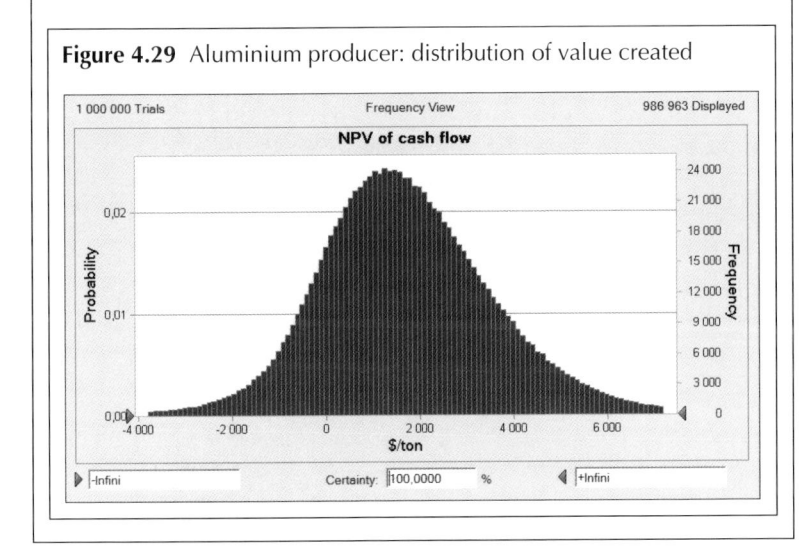

Figure 4.29 Aluminium producer: distribution of value created

> the operations and emissions risk are asymmetrical: they only reduce the value of the project. The standard deviation is $\sigma_{VC} = 1,959$ US\$/ton, quite large, due to the various sources of uncertainty on the project. The price risk alone contributes 1,759 US\$/ton to the standard deviation. Furthermore there is a 19% chance of the project destroying value.

4.4 SPECIFICITY OF ENTERPRISE RISK ANALYSIS

4.4.1 The peculiar analytics of enterprise risk management

As a risk management professional in a leading metals and mining company headquartered in Montreal, I have found it challenging to recruit quantitative analysts well-versed in enterprise risk analysis. Most graduates of the risk management or mathematical finance programs I have interviewed were very familiar with stochastic processes used in financial markets, but had no or limited experience directly relevant to the task at hand. This does not mean that the programs or the students were not good. On the contrary, I have found many extremely solid quantitative analysts among the graduates. This simply shows that (1) enterprise risk analysis requires slightly different analytical techniques than financial markets risk analysis, and (2) finance and risk management programs have yet to teach these techniques.

I believe there are two main specificities to enterprise risk analytics. First, probability distributions used in enterprise risk management differs from the more developed financial markets risk management distributions, such as the Black–Scholes model of stock price behaviour. Enterprise price risk analysis is mostly concerned with long-term annual averages of prices. Daily, weekly, even monthly variations in oil prices are not relevant to determine the equity level of Exxon/Mobil. However, the probability that oil price falls below US\$20/bbl on average for three to five years is a highly relevant metric. The mathematical models that are used for short-term pricing (eg, next day) are not always appropriate to predict long-term evolution: for example, the Black–Scholes diffusion model – widely used in financial markets – assumes that prices grow indefinitely, which might be appropriate for a few days, but certainly not for a few years, where mean-reversion is likely to set in.

Additionally, as we have seen above, invested capital distributions often exhibit jumps. I believe this is also the case for profitability distribution, in particular for smaller firms, that are heavily dependent on the success of one venture. Smooth distributions, that assume a small change from one period to the next are probably not the best representation. I have found very few studies that examine this issue. I believe this is a very promising avenue for future research.

Secondly, enterprise risk analysis requires robust mathematics, but also a solid business sense. Enterprise risk analysts can rarely obtain long series of historical data, such as daily prices. For example, to evaluate the risk of failure at a specific plant, the analyst will likely have only a few years worth of monthly production data. The data will then have to be cleaned up, interviews of plant personnel conducted to understand them, and also leverage data from other comparable plants.

4.4.2 The black swan paradox

One cannot discuss risk analysis without mentioning the "black swan paradox". In his 2005 book *Fooled by randomness,* Salim Taleb explains how he built his successful trading career precisely by hunting crises that allude others' VaR models. This limitation arises from the "Black swan" problem introduced by Karl Popper. Simply put: "one cannot conclude definitely that black swans do not exist simply by observing a white swan population".

This notion, while simple, is highly powerful. Our ability to predict different futures is limited by our past experience. Can a quantitative analyst ever be absolutely confident that he has included all possible scenarios in his models? Probably not.

Taleb is therefore highly skeptical about a risk analyst's ability to correctly anticipate worst-case scenarios. However, I am not as pessimistic as Taleb, for two reasons.

First, there are often warning signs for the courageous observer. Adverse events rarely happen without any warning. In the LTCM example discussed in Chapter 3, some other trading houses had correctly anticipated the risk of Russian default. Taleb shows that many spectacular trading failures do not come from the black swan alone, but from the combination of a rapid market evolution with unwillingness by traders to accept that their previous view turned out to be wrong, and to cut losses.[17] In the power spike price case in the US in 1998 and 1999, some traders had anticipated the spike as the summer was getting warmer, and covered their position at a loss, which turned out to be lower than the enormous loss suffered by uncovered players. Similarly, in the 2000 California electric power crisis, astute traders had anticipated the shortage of gas, and bought the pipeline capacity forward.

Second, analysis of historical data is not the only source to develop distributions of future events. Enterprise risk analysts can – and should – engage management in developing probability trees, identifying and quantifying all risks. This technique has been used extensively by engineers, in particular in nuclear reactors design, and can be applied to enterprise operations and business risk analysis.

One implication of the black swan paradox is that risk metrics that include all possible losses, such as risk capital discussed in Chapter 5, are preferable to metrics that truncate the worst-loss at a predefined level, such as VaR or Economic Capital, reviewed in Chapter 3.

APPENDIX

4.A COAL-FIRED PLANT PROFIT UNDER EMISSION TRADING

Green (2006) states that producing electric power using one MWh of coal generates 0.3395 tons of carbon (rounded to 0.4) in the example, and that producing electric power using one MWh of gas generates 0.19635 tons of carbon (rounded to 0.2) in the example. Then, denoting p_{car} the (expected) price of a ton of carbon, the marginal cost of producing power using coal including the carbon permit is: $\alpha_{coal} \cdot (0.4 \cdot p_{car} + p_{coal})$. Similarly, the marginal cost of producing power using gas is: $\alpha_{gas} \cdot (0.2 \cdot p_{car} + p_{gas})$. At equilibrium, the price of carbon is set so that both costs are equal, to allow for switching:

$$\alpha_{coal} \cdot (0.4 \cdot p_{car} + p_{coal}) = \alpha_{gas} \cdot (0.2 \cdot p_{car} + p_{gas})$$

We immediately have:

$$p_{car} = \frac{\alpha_{gas} \cdot p_{gas} - \alpha_{coal} \cdot p_{coal}}{0.4\alpha_{coal} - 0.2\alpha_{gas}}$$

Profit for the coal-fired producer is:

$$\begin{aligned}
\pi &= \alpha_{coal} \cdot (0.4 \cdot p_{car} + p_{coal}) - \alpha \cdot (0.4 \cdot p_{car} + p_{coal}) \\
&= (\alpha_{coal} - \alpha) \cdot (0.4 \cdot p_{car} + p_{coal}) \\
&= (\alpha_{coal} - \alpha) \cdot \left(0.4 \cdot \frac{\alpha_{gas} \cdot p_{gas} - \alpha_{coal} \cdot p_{coal}}{0.4\alpha_{coal} - 0.2\alpha_{gas}} + p_{coal}\right) \\
&= \frac{(\alpha_{coal} - \alpha)}{0.4\alpha_{coal} - 0.2\alpha_{gas}} \cdot (0.4\alpha_{gas} \cdot p_{gas} - 0.2\alpha_{gas} \cdot p_{coal}) \\
&= \frac{\alpha_{coal} - \alpha}{2\frac{\alpha_{coal}}{\alpha_{gas}} - 1} \cdot (2p_{gas} - p_{coal})
\end{aligned}$$

4.B THE ALUMINIUM SMELTER EXAMPLE

As suggested by the academic literature (eg, Schwartz (1997)), the logarithm of the aluminium price (US$ per ton) and the

US$/CA$ exchange rate (US$ per CA$) are both assumed to follow mean reverting processes, as described by Equation (1). The time step is taken to be one month. The parameters are estimated here in two steps: (1) for each price $i = 1, 2$, the parameters μ_i, κ_i and σ_i are estimated using Ordinary Least Squares, and (2) the correlation coefficient ρ of the normal disturbances is estimated later. This proves to be easier to implement. Alternatively, one could estimate all parameters simultaneously using Maximum Likelihood Estimation. The resulting estimates are:

	p_{Al}	$p_{\frac{US\$}{CA\$}}$
μ_i	7.548	−0.250
κ_i	0.300	0.106
σ_i	0.300	0.078

and $\rho = 0.281$

The resulting monthly prices are then averaged, to produce a yearly average price. The distribution of average aluminium price is shown in Figure 4.30 and the distribution of average exchange rate is as shown in Figure 4.31.

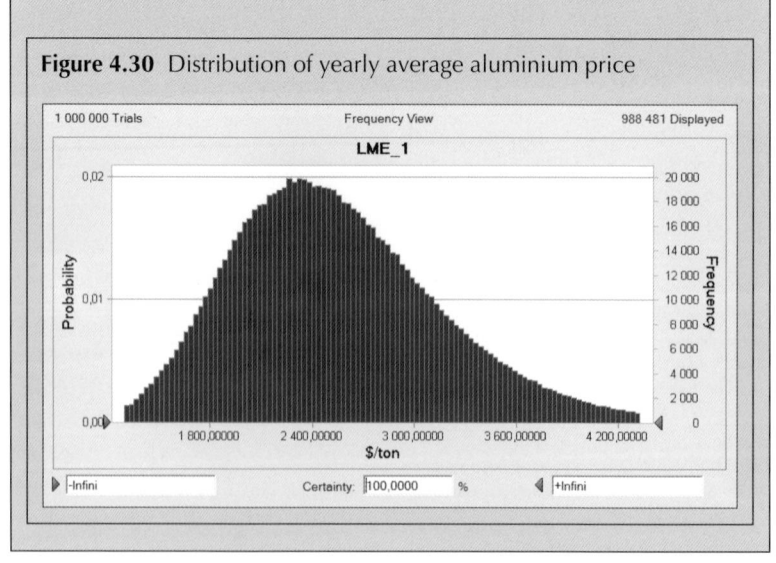

Figure 4.30 Distribution of yearly average aluminium price

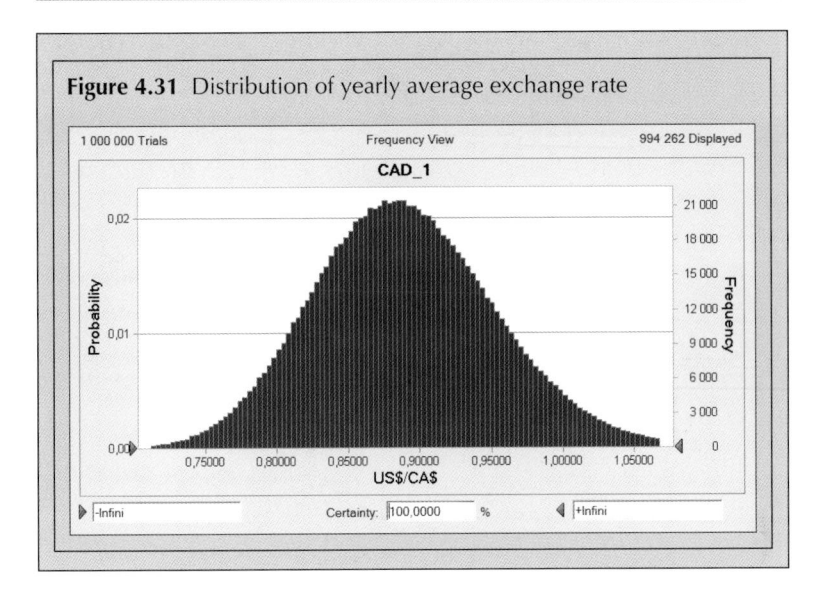

ENTERPRISE RISK ANALYSIS

Figure 4.31 Distribution of yearly average exchange rate

1 I am grateful to Laurent Antras, Michel Allain, and Alexandru Nichifor, who developed the OSG case as a risk management term-paper.
2 The maximum extreme value is the best fit for the Chi-square and the Anderson–Darling test.
3 See for example the statistical tests conducted in Schwartz (1997) and Bernard et al (2006).
4 "Return to founder", *The Economist*, 1 February 2007.
5 Foster and Kaplan (2001).
6 Kennedy (1990).
7 This distribution is the discrete approximation of the solution to the continuous differential equation defining a mean-reverting process.
   Other specifications can be used. For example, academic researchers have found that the logarithm of oil price exhibits "better" mean reversion than the price itself. Therefore, the logarithm of profitability for an oil company may also exhibit a "better" mean reversion than the profitability itself.
8 Since $E[\rho_{t+1}/\rho_t] = \rho_t$, $d/dt E[\rho_{t+1}/\rho_t] = 1 > 0$.
9 The Student-*t* distribution is a best fit for the Chi-square, Anderson–Darling, and Kolmogrov–Smirnov tests.
10 In practice, an additional risk is the spread between the price it pays for its coal and the price paid for coal by the marginal power producer. On average, that spread should be equal to zero.
11 Due to lags in the passthrough mechanism, they are likely to have a time-spread exposure.
12 Accountants define balance sheet translation risk as the risk associated with translation of foreign asset (book) values in domestic currency at the end of the period to produce consolidated financial statements.
13 This metric is common practice in the industry. It corresponds to the capital cost of producing one ton of aluminium every year for 30 years, the useful life of the assets.
14 Marshall (2005).
15 This process is known as a Bernouilli process. The annual duration of interruption is a binomial distribution with 12 trials and $p = 0.05$ probability of success at each trial. The parameters are selected to create a visible impact on profitability. They do not represent actual probabilities I have observed.

16 I am grateful to Alejandra Barrientos, Ludovic Couturier, Geoffrey Dapoigny and Hui Lou for developing that original example.
17 This behaviour is consistent with psychological biases explored for example by Kahneman and Tversky, and since confirmed by modern psychological research.

5

Risk Capital

This chapter discusses risk capital, an extremely powerful risk metric. As was mentioned in Chapters 1 and 2, risk capital is the *price of risk*: the minimum "hypothetical" insurance premium that insures that the assets of the firm can be financed using risk free debt. Risk capital can be used to address many practical risk management issues, such as project valuation and performance management.

The approach proposed here integrates and expands upon two existing concepts: (1) risk capital, introduced by Robert Merton and André Perold in their seminal article[1] for a one-period financial portfolio, and (2) the KMV dynamic equity-based credit risk measurement model discussed in Chapter 4.

Section 5.1 briefly presents Merton and Perold's one-period model, and applies it to three simple examples. Section 5.2 discusses the relationship between investment and risk capital: sources and adequacy of risk capital, and implications for cost of capital for a project/business. Section 5.3 applies risk capital for (*ex ante*) project valuation and (*ex post*) performance management in the one-period case.

Section 5.4 extends risk capital to multi period firms and projects. We first derive the multi period expression of risk capital, and apply it to two examples: (1) a "stylised" example where closed form solutions are available, that helps us enhance our intuition, and (2) the aluminium producer introduced in Chapter 4.

Section 5.5 compares Risk Capital to Economic Capital introduced in Chapter 3. Finally Section 5.6 concludes and discusses avenues of future research.

Appendix 5.A derives the beta of the (hypothetical) insurance contract as a function of the beta of the underlying assets.

5.1 THE BASIC MODEL
5.1.1 Derivation

In their seminal article, Robert Merton and André Perold introduce risk capital as an economic measure of volatility. They provide the following definition:

> "the smallest amount that can be invested to insure the value of the firm's net assets against a loss in value relative to the risk-free investment of those net assets."

Derivation of the expression for risk capital in the simplest setting – the one-period tax-less environment introduced by Merton and Perold – is presented below.

At date $t = 0$, an asset A is built (or bought), requiring investment I. The asset is fully financed by a loan. At date $t = 1$, this asset, has a value V_A, a random variable. If the value of the asset is high enough, the lenders receive payment of the principal I plus interest on the loan, and the equity holders receive the residual value. If the value of the asset is not sufficient, the lenders receive the full value V_A, and the equity holders receive no payment.

Consider now that there exists a "hypothetical" insurance contract, that fully guarantees the loan. The lenders then have no risk, hence demand only the risk-free rate r_f. In practice, the insurance contract can be a formal contract with a third party, a parent guarantee, or implicitly provided by the stakeholders.

The payoffs to all parties are as follows:

❏ If V_A exceeds the investment cost (equal to the loan amount) I plus the risk-free interest on the loan $r_f \cdot I$, the insurer makes no payment. The lenders receive $(1 + r_f) \cdot I$. The equity owners receive $V_A - (1 + r_f) \cdot I \geq 0$.
❏ If V_A is smaller than the investment cost I plus the risk-free interest on the loan $r_f \cdot I$ (ie, $A < (1 + r_f) \cdot I$), the insurer pays the shortfall: $((1 + r_f) \cdot I - V_A)$. The lenders receive $(1 + r_f) \cdot I$, hence are fully insured. The equity owners receive nothing.

Table 5.1 Payoffs in different cases

Case	Lender	Insurer	Equity holder	Total
$V_A \geq (1 + r_f) \cdot I$	$(1 + r_f) \cdot I$	0	$V_A - (1 + r_f) \cdot I$	V_A
$V_A < (1 + r_f) \cdot I$	$(1 + r_f) \cdot I$	$-((1 + r_f) \cdot I - V_A)$	0	V_A
Average	$(1 + r_f) \cdot I$	$E[V_A - (1 + r_f) \cdot I /$ $V_A < (1 + r_f) \cdot I]$ $Pr(V_A < (1 + r_f) \cdot I)$	$E[V_A - (1 + r_f) \cdot I /$ $V_A \geq (1 + r_f) \cdot I]$ $Pr(V_A \geq (1 + r_f) \cdot I)$	$E[V_A]$

These payoffs are summarised in Table 5.1. The expected payment from the insurance – denoted $E[p]$ – is then:

$$E[p] = Pr(V_A < (1 + r_f) \cdot I) \cdot E[(1 + r_f) \cdot I - V_A / V_A < (1 + r_f)]$$
$$= E[\max((1 + r_f) \cdot I - V_A, 0)]$$

Assuming the insurance sector is competitive, insurers make no profit[2]. The insurance premium is equal to the present value of the expected payment:

$$R^K = \frac{E[\max((1 + r_f) \cdot I - V_A, 0)]}{1 + \bar{r}} \quad (1)$$

where $\bar{r}$ is the discount rate for the insurance payments.

The risk capital depends only on the investment cost I, the risk-free rate r_f, and the (left tail) of the distribution of asset value V_A. It is an absolute metric: there is no need to specify a holding period, or a confidence level. Risk capital is simply the value of risk.

We observe from Equation (1) that providing risk capital is equivalent to selling a European put on the value of asset, at strike price $(1 + r_f) \cdot I$. In the particular case where the asset value V_A is distributed log-normally, we can use the Black and Scholes option pricing formula.

Merton and Perold's elegant notion presents multiple advantages:

❏ It includes the *full distribution of possible losses*, not only losses limited to a given confidence level, as is the case for VaR (discussed in Chapter 3). This is critical when extremely damaging yet highly infrequent "spikes" can occur.

- It illustrates the *different functions of capital*: (1) purchase equipment, plant, facilities at no risk (investment capital), and (2) purchase insurance against adverse events (risk capital).
- Since risk capital is the cost of a "hypothetical" insurance contract and can also be expressed as the value of a put option, it illustrates the *equivalence between insurance and hedging* as contributors to the risk capital balance.
- It converts volatility, which is not priceable into a capital measure, which is *price-able*. This makes it possible to formally include risk considerations in the project valuation and performance processes.
- It is a *universal risk metric*: risk capital as a percentage of an asset value can be compared to an insurance premium as a percentage of an asset value and/or to a Credit Default Swap premium as a percentage of the nominal position and/or to an option premium.

5.1.2 Discount rate for the insurance payments

As shown in Appendix 2.D, the discount rate $\bar{r}$ is determined by the systematic risk of the insurance payments p. Specifically, denote r^p and r^M respectively the returns on the insurance payments and the market index, and $\beta_p = cov(r^p, r^M)/\sqrt{var(r^M)}$ the beta of the insurance payment. The CAPM yields:

$$\bar{r} = r_f + \beta_p \cdot (E[r_M] - r_f)$$

Suppose the (returns on the) payments are positively correlated with the market returns: $\beta_p \geq 0$. The payments provide a natural hedge to the "insurance company", as they constitute a positive-β liability that offset the risk of the positive-β assets held by the "insurance company". Therefore, the "insurance company" will require a lower premium, which is captured in a higher discount rate.

Denote β_A the beta of the asset. Derivations presented in Appendix 5.A show that:

$$\beta_p \approx \Delta \cdot \frac{E[V_A]}{R^K} \cdot \beta_A \qquad (2)$$

where $\Delta = \partial R^K / \partial V_A$ is the derivative of the risk capital with respect to the value of the underlying asset. Since risk capital is the value of a put option on the underlying asset, Δ has the usual interpretation. In particular Δ is negative, hence the beta of the insurance payment is of opposite sign to the beta of the assets: when the returns on the assets are high, the returns on the payments are lower.

Our approximation is exact when the investment asset is uncorrelated with the market, ie, $\beta_A = 0$. Then, $\beta_p = \beta_A = 0$ and $\bar{r} = r_f$: the expected payment from insurance is discounted at the risk free rate in Equation (1).

5.1.3 Trading example

A trading company purchases US$100 *million* worth of pork bellies, for delivery in 12 months. Denote V_A the value of this contract at the delivery date. The traders expect V_A = US$110 *million*, hence, at delivery, they expect to buy the pork bellies for US$100 *million* as agreed, sell them for US$110 *million*, and net US$10 *million*. The risk analysis group determines that the delivery price of the pork bellies twelve months forward is normally distributed, with average $E[V_A]$ = US$100 *million* (in that case, the expected spot price is equal to the forward price) and standard deviation σ_{V_A} = US$30 *million*. Furthermore, pork bellies returns are uncorrelated to the market, hence the expected payment is discounted at the risk free rate $r_f = 5\%$.

Since the physical investment for a trading company is negligible, payment under the "hypothetical" insurance contract is triggered when the value of the portfolio is negative, ie, $V_A <$ US$100 *million*. Equation (1) becomes:

$$R^K = \frac{E[\max(100 - V_A, 0)]}{1 + r_f}$$

Since $E[V_A]$ = US$100 *million*, the put option is at-the-money: the probability of default is 50%. Since V_A is normally distributed, one can show that $\max(100 - V_A, 0) \simeq 0.4\sigma_{V_A} = 0.4 \times 30 =$ US$7.5 *million*. Then $R^K =$ US$7.1 *million*.

5.1.4 Industrial example

A firm invests $I =$ US$100 *million* at the beginning of the year. At the end of the year, it expects the assets to be worth $V_A =$ US$110 *million* (ie, generating a 10% return). The returns on the asset are uncorrelated with the market, hence the expected payment is discounted at the risk-free rate $r_f = 5\%$. The payment required by the lenders is therefore US$105 *million* = US$100 *million* + 5% × US$100 *million*. The insurance payment is triggered when $V_A <$ US$105 *million*. Equation (1) becomes:

$$R^K = \frac{E[\max(105 - V_A, 0)]}{1 + r_f}$$

The risk analysis group determines the asset value is normally distributed, with average $E[V_A] =$ US$110 *million* and standard deviation $\sigma_{V_A} =$ US$30 *million*. Numerical simulations then show that $\Pr(V_A < 105) = 44\%$, $E[\max(105 - V_A, 0)] =$ US$9.6 *million*, and $R^K =$ US$9.2 *million*.

5.1.5 Bernoulli example

We now introduce a stylised example, for which we can obtain closed form solutions. We gain in insight as we lose in realism.

Consider the following firm: today, we invest an amount $I = 1$ in an asset (eg, a new technology), that has value u at the end of the first (and unique) period of our analysis. We assume u follows a binary distribution:[3] with probability $(1 - \phi)$ the technology is successful and produces $u = 1 + x$, and with probability ϕ it is unsuccessful and produces $u = 0$. The returns on the asset are uncorrelated to the market returns, hence the payment from insurance are discounted at the risk free rate.

Denote w the cost of capital of this project. We will invest in the firm if (and only if) we expect it to be value-creating:

$$\frac{E[u]}{1 + w} - 1 \geq 0$$

⇔

$$(1 - \phi) \cdot (1 + x) \geq 1 + w$$

which we assume holds.

At the end of the period, the asset is worth more than the debt plus the risk free interest if (and only if): $u \geq 1 + r_f$. We assume this holds if $u = 1 + x$. Of course, this does not hold if $u = 0$. The payment from insurance, denoted p, is then:

$$p = \begin{cases} 0 & \text{if } u = 1+x \quad (prob = 1 - \phi) \\ 1 + r_f & \text{if } u = 0 \quad\;\; (prob = \phi) \end{cases}$$

The expected payment from insurance at the end of the period is:

$$E[p] = \phi \cdot (1 + r_f)$$

The risk capital is therefore the discounted value of expected payment:

$$R^K = \phi$$

If the project has a $\phi = 1\%$ chance of failure, $R^K = 1\%$ of the investment (normalised to one in this example). In this simple model, the risk capital depends only on the probability of failure ϕ. In particular, it does not depend on the profit if the project is successful (x). This is a general feature: only the left tail matters to determine risk capital.

5.2 INVESTMENT CAPITAL AND RISK CAPITAL
5.2.1 Source and adequacy of risk capital

Companies do not explicitly report risk capital in their balance sheet. Where is it then? The simple answer is: debt holders, equity holders, and stakeholders all provide risk capital. When debt is issued with a positive probability of default, the debt holders provide risk capital remunerated by the spread over the risk-free rate. Equity holders also provide risk capital, remunerated by the potential upside. Suppliers provide risk capital, through payment terms and credit terms.

One can naturally ask whether a firm has enough risk capital. The answer is yes: there is always enough risk capital. At the end of the day, someone will cover the firm's losses. A more appropriate question is: "who provides risk capital?"

If the risk capital is lower than the investment (physical) capital, then investors (ie, stock- and bond-holders) provide sufficient risk capital. This is the case for most industrial firms, where the worst that can happen is the net value of the assets falling to zero. For example, during the 1998–2000 bubble in the power industry too many power plants were built. As a result, some peaking assets in the Midwest of the US were never used. Their value was therefore equal to zero. By providing physical capital, investors have provided all the risk capital that was required.

On the other hand, if risk capital is larger than investment capital, then investors' contributions to risk capital are not sufficient. This can happen in a trading business, where the liabilities created by a portfolio of derivatives can far exceed the physical capital required to create that portfolio. As one trader famously observed:

> You do not need up-front capital to sell options. They pay you for it.

This situation can also happen if an industrial firm faces large liabilities (eg, asbestos litigation) which could exceed the value of the assets. In these cases, risk capital is provided by external sources: trading counterparties in the first case, and society at large in the second.

5.2.2 Resulting cost of capital

As seen in Appendix 2.D, the cost of capital can be expressed as a function of the unlevered expected return on the asset $E[r_A^*]$, the tax rate τ, and the market values of debt $E[B]$ and asset $E[V_A]$:

$$w = E[r_A^*] \cdot \left(1 - \tau \cdot \frac{E[B]}{E[V_A]}\right)$$

We consider the following capital structure:

(1) Debt holders provide risk-free debt to finance the physical investment (value I) and simultaneously sell a put on the assets, at strike price $K = (1 + r_f) \cdot I$. The market value of the debt, denoted $E[B]$ is therefore the face value of the debt I, less the value of the put option:

$$E[B] = I - R^K$$

Since debt is now risky, the promised yield to maturity on debt, denoted r_B, exceeds the risk free rate:

$$r_B = \frac{r_f \cdot I}{I - R^K} = \frac{r_f}{1 - \frac{R^K}{I}} \geq r_f$$

(2) Equity providers then provide the shortfall R^K to finance the investment. In terms of risk, they purchase the put option from the debt holders. They are residual claimants on the value of the assets, as long as the assets are worth more than the face value of debt, after which they put the assets to the debtors.

The balance sheet of the firm at market value is then:

Assets	Liabilities	
V_A	$I - R^K$	Debt
	$V_A - I + R^K$	Equity
V_A	V_A	Total

The market value of equity is the value of the assets net of the investment cost ($V_A - I$), plus the value of the put option R^K. Using the call-put parity, the value of the equity is the value of a call on the value of the assets, at strike price $K = (1 + r_f) \cdot I$.

We immediately have:

$$w = E[r_A^*] \cdot \left(1 - \tau \cdot \frac{I - R^K}{E[V_A]}\right) \quad (3)$$

Equation (3) allows the risk analyst to estimate the cost of capital for a project, fully taking the risk profile into account. As shown in Example 5.1, this approach can be used to select among projects with differing risk.

We observe:

$$\frac{\partial w}{\partial R^K} = E[r_A^*] \cdot \frac{\tau}{E[V_A]} \geq 0$$

Everything else being held constant, reducing the risk capital reduces the cost of capital, hence, everything else being equal, increases the value of the project. This illustrates the mechanics of the substitution of risk transfer instruments for equity discussed in Chapter 2: since the project is less risky, the market value of the debt is higher, hence the cost of capital is lower.

CORPORATE RISK MANAGEMENT FOR VALUE CREATION

Equation (3) does not lead to a U-shaped cost of capital. It is applicable only when financial flexibility is not an issue. For example, if a firm needs to select among two investment opportunities with different risk profiles, as is the case in Example 5.1, the appropriate discount rates are given by Equation (3) as long as the opportunities are small enough that failure in one does not jeopardise the financial flexibility of the firm. If the opportunities are too large (eg, a significant merger or acquisition), we must use the more comprehensive analytical framework described in Chapter 6.

> **Example 5.1** A firm considers two projects: project A generates perpetual ROIC $\rho_A = 10\%$ and has risk capital $R_A^K = 10\%$, while project B generates perpetual ROIC $\rho_B = 13\%$ and has risk capital $R_B^K = 40\%$. The unlevered expected returns are $E[r_A^*] = 10\%$ on project A, and $E[r_B^*] = 12\%$ on project B. The investment is normalised to $I = 1$.
> From Appendix 2.D, we know that:
>
> $$E[V_A] = 1 + \frac{\rho_A - w_A}{w_A} = \frac{\rho_A}{w_A}$$
>
> Then, substituting in Equation (3):
>
> $$E[V_A] = \frac{\rho_A}{E[r_A^*] \cdot \left(1 - \tau \cdot \frac{1 - R^K}{E[V_A]}\right)}$$
>
> We face the circularity problem familiar in valuation: the (expected) value of the firm depends on the cost of capital, which itself depends on the (expected) value of the firm. Fortunately, a closed form solution is available in this case:
>
> $$E[V_A] \cdot \left([r_A^*] \cdot \left(1 - \tau \cdot \frac{1 - R^K}{E[V_A]}\right)\right) = \rho_A$$
>
> $\Leftrightarrow$
>
> $$E[V_A] \cdot [r_A^*] = \rho_A + E[r_A^*] \cdot \tau \cdot (1 - R^K)$$
>
> $\Leftrightarrow$
>
> $$E[V_A] = \frac{\rho_A}{E[r_A^*]} + \tau \cdot (1 - R^K)$$

The value of the firm is the constant ROIC, discounted at the unlevered cost of capital, plus the present value of the tax shield, which is the tax rate times the market value of the debt.
Then:

$$E[V_A] \geq E[V_B] \Leftrightarrow \frac{\rho_A}{E[r_A^*]} - \frac{\rho_B}{E[r_B^*]} \geq \tau \cdot \left(R_A^K - R_B^K\right)$$

Substituting in the values from the example:

$$\frac{\rho_A}{E[r_A^*]} - \frac{\rho_B}{E[r_B^*]} = 1 - 1.083 = -0.083$$
$$\geq -0.12 = -0.4 \cdot 0.3 = \tau \cdot \left(R_A^K - R_B^K\right)$$

Project A is preferred to project B, even though its ROIC is lower.

5.3 ONE-PERIOD PROJECT VALUATION AND PERFORMANCE MEASUREMENT

5.3.1 Bernoulli example

We now use the cost of capital Equation (3) to value the Bernoulli assets. We previously found that the risk capital is:

$$R^K = \phi$$

Remembering that the investment capital is normalised to $I = 1$, Equation (3) becomes:

$$w = r_f \cdot \left(1 - \frac{\tau \cdot (1 - \phi)}{E[V_A]}\right)$$

The expected value of the firm as of today is then:

$$E[V_A] = \frac{(1 - \phi) \cdot (1 + x)}{1 + w} = \frac{(1 - \phi) \cdot (1 + x)}{1 + r_f \cdot \left(1 - \frac{\tau \cdot (1 - \phi)}{E[V_A]}\right)}$$

We face the circularity problem again: the (expected) value of the firm depends on the cost of capital, which itself depends on the (expected) value of the firm. A bit of algebra leads to:

$$E[V_A] = \frac{(1 - \phi) \cdot (1 + x + \tau \cdot r_f)}{1 + r_f}$$

The value of the project is the expected of the value of the project at date $t = 1$ ($(1 - \phi) \cdot (1 + x)$), plus the expected tax shield ($(1 - \phi) \cdot \tau \cdot r_f$), discounted at the risk-free rate.

With $x = 20\%$, $\phi = 10\%$, $r_f = 5\%$ and $\tau = 40\%$, we find $E[V_A] = 1.05$.

We observe that:

$$w = r_f \left(1 - \tau \frac{1 + r_f}{1 + x + \tau r_f}\right)$$

The cost of capital is independent of the default probability, since the market values of the assets and of the debt are proportional to $(1 - \phi)$

We also observe that:

$$\frac{dE[V_A]}{d\phi} = -\frac{1 + x + \tau \cdot r_f}{1 + r_f} < 0$$

As expected, reducing the probability of failure increases the expected value of the project, through two channels: (1) it increases the expected value of the project at date $t = 1$ and (2) it increases the expected value of the tax shield.

5.3.2 Trading example

Consider the pork bellies trading business discussed in Section 5.1. Suppose the traders were right, and they realised NOPLAT $\pi = US\$10\ million$. If the bank does not allocate investment capital to that particular trade ($I = 0$), the apparent EP is then $\widetilde{EP} = NOPLAT = US\$10\ million$, and the traders receive a hefty bonus.

RISK CAPITAL

As observed by Merton and Perold, risk capital is missing in this description of the situation. Counterparties will not enter the trade, unless they receive a guarantee that someone will pay them, should that be required. In most cases, the guarantee is provided by the parent company of the trading business, and not explicitly accounted for.

If the guarantee was external, and assuming the insurance market was perfect, it would cost exactly R^K, the risk capital. This expense would have to be subtracted from the NOPLAT π. The NOPLAT would then be $\pi - R^K$. Equity holders in the trading business would have to provide cash to purchase the guarantee. This capital would have to be remunerated. Since pork bellies are uncorrelated with the market, the required return would be $R = r_f$. The EP would then be:

$$EP = \pi - R^K - r_f \cdot R^K$$

As Merton and Perold observe, there is no reason why the economics of a business with a parent guarantee should be any different from the economics of the business with an external guarantee. The EP given by the above equation is the true EP of the trading business.

Assuming that the risk free rate is $r_f = 5\%$, and recalling that risk capital $R^K = US\$7.1\ million$, we have:

$$EP = 10 - 7.1 \cdot 1.05 = US\$2.55\ million$$

The real EP remains positive, since the trade is truly profitable. However, the true profitability is significantly reduced by including the cost of the insurance premium. For example, if the NOPLAT is only $\pi = US\$5\ million$, the trade appears to create value, while it is in fact destroying value when risk capital is properly taken into account.

If the trade generates negative profits, traders are insured. The *ex post* EP on the negative profit trade is:

$$EP = -\left(1 + r_f\right) \cdot R^K$$

We also note that charging for risk capital does not distort trading behaviour *ex ante*.

The expected EP from the trade is:

$$E[EP] = E[\pi / \pi \geq 0] \cdot \Pr(\pi \geq 0) - R^K - r_f \cdot R^K$$
$$= E[\pi] - r_f \cdot R^K$$

since

$$E[\pi] = E[\pi / \pi \geq 0] \cdot \Pr(\pi \geq 0) + E[\pi / \pi < 0] \cdot \Pr(\pi < 0)$$
$$= E[\pi / \pi \geq 0] \cdot \Pr(\pi \geq 0) - R^K$$

Ex ante, the traders pay the capital charge of the risk capital only. With the assumptions described above, the trade is EP positive as long as:

$$E[\pi] \geq r_f \cdot R^K = US\$355{,}000$$

This example illustrates how risk capital can be used to control trading activity: evaluating performance *ex post* as we discussed here, but also setting limits *ex ante*. Determining position limits in then simply allocating risk capital.

It is particularly important when the commodity traded presents a very "fat" left tail. For example, alumina or power prices, where prices can sometimes exhibit spikes caused by physical events: a hurricane in Australia – a country with significant alumina production – could shut down a harbour for a few weeks, cause a shortage on the spot market, and, if the market is generally tight, send the prices skyrocketing as it did at the end of 2005 and early in 2006. Similarly, an outage of a major electric power plant in a tight market can send the prices up to 500 higher than average, as it occurred in the summers of 1998 and 1999 in the Midwest of the US.

None of these would be picked up in the traditional VaR analysis, however, they would be included in the risk capital, which includes the entire left tail.

5.4 RISK CAPITAL FOR A MULTI-PERIOD FIRM

This section generalises the risk capital notion to a more realistic multi-period environment. The general model is presented, then risk capital is estimated for various cases. We then show how risk capital can be used for capital allocation decisions in the multi-period case.

5.4.1 General framework

For $t \geq 1$, we define period t as running between dates $(t-1)$ and t. I_{t-1} is the invested capital at date $(t-1)$ generating free cash flows x_t during period t. V_{A_t} is the value of the investment assets at date t. Denote r_f the risk free rate. We assume here that, if the firm defaults, it does not generate enough EBIT to create a tax shield on its interest payment. This possibly leads to a slight overestimation of the risk capital, since a portion of the interest payment may be tax deductible. In practice, analysts will determine the size of the tax shield in their simulations. The effective interest rate on the risk free debt is simply r_f. The debt to be paid at date t is then $(1 + r_f) \cdot I_{t-1}$.

We conduct the analysis at date $t = 0$. In the general formulation, the firm operates an infinite number of periods.

The multi-period "hypothetical" insurance contract builds on the insight presented in the counterparty risk analysis section in Chapter 4: if the value of the firm at date t, denoted V_{A_t} falls below the value of the debt (including interest dues) $(1 + r_f) \cdot I_{t-1}$, the shareholders default, and put the assets to the creditors. The default condition at date t is then:

$$V_{A_t} < (1 + r_f) \cdot I_{t-1}$$

We now derive the expression for risk capital. To simplify the notation, it is helpful to define two events: ND_t is the event "no default up to and including date t" and d_t is the event "no default up and until date $(t-1)$ *and* default at date t". Alternatively, d_t is the default at date t, *conditional on* no default up and until date $(t-1)$.

Denote $\phi_t = \Pr(d_t)$ the probability of default at date t, conditional on no default up and until date $(t-1)$. We immediately observe that, conditional on ND_{t-1}, no default at date t occurs with probability $(1 - \phi_t)$. Hence $\Pr(ND_t) = \Pr(ND_{t-1}) \cdot (1 - \phi_t)$.

For every date $t \geq 1$, three situations can occur. First, the firm has already defaulted, hence there is no insurance payment.

Second, if the firm has not defaulted until date $(t-1)$, and if $V_{A_t} \geq (1+r_f) \cdot I_{t-1}$ no insurance payment is made, and we move to the next period. Third, still conditional on no default up and until date $(t-1)$, if $V_{A_t} < (1+r_f) \cdot I_{t-1}$, the insurance pays $(1+r_f) \cdot I_{t-1} - V_{A_t}$ and the insurance contract terminates. The expected payment[4] at date t, denoted $E[p_t]$ is equal to:

$$E[p_t] = \begin{cases} E[\max((1+r_f) \cdot I_{t-1} - V_{A_t}, 0) / ND_{t-1}] & \text{if } ND_{t-1} \\ 0 & \text{otherwise} \end{cases} \quad (4)$$

As previously, the risk capital is equal to the discounted sum of the expected insurance payments:

$$R^K = \sum_{t=1}^{\infty} \frac{\Pr(ND_{t-1}) \cdot E[p_t]}{(1+\bar{r})^t} \quad (5)$$

where the discount rate $\bar{r}$ is determined according to Equation (2) presented in Section 5.1.

The value of the firm is the present value of the expected FCFs. As mentioned before, three situations can occur. First, with probability $(1 - \Pr(ND_{t-1}))$ the firm has already defaulted in the past, and no cash flow occurs. Also with probability $\Pr(ND_t) = \Pr(ND_{t-1}) \cdot (1 - \phi_t)$ no default occurs, and the investors receive $E[x_t/ND_t]$. Finally, with probability $\Pr(ND_{t-1}) \cdot \phi_t$, default occurs and the investors receive 0.

The expected value of the firm is:

$$E[V_A] = \sum_{t=1}^{\infty} \Pr(ND_{t-1}) \cdot \frac{(1-\phi_t) \cdot E[x_t/ND_t] \cdot I_{t-1}}{(1+w)^t} \quad (6)$$

where w is the cost of capital for the firm as given by Equation (3).

Except for simple specifications (such as the Bernoulli example presented below), there exists no general closed-form solution for the system of Equations (2), (3), (4), (5) and (6) for three reasons: (1) Equation (4) takes into account the history of the asset values, (2) distributions are not always log normal, and (3) we face the cyclicality issue familiar to valuation practitioners: the value V_{A_t} is a function of the rate used to discount the future cash flows, which itself depends on the risk capital as can be seen from Equation (3). Risk capital is then a function of the value V_{A_t} as can be seen from Equations (2), (4) and (5).

Therefore we have to resort to Monte Carlo simulations, as will be shown in the aluminium company example below. We develop for each date $t \geq 1$ a distribution of the value of the firm *at date t*, for example using DCF or EP valuation. Then we compare the value of the firm to the value of the risk-free debt. We then conduct multiple simulations until we reach convergence to resolve the cyclicality issue. In practice, less than five simulations are required.

As mentioned earlier, the approach we propose builds on the same insight as the KMV credit risk measurement approach. However, there are a few differences, which reflect the differing purposes: the credit risk measurement literature is primarily concerned with estimating the probability of default, while we are concerned with estimating the (NPV of the) cost of default. Additionally, we are mainly concerned with *ex ante* project evaluation, not continuous evolution. Therefore, we use a discrete-time model, and our primary random variables are the FCFs or the EPs generated by the firm at each date, while KMV uses a continuous-time model, and their primary random variable is the value of the asset V_{A_t}.

We now apply the approach to two examples.

5.4.2 Bernoulli example

We first examine a stylised example where closed-form solutions are available. The main features of this example are independence and stationarity, ie, all the key parameters are independent of time and constant. Specifically, we assume that in any given year, a negative value shock can occur, in which case the firm's value drops to zero. We assume that these shocks are uncorrelated with each other and with the market returns, and that their probability of occurrence is constant and equal to ϕ.

For example, in any year, there is a small probability that a new technology be introduced that renders ours completely obsolete (eg, the personal computer for the typewriter), or that a new regulation be introduced that completely eliminates our value creation source (eg, US congress prohibits drugs imports from Canada into the US).

If the shock does not occur, the firm generates constant expected free cash flow per unit of invested capital $E[x_t/ND_t] = x$, and the firm grows at constant rate g, which implies:

$$I_t = (1 + g) \cdot I_{t-1}$$

Since we are valuing the firm over an infinite horizon, g has to be smaller than the appropriate discount rate. Specifically, we assume $g < r_f$. For simplicity, we normalise $I_0 \equiv 1$.

The expected payment Equation (4) simplifies to:

$$E\left[p_t / ND_{t-1}\right] = (1 + g)^{t-1} \cdot \phi \cdot \left(1 + r_f\right)$$

and Equation (5) becomes:

$$R^K = \sum_{t=1}^{\infty} (1 - \phi)^{t-1} \cdot (1 + g)^{t-1} \cdot \frac{\phi \cdot (1 + r_f)}{(1 + r_f)^t}$$

$$= \frac{\phi \cdot (1 + r_f)}{r_f + \phi - g \cdot (1 - \phi)}$$

As expected, the risk capital increases with the probability of default:

$$\frac{\partial R^K}{\partial \phi} = \frac{(1 + r_f) \cdot (r_f - g)}{(r_f + \phi - g \cdot (1 - \phi))^2} > 0$$

We also have

$$R^K\big|_{\phi=0} = 0 \quad \text{and} \quad R^K\big|_{\phi=1} = 1$$

If there no chance of default, there is no risk capital. If default is certain, all capital is risk capital.

We also observe that the risk capital increases with the growth rate:

$$\frac{\partial R^K}{\partial g} = \frac{\phi \cdot (1-\phi)(1+r_f)}{\left(r_f + \phi - g \cdot (1-\phi)\right)^2} \geq 0$$

The relationship between risk and growth is central, and found in many chapters in this book: simply put, higher growth anticipation means higher risk. This explains (in part) why firms with no growth potential, for example single asset SPVs, can support higher leverage than firms with strong growth potential.

We now turn to the value of the firm. Conditional on no default up to and including $(t-1)$, the expected cash flow from the firm at date t is:

$$E[x_t / ND_{t-1}] = (1+g)^{t-1} \cdot (1-\phi) \cdot x$$

Equation (6) then becomes:

$$E[V_A] = \sum_{t=1}^{\infty} \frac{(1-\phi)^t \cdot (1+g)^{t-1} \cdot x}{(1+w)^t} = x \cdot \frac{1-\phi}{w + \phi - g \cdot (1-\phi)}$$

We now turn to the cost of capital. We assume that the creditors accept *ex ante* to finance all new invested capital, should it be required. Denote $E[I]$ the expected invested capital in the firm. We have:

$$E[I] = 1 + \frac{(1-\phi) \cdot g}{1+r_f} + \frac{(1-\phi)^2 \cdot g \cdot (1+g)}{(1+r_f)^2} + \dots$$

$$+ \frac{(1-\phi)^t \cdot g \cdot (1+g)^{t-1}}{(1+r_f)^t} + \dots$$

$$= 1 + \frac{g}{1+g} \sum_{t=1}^{\infty} \left(\frac{(1-\phi) \cdot (1+g)}{1+r_f} \right)^t$$

$$= \frac{r_f + \phi}{r_f + \phi - g \cdot (1-\phi)}$$

The debt is discounted at the risk free rate since the returns on the shocks are uncorrelated with the market.

The market value of debt is then:

$$E[B] = E[I] - R^K$$

or

$$E[B] = \frac{r_f \cdot (1 - \phi)}{r_f + \phi - g \cdot (1 - \phi)}$$

and

$$\frac{E[B]}{E[I]} = \frac{r_f \cdot (1 - \phi)}{r_f + \phi}$$

The market value of debt per unit of physical investment is independent of the growth rate, and depends only on the risk free rate and on the probability of negative shock. With $\phi = 1\%$ and $r_f = 5\%$, we have $E[B]/E[I] = 82.5\%$. If we further assume $g = 3\%$, we have: $E[I] = 1.98$.

Since

$$w_A = r_f \cdot \left(1 - \tau \cdot \frac{E[B]}{E[V_A]}\right)$$

the expected value of the firm is:

$$E[V_A] = \frac{(1 - \phi) \cdot x}{r_f \cdot \left(1 - \tau \cdot \frac{E[B]}{E[V_A]}\right) + \phi - g \cdot (1 - \phi)}$$

Simple algebra leads to:

$$E[V_A] = \frac{(1 - \phi) \cdot x + \tau \cdot r_f \cdot E[B]}{r_f + \phi - g(1 - \phi)}$$

The expected value of the firm is the sum of the discounted sum of the expected free cash flow generated by the assets, plus the discounted sum of the expected tax shield, which is the market value of the debt times the risk free rate times the tax rate. With the previous numerical assumptions and $x = 10\%$, we have $E[V_A] = 4.35$, and $E[V_A]/E[I] = 2.2$.

Of course, reducing the probability of default increases the expected value of the firm:

$$\frac{dE[V_A]}{d\phi} = -\frac{1}{(r_f + \phi - g \cdot (1 - \phi))^2} \cdot \left((1 + r_f) \cdot x + \tau \cdot r_f^2 \cdot \left(\frac{(1 + r_f) + (1 - \phi) \cdot (1 + g)}{(1 + r_f) - (1 - \phi) \cdot (1 + g)} \right) \right)$$
$$< 0$$

The first term is an "expected cash flows effect": as the probability of negative shock decreases, the expected cash flows generated by the assets increase. The second term is a true "reduced risk" effect: as the probability of negative shock decreases, the expected value of the tax shield increases, for two reasons: the tax shield is more likely, and it is also larger.

5.4.3 Aluminium producer example

In this case, we assume a finite life for the asset (30 years). As before, we run a Monte Carlo simulation with one million scenarios to estimate the values. Since the discount rate of the risk capital is a function of the value of the firm and of the value of risk capital, we need a few iterations to get convergence.

The probability that default occurs in a given year, is presented in Figure 5.1.

First, we observe that half of the projects never default. The cumulative probability of default is therefore 50%. Second, the biggest default risk is in the first year. This illustrates the critical importance of the construction risk: if the construction cost overrun is significant, the project defaults immediately. If on the other hand construction cost overrun is under control, default in later years, that will then be driven by price risk, is much less likely. The resulting average time to default is 20 years. Since half of the project never defaulted, the median is much higher, at 30 years.

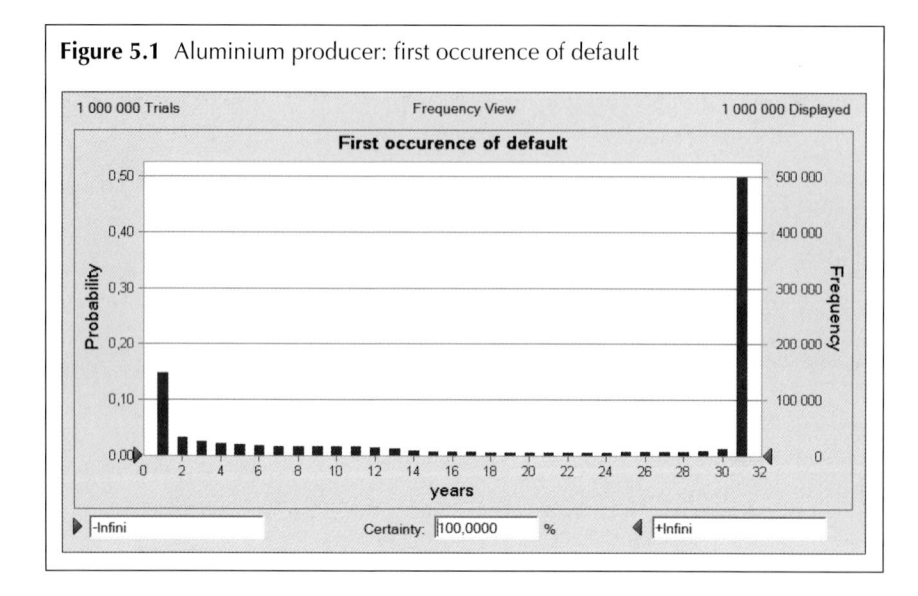

Figure 5.1 Aluminium producer: first occurence of default

[Figure: Histogram showing first occurence of default over years, 1 000 000 Trials, Frequency View, 1 000 000 Displayed. Probability on left axis (0.00 to 0.50), Frequency on right axis (0 to 500 000), years on x-axis (0 to 32).]

As we did in Chapter 4, we assume that the unlevered β of our aluminium producer is $\beta_A = 1$. After a few iterations we find: $\beta_p = -0.30$. Then with a risk free rate $r_f = 5\%$ and market risk premium $E[r^M - r_f] = 5\%$, we have $\bar{r} = 3.51\%$. The distribution of risk capital is displayed in Figure 5.2.

The expected insurance payment is $R^K = 200$ US$/ton. It is helpful to express it as a percentage of the value of the (average) invested capital. We have $R^K = 5.7\% \cdot I$. Since the aluminium producer in the configuration we have selected is highly value-creating, default is very unlikely, and the risk capital is low. Of course, if the firm was less profitable, the risk capital would be higher as a fraction of invested capital.

When we use these values in the cost of capital Equation (3), we find that the cost of capital is $w = 8.73\%$, slightly lower than the initial value of $w = 8.9\%$. We then use $w = 8.73\%$ as the discount rate, and run a few simulations until we obtain convergence. After less than five simulations, we obtain:

$$\begin{cases} R^K = 180 \text{ US\$}/ton \\ E[VC] = 1,740 \text{ US\$}/ton \\ w = 8.74\% \end{cases}$$

Figure 5.2 Aluminium producer: risk capital

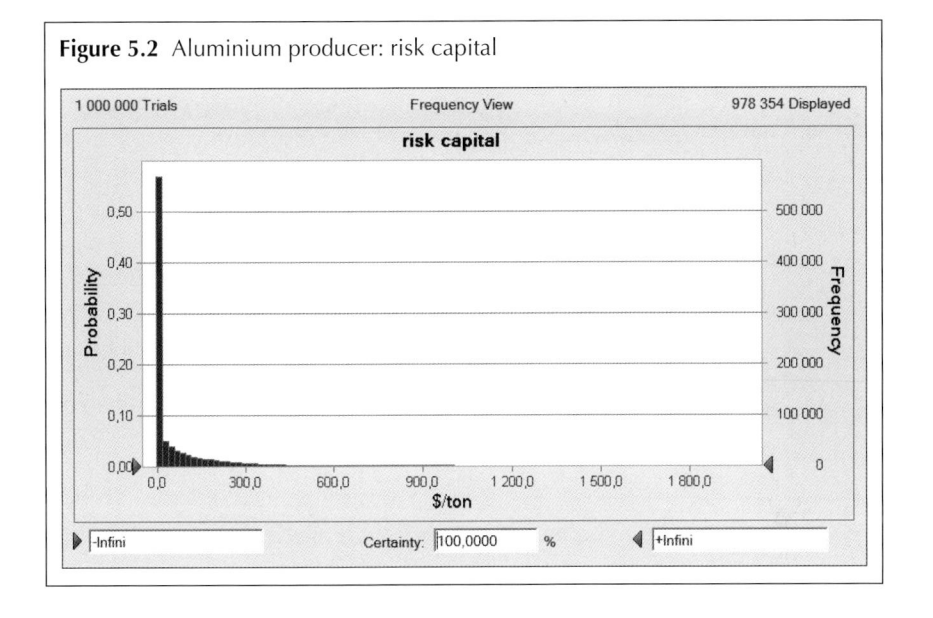

The risk capital is slightly lower than our initial estimate (-10%). The value created is slightly higher ($+3\%$): we had a slightly higher cost of capital than was required: $w = 8.9\%$ initially compared with $w = 8.74\%$ at convergence. Of course, the development team should not take these numbers at face value, and "book" the value created immediately. However, this suggests there may be an opportunity to challenge the cost of capital assumptions.

Finally, we can examine the impact of risk transfer activities. Specifically, we evaluate (1) taking an insurance against construction costs overruns (eg, structuring the construction contract as a fixed-price contract) and (2) selling forward the full production for the first five years of the project. As usual, we run a few simulations until we reach convergence. We find:

$$\begin{cases} R^K = 50 \text{ US\$}/ton \\ E[VC] = 1,770 \text{ US\$}/ton \\ w = 8.69\% \end{cases}$$

Risk transfer has a dramatic impact on the risk capital, however it has only a small impact on value creation. Since the initial risk capital is only a small fraction of invested capital, a reduction in risk capital has only a small impact on the cost of capital, hence on the value created.

If risk capital was a larger fraction of initial capital, a reduction in risk capital would have a larger impact on valuation. But then, we would have to take financial flexibility into account, and use the more comprehensive analytical framework presented in Chapter 6.

5.5 LINK WITH ECONOMIC CAPITAL

As discussed in Chapter 3, academics and practitioners, in particular financial institutions, use Economic Capital to measure risks. Two questions naturally arise: (1) how do these measure compare numerically? and (2) which one to use?

5.5.1 How do these measures compare numerically?

Consider the one-period trading firm discussed in Section 5.1.3. To compute Economic Capital, the trading company's debt rating is required. Suppose the firm is A1-rated, which corresponds to a 0.05% probability of default. The Economic Capital, denoted R for reserve, is the amount required at the beginning of the year to ensure that the firm will meet its obligations up to the default probability implied in its credit rating when the contracts expire. In other words, the value of the reserves available at year end must equal the 0.05% worst loss on the portfolio. Then, the firm would default only when the loss exceeds the 0.05% worst case.

Since the returns are normally distributed, the 0.05% worst loss, denoted W_1, is simply proportional to the standard deviation. A table of the normal distribution gives: $W_1 = 3.3\sigma = US\$99$ *million*.

The firm invests this reserve at the risk-free rate during the year. If the initial reserve is R at the beginning of the year, it is worth $(1 + r_f) \cdot R$ at the end of the year. We immediately have:

$$R = \frac{W_1}{1 + r_f} = US\$94 \text{ million}$$

The firm needs to hold reserve equal to 94% of the nominal value of the contracts. This number is more than ten times higher than the risk capital number estimated above. How can that be?

The explanation to this apparent paradox is that risk capital is a flow (an annual payment) while Economic Capital is a stock (an invested quantity). We need to compare the risk capital with the cost, denoted C, the trading company's parent (or any other firm) will charge the trading company to provide it with economic capital. If the parent's cost of capital is 8%, it will charge the trading company $C = 8\% \times 94 = US\$7.5$ *million*, which is very close to the risk capital.

The closeness is an artefact of the numbers used in the example, in particular the credit rating and the parent's cost of capital. More generally, these two numbers are of the same magnitude for the normal distribution. Denote r the parent's cost of capital (8% in our example) and m the multiple of the standard deviation required to reach the desired default probability. We have:

$$C = \frac{r \times m}{1 + r_f} \cdot \sigma$$

If the expected value of the assets is close to the required payment to the lenders, we have $R^K \approx 0.4 \cdot \sigma$. We have seen in Chapter 3 that $3 \leq m \leq 4$ for most investment grade ratings. Then, with $r \approx 10\%$ we have: $r \times m/1 + r_f \approx 0.3 - 0.4$, hence $C \approx R^K$.

5.5.2 Which measure to use?

As was discussed above, both metrics are mutually consistent. Risk capital is numerically close to the cost of holding Economic Capital for the normal distribution.

The answer therefore depends on the purpose, as Economic Capital and risk capital answer different questions.

Economic Capital measures *capital adequacy*: whether a firm has enough liquid assets to maintain its target credit rating, given the volatility of its portfolio. While it applies to all firms, it is particularly relevant for financial firms, for which capital adequacy is critical.

Risk capital measures the *cost of the risk* embedded in a portfolio of projects and/or assets. It provides a common metric for all risks facing a corporation. It is particularly relevant for risk-adjusted capital budgeting and performance management. As discussed in

Section 5.4, it can be used to value risk management activities in certain instances.

In addition, risk capital is well-suited to control (ie, set limits) and manage trading businesses where "fat tails" are likely.

5.6 CONCLUDING REMARKS

This chapter has introduced and developed a new concept, multi-period risk capital, that measures the risk of a project or a firm over its useful life. As was discussed, risk capital and Economic Capital – widely used by financial institutions – are consistent, even though they have different uses. Risk capital provides a simple – yet theoretically sound – approach to risk-adjust the capital budgeting and performance management processes.

I believe risk capital provides a fertile field for further research and analysis. For example, one would like to estimate risk capital for different firms (expanding on the individual analyses presented in this chapter), and for different industries. One subject of particular interest would be the evolution of risk capital over time, as industries structure change, new technologies are introduced, etc.

APPENDIX

5.A DERIVATION OF THE β OF THE INSURANCE PAYMENTS

We first observe that β_p, which is the β of the insurance payments from the insured firm's perspective, is also the β used by the hypothetical insurance company to price the contract. Consider first the insured firm's perspective. Denote $E_t[p]$ the expected value of the insurance payment at date t, hence the expected value of the insurance asset from the insured firm's perspective. The expected return on the insurance asset is:

$$r_p = \frac{dE_t[p]}{E_t[p]}$$

Consider now the insurer's perspective. It holds a liability to pay $E_t[p]$, which is equivalent to holding an asset worth $-E_t[p]$. The return on that asset is then:

$$r_{-p} = \frac{d(-E_t[p])}{-E_t[p]} = r_p$$

The return required by the insurer to hold that asset is then:

$$\bar{r} = r_f + \beta_p \cdot (E[r_M] - r_f)$$

We now estimate[5] β_p. We follow the presentation from Copeland et al (2003, pp 579–88). Denote V_A the value of the firm, and p the value of the put option. For a small increment of time δt, only the incremental change in the value of the underlying asset matters for the change in value of debt:

$$\delta p = \frac{\partial p}{\partial V_A} \cdot \delta V_A$$

Taking the limit as as $\delta t \to 0$ and after a few manipulations:

$$r_p = \frac{dp}{p} = \frac{\partial p}{\partial V_A} \cdot \frac{dV_A}{V_A} \cdot \frac{V_A}{p} = \frac{\partial p}{\partial V_A} \cdot \frac{V_A}{p} \cdot r_{V_A}$$

Then:

$$\beta_p = \Delta \cdot \frac{V}{p} \cdot \beta_{V_A}$$

where $\Delta = \partial p / \partial V$. The above equation holds in continuous time. To implement the approach in practice, we need to use an expected value. We make the simplifying assumption that:

$$\beta_p \approx \Delta \cdot \frac{E[V_A]}{R^K} \cdot \beta_V$$

In general, Δ can be a complex function. We therefore assume that Δ can be computed using the formula available for the Black–Scholes model, even though the distribution of value of assets may not satisfy the log-normality assumptions. If V_A is lognormally distributed:

$$\Delta = N(d_1) - 1$$

where $N(\cdot)$ is the cumulative standard normal distribution, and:

$$d_1 = \frac{\ln(E[V_A]/D) + r_f \cdot T}{\sigma\sqrt{T}} + \frac{1}{2}\sigma\sqrt{T}$$

where σ is the annualised standard deviation of returns on the asset, and T the time of expiry of the contract.

In the aluminium producer example discussed in the main text, we take $T = 30$ years, and we assume $\sigma = 20\%$. We have:

$$d_1 = 2.28 \quad N(d_1) = 0.99 \quad \beta_p = -0.30 \quad \bar{r} = 3.51\%$$

Finally, we may encounter situations where $\beta_p < -1$, which – assuming $r_f = (E[r_M] - r_f) = 5\%$ – would lead to a negative required return. In these instances, we choose $\bar{r} = 0$: insurance payments are not discounted.

1. Merton and Perold (1993).
2. As Merton and Perold point out, in the case where the insurance premium is real, it may not be actuarially fair. Since we are mostly concerned here with internal insurance, we assume that the premium is fair.
3. A binary distribution is also called a Bernoulli distribution, hence the name of the example.
4. Technically, p_t is the expected payment as of date t, then we take the expectation of date $t = 0$ to compute the risk capital. Since we end up taking expectations at $t = 0$, we omit that step in the main text.
5. I am grateful to Vladimir Antikarov who suggested this derivation.

6

Risk Management Strategy

This chapter presents a simple financial model where the optimal risk management strategy is determined, and the value created by risk management quantified. It builds on earlier academic work, most notably the seminal article by Froot *et al* (1993), and the more recent work by Rochet and Villeneuve (2006).

The value of this chapter for practitioners is twofold: first, it describes a simple framework that firms can apply. As discussed in the introductory Chapter 1, the theoretical literature on risk management, while rich in insight, is not readily applicable for practitioners. For example, a series of articles assume a specific form of a firm's utility and use an exogenous "coefficient of risk aversion" to derive a risk management strategy, which is highly impractical for most firms. By contrast, the framework discussed here can be simply added on to the (deterministic) strategic plan, as was the case for example at Alcan. The "risk appetite" is determined endogenously as a function of characteristics of the firm's business environment that are observable to the management team, such as the cost of capital environment and the investment opportunities.

This chapter provides quantitative results on the optimal risk management strategy and on the value of risk management. Corporate treasurers and recent corporate finance textbooks recognise that equity and hedging are partially substitutable in insuring the firm against adverse cash flow shocks. For example, Pettit (2007) mentions that:

"we have witnessed a resurgence of interest in the economic substitution of risk management for equity, such as de-risking business assets and cash flows to create more debt capacity to repurchase equity."

However, practitioners cannot rely on clear rules to determine the appropriate equity/hedging mix for their firm. This chapter provides such rules, and shows that the mix varies enormously depending on a firm's business environment, and quantifies the appropriate level for each.

In order to keep the exposition simple, and to illustrate the main concepts and effects, this chapter presents a two-period model. Risk management professionals can expand this analysis to include multiple periods. For example Alcan, a leading aluminium and packaging company, has used a similar model for ten years plus the continuing value.

This chapter is structured as follows: Section 6.1 presents the analytical framework. Section 6.2 derives and discusses the optimal risk management strategy. As soon as realistic features are included in risk management analyses, Monte Carlo simulations are required to determine the best strategy. Section 6.3 therefore presents the Monte Carlo simulations for the "base case". Section 6.4 examines the impact of changing key characteristics of the firm's business environment on the strategy and the value created. Finally, Section 6.5 concludes and highlights avenues for future analysis. As in other chapters, the supporting derivations are included in the Appendix.

6.1 A SIMPLIFIED RISK MANAGEMENT ANALYSIS FRAMEWORK

A firm's business environment is affected by two distinct sources of uncertainty: first, the profitability of its invested capital, and second, investment opportunities it may face. The former is well understood, and has been discussed at length in Chapter 4. The latter is a little less obvious, and recognises the fact that senior managers do not know in advance how much unplanned growth capital (i.e., over and above what has already been included in the capital plan: maintenance capital expenditure, planned expansion, etc) may be required. For example, senior managers do not know whether or precisely when an acquisition or a merger opportunity will arise, as these are often contingent on numerous factors, including regulatory conditions, other mergers and acquisitions in the industry, etc. Similarly, senior managers have only imperfect foresight on which projects in the firm's pipeline of opportunities will actually materialise, as it also often depends on numerous factors: technical readiness, regulatory approval, community approval, etc.

As unplanned opportunities arise, firms determine their level of investment, given their financial flexibility and the profitability of the opportunity. Obviously, financial flexibility ensures that the firm is able to capture all profitable investment opportunities whenever they arise. However, financial flexibility is costly. This is precisely the trade-off captured in this analysis.

6.1.1 Main elements of the framework

Timing

At date $t = 0$, the firm invested capital is I. The firm selects its risk management strategy: its capital structure and its hedging ratio.

At date $t = 1$ the Return On Invested Capital (ROIC) in period 1, denoted x_1, is realised. For simplicity, we normalise $I \equiv 1$. The NOPLAT realised during period 1 is then:

$$\pi_1 = x_1$$

Also at date $t = 1$, an unplanned investment opportunity arises. The magnitude of the opportunity i is expressed as a fraction of the initial invested capital. Denote y the ROIC of the opportunity. The firm decides the amount of its investment in the opportunity denoted g, again expressed as a fraction of the initial invested capital. The firm's investment cannot exceed the opportunity: $g \leq i$.

Note that i, g, and b can take positive or negative values. Negative investment ($g < 0$) corresponds to divestiture, either to capture an attractive sale opportunity ($i < 0$), or to respond to adverse cash flows (forced divestiture). In the later case, the firm may accept a lower return than it would achieve by holding the assets. Similarly $b \leq 0$ means that the firm repays a portion of its debt.

The model captures both sides of financial flexibility: it enables the firm to seize growth opportunities, and it protects the firm when facing profitability downsides.

Throughout this chapter, we suppose the firm decides not to issue shares. As discussed in Chapter 2, this is consistent with empirical evidence as well as theoretical models. Further work not presented in this book will relax this assumption, and identify situations were share issuance is optimal for firms.

At date $t = 2$, the profitability from both investments is realised. Denote x_2 the return on the initial invested capital during period 2. The NOPLAT realised in period 2 is then:

$$\pi_2 = x_2 + y \cdot g$$

As of date $t = 0$, the profitability of initial invested capital x_1 and x_2, the magnitude i and profitability y of the investment opportunity are unknown. As of date $t = 1$, the first period profitability x_1, and the magnitude of the investment opportunity i are known. The profitability y of the investment opportunity and x_2 of the initial investment are unknown.

Cost of capital
As was discussed in Chapter 2, empirical evidence as well as theoretical work indicate that the cost of capital is a U-shaped (ie, convex) function of the leverage ratio.

Accordingly, we assume that the cost of capital $w(\cdot)$ is a convex function of the leverage ratio at date t, denoted λ_t. We denote $\bar{\lambda}$ the cost minimising leverage: $w(\lambda)$ decreases on the left of $\bar{\lambda}$ and increases on the right.

Value of the firm
We introduce Π_t the Economic Profit – or value created – during period t. Π_t is the profit less the capital charge:

$$\begin{cases} \Pi_1 = \pi_1 - w(\lambda_0) = x_1 - w(\lambda_0) \\ \Pi_2 = \pi_2 - w(\lambda_1) \cdot (1 + g) = x_2 + y \cdot g - w(\lambda_1) \cdot (1 + g) \end{cases}$$

The expected value of the firm V is then the expectation of the discounted value of the EPs,[1] plus the initial invested capital:

$$V = I + \frac{1}{1 + w(\lambda_0)} E\left[\Pi_1 + \frac{\Pi_2}{(1 + w(\lambda_1))}\right]$$

Cash budget constraint at date $t = 1$
At date $t = 1$, the free cash flow is equal to the financing flow. For simplicity, we assume maintenance capital expenditures are equal to depreciation. The free cash flow is then equal to the NOPAT π_1 less the growth investment g. If we denote r the after-tax initial cost of debt, the budget constraint is:[2]

$$\pi_1 - g = r\lambda_0 - b$$

or:

$$b = g + r\lambda_0 - \pi_1$$

The firm's borrowing need is the investment plus interest payments on existing debt less the after-tax operating cash flows. In general, the initial cost of debt r depends on the initial leverage ratio. However, as we will see, the optimal strategy has the firm select an initial leverage ratio on the left of the minimum cost of capital, where the cost of debt is constant.

The leverage at $t = 1$ is then:

$$\lambda_1 = \frac{\lambda_0 + b}{1 + g}$$

substituting in the budget constraint:

$$\lambda_1 = \frac{(1 + r)\lambda_0 + g - \pi_1}{1 + g}$$

or

$$1 - \lambda_1 = \frac{1 + \pi_1 - (1 + r)\lambda_0}{1 + g} \qquad (1)$$

By construction $\lambda_1 \leq 1$. If the profitability shock is so adverse that borrowing needs are such that the leverage would exceed 1, the firm does not pursue the investment, or even sells assets to maintain leverage below unity.

We immediately verify that the leverage in increasing in the investment level:

$$\frac{\partial \lambda_1}{\partial g} = \frac{1 - \lambda_1}{1 + g} \geq 0 \qquad (2)$$

Hedging technology

The hedging strategies considered in this chapter simply reduce volatility. Denote η the hedging ratio, and z_1 the underlying profitability. For example, for an oil company z_1 is the price of oil times the annual production, and η is the fraction sold forward. The actual profitability x_1 is:

$$x_1 = \eta \cdot E[z_1] + (1 - \eta) \cdot z_1$$

One can easily verify that hedging does not affect expected profitability: $E[x_1] = E[z_1]$ for all values of η. However, as expected, hedging reduces profitability volatility:

$$var(x_1) = (1 - \eta)^2 \cdot var(z_1)$$

Finally, we observe that:

$$\frac{d\pi_1}{d\eta} = \frac{dx_1}{d\eta} = E[z_1] - z_1$$

Then:

$$E\left[\frac{d\pi_1}{d\eta}\right] = 0$$

As is well known, hedging per se does not create value.

6.1.2 Optimal investment decision

At date $t = 1$, the firm selects the level of investment that maximises the value created[3]:

$$\max_g E[\Pi_2(g)] = E[x_2 + y \cdot g - w(\lambda_1) \cdot (1 + g)]$$
$$st : g \leq i$$

We first solve the unconstrained problem, then determine whether the constraint is met. Denote $\hat{g}$ the solution of the unconstrained problem, and g^* the optimal investment level. Since the derivations inform the intuition, they are presented in the main text.

The first derivative of $E[\Pi_2]$ with respect to g is:

$$\frac{dE[\Pi_2]}{dg} = E[y] - w(\lambda_1) - (1 + g) \cdot \frac{dw}{dg}$$
$$= E[y] - w(\lambda_1) - (1 - \lambda_1) \cdot w'(\lambda_1)$$

since, using Equation (2), we have

$$\frac{dw}{dg} = w'(\lambda_1) \cdot \frac{\partial \lambda_1}{\partial g} = w'(\lambda_1) \cdot \frac{1 - \lambda_1}{1 + g}$$

The first-order condition for the (unconstrained) optimum is then:

$$(1 - \lambda_1) \cdot w'(\lambda_1) = E[y] - w(\lambda_1) \qquad (3)$$

The second order derivative is:

$$\frac{d^2 E[\Pi_2]}{dg^2} = -\left(2 \cdot \frac{dw}{dg} + (1+g) \cdot \frac{d^2 w}{dg^2}\right)$$

$$= -\frac{1}{1+g} \cdot \left((1-\lambda_1)^2 w''(\lambda_1) + (1-\lambda_1) \cdot w'(\lambda_1)\right)$$

The firm invests in the project only if it is value-creating: $E[y] - w(\lambda_1) \geq 0$. Then, at the optimum $(1 - \lambda_1) \cdot w'(\lambda_1) = E[y] - w(\lambda_1) \geq 0$. Then, since $w(\cdot)$ is convex, we have $d^2 E[\Pi_2]/dg^2 < 0$ at the optimum: the objective function is locally concave, and the optimum is a maximum.

The firm invests as long as the marginal return $y - w(\lambda_1)$ on the marginal investment remains higher than the incremental cost of capital dw/dg applied to all of the invested capital $(1 + g)$. This is very consistent with corporate practices. Firms take into account the impact of new investments of their cost of capital, as it applies to their entire capital base. For example, if a firm is downgraded, it increases the cost of new debt issuance, hence increases the average cost of debt, but it can also have an impact on the cost of existing debt, through covenants, etc. This effect is critical as will be seen below, and constitutes a key difference with previous academic work, in particular Froot *et al* (1993), that take into account only the incremental cost of incremental capital.

Let us now turn to the constraint. If $\hat{g} < i$, then $g^* = \hat{g} < i$. The firm lacks the financial flexibility to capture the full investment opportunity. *The firm is financially constrained.* For example, M&A deals are often considered and not pursued because they weaken a firm's financial stability.

Denote $\hat{\lambda}_1$ the leverage ratio of the financially constrained firm. $\hat{\lambda}_1$ is not a random variable, rather it is determined by Equation (3) and depends only on the shape of the cost of capital and on the expected profitability of the new investment. Then, the optimal investment $\hat{g}$ is a random variable determined using Equation (1), and depends on the constrained leverage $\hat{\lambda}_1$, the realised profitability π_1, and the initial leverage λ_0.

If $\hat{g} \geq i$, then $g^* = i$. The firm can capture the full investment opportunity. In fact, it has unused financial flexibility. For this reason, *the firm is opportunity constrained*. Firms that return large sums to their shareholders, often as extraordinary dividends (eg, Microsoft in 2004) or as large share buy-back, are opportunity constrained.

Since the investment is constant, the actual leverage λ_1 is a random variable determined from Equation (1) by the realised profitability π_1 and the initial leverage λ_0.

Finally, we observe that $\lambda_1 \leq \hat{\lambda}_1$ since from Equation (2), λ_1 is increasing in the investment level g and $i \leq \hat{g}$.

6.2 OPTIMAL RISK MANAGEMENT STRATEGY

At $t = 0$, the firm chooses its risk management strategy to maximise the expected value created $VC = V - I$. The risk management strategy is composed of two elements: an initial leverage ratio λ_0^* and a hedging ratio η^*. The firm's problem is therefore:

$$\max_{\lambda_0, \eta} VC = \frac{1}{1 + w(\lambda_0)} \cdot E\left[\Pi_1 + \frac{\Pi_2}{(1 + w(\lambda_1))}\right]$$

The derivations are presented in Appendix 6.A. We examine both elements of the risk management strategy in turn.

6.2.1 Optimal capital structure

We have:

$$\frac{\partial VC}{\partial \lambda_0} = -\frac{1}{1 + w(\lambda_0)} \cdot \left(w'(\lambda_0) \cdot (1 + VC) + (1 + r) \cdot \left(E\left[\frac{w'(\lambda_1)}{1 + w(\lambda_1)} \left(1 + \frac{\Pi_2}{(1 + w(\lambda_1)) \cdot (1 + i)} \right) \bigg/ \Omega^{OC} \right] \cdot \Pr(\Omega^{OC}) \right) \right)$$

(4)

where Ω^{FC} is the event "the firm is financially constrained" and Ω^{OC} is the event "the firm is opportunity constrained".

An increase in initial leverage has three impacts:

(1) It changes the first-period cost of capital, hence the value created.
(2) If the firm is financially constrained, it reduces the investment level (as can be seen in Equation (1)), hence reduces the value created.
(3) The impact if the firm is opportunity constrained is a priori ambiguous. If the opportunity is such that $\lambda_1 > \bar{\lambda}$, then $w'(\lambda_1) \geq 0$: an increase in initial leverage reduces the value created, as when the firm is financially constrained. Consider now the case where the opportunity is such that $\lambda_1 < \bar{\lambda}$. For example, a scenario where there is no investment opportunity, and the cash flow generated exceeds the required interest payments. Then, $w'(\lambda_1) < 0$: everything else being equal, an increase in initial leverage increases the value created.

When the firm selects its capital structure *ex ante*, it trades-off these three effects, taking into account the (*ex ante*) probability of having to select $\lambda_1 < \bar{\lambda}$.

Selecting the cost minimising initial leverage is not always optimal. If $w'(\lambda_0) = w'(\bar{\lambda}) = 0$, we have:

$$\left.\frac{\partial VC}{\partial \lambda_0}\right|_{\lambda_0 = \bar{\lambda}} = -\frac{1+r}{1+w(\bar{\lambda})}\left(\frac{w'(\hat{\lambda}_1)}{1+w(\hat{\lambda}_1)} \cdot \Pr(\Omega^{FC}) + E\left[\frac{w'(\lambda_1)}{1+w(\lambda_1)} \cdot \left(1 + \frac{\Pi_2}{(1+w(\lambda_1))\cdot(1+i)}\right)\middle/\Omega^{OC}\right]\cdot \Pr(\Omega^{OC})\right)$$

Then, if the firm expects "more" states of the world for which $\lambda_1 > \bar{\lambda}$, the expectation is positive, and $\partial VC/\partial \lambda_0|_{\lambda_0 = \bar{\lambda}} < 0$. But then, decreasing leverage raises the value created, and $\lambda_0 = \bar{\lambda}$ cannot be optimum. The intuition is clear: the firm selects a more conservative capital structure if it believes unplanned investment opportunities can be larger.

The firm can select an initial leverage to the right on the minimum, ie, $\lambda_0 > \bar{\lambda}$. While it does not happen in most realistic examples, it is possible, if the firm expects more states of the world for which $w'(\lambda_1) < 0$, for example if there is no unplanned investment opportunity. Then, since $w'(\hat{\lambda}_1) > 0$ the firm select λ_0 such that $w'(\lambda_0) > 0$, ie, $\lambda_0 > \bar{\lambda}$ at the optimum.

We now discuss how changes in the firm's environment will affect the optimal leverage ratio. To simplify, suppose for example that the investment opportunity is a binary variable: it arises with probability p, in which case the firm is always financially constrained and $\lambda_1 = \bar{\lambda}_1$ while, with probability $(1 - p)$, no opportunity arises and $w'(\lambda_1) < 0$. Concentrating on the second period effect, we have:

$$A = -\left(\begin{array}{l} p \cdot \dfrac{w'(\hat{\lambda}_1)}{1 + w(\hat{\lambda}_1)} \\ + (1-p) \cdot E\left[\dfrac{w'(\lambda_1)}{1 + w(\lambda_1)} \cdot \left(1 + \dfrac{\Pi_2}{(1 + w(\lambda_1)) \cdot (1 + i)}\right) \bigg/ \text{no opportunity} \right] \end{array} \right)$$

An increase in the probability of an investment opportunity increases the weight of the first term, which is positive, hence everything else being equal, reduces the optimal initial leverage. Conversely, the optimal initial leverage increases if the probability of an investment opportunity decreases.

Consider now an increase in the slope of the cost of capital on the right of the minimum: $w'(\hat{\lambda}_1)$ is larger. Then, everything else being equal, the optimal initial leverage decreases.

6.2.2 Optimal hedging ratio
We have:

$$\frac{\partial VC}{\partial \eta} = \frac{1}{1 + w(\lambda_0)} \cdot \left(\begin{array}{l} \dfrac{w'(\hat{\lambda}_1)}{1 + w(\hat{\lambda}_1)} E\left[E[z] - z_1 / \Omega^{FC}\right] \cdot \Pr(\Omega^{FC}) \\ + E\left[\dfrac{w'(\lambda_1)}{1 + w(\lambda_1)} \cdot \left(1 + \dfrac{\Pi_2}{(1 + w(\lambda_1)) \cdot (1 + i)}\right) \right. \\ \left. \cdot (E[z] - z_1) / \Omega^{OC} \right] \cdot \Pr(\Omega^{OC}) \end{array} \right)$$

(5)

As previously discussed, an increase in the hedging ratio η does not change the value created in the first period.

To understand the impact on the second period, we first observe that, since the firm is more likely to be financially constrained for adverse cash flow shocks, $E[E[z] - z_1/\Omega^{FC}] = E[z] - E[z_1/\Omega^{FC}] > 0$. Similarly, $E[E[z] - z_1/\Omega^{OC}] = E[z] - E[z_1/\Omega^{OC}] < 0$.

Then, if the firm is financially constrained, increasing the hedging ratio increases the investment level *on average*, hence increases the value created.

However, full hedging is not always optimal. Suppose the firm is opportunity constrained. As for the leverage ratio, we need to consider two cases: if the realised opportunity is such that $\lambda_1 \geq \bar{\lambda}$, then $w'(\lambda_1) \geq 0$. If the realised opportunity is such that $\lambda_1 < \bar{\lambda}$, then $w'(\lambda_1) < 0$. The expectation over Ω^{OC} can then be positive or negative. If it is positive, then an increase in the hedging ratio increases the value created, and the firm hedges perfectly.

Suppose now the expectation is negative. We show in Appendix 6.A that, for very realistic values of the parameters, we have:

$$\lim_{\eta \to 1} \Pr(\Omega^{FC}) = 0$$

Then:

$$\lim_{\eta \to 1} \frac{\partial VC}{\partial \eta} = \frac{1}{1 + w(\lambda_0)} \cdot E\left[\frac{w'(\lambda_1)}{1 + w(\lambda_1)} \cdot \left(1 + \frac{\Pi_2}{(1 + w(\lambda_1)) \cdot (1 + i)}\right) \cdot (E[z] - z_1) \right] < 0$$

But then, reducing the hedging ratio increases the value created: full hedging is not optimal. This contrasts with a fundamental result of the risk management literature, in particular Froot *et al* (1993) and Holmström and Tirole (2000), who show that full hedging is optimal if the profitability is uncorrelated to the investment opportunities. Here the possibility of *not* facing a unplanned investment opportunity drives the decision not to fully hedge.

RISK MANAGEMENT STRATEGY

As previously, we can discuss how changes in the firm's environment will affect the hedging ratio. We consider the same simplified opportunity set:

$$\frac{\partial VC}{\partial \eta} = \frac{1}{1 + w(\lambda_0)} \left[p \cdot \frac{w'(\hat{\lambda}_1)}{1 + w(\hat{\lambda}_1)} \cdot \left(E[z] - E[z_1 / \Omega^{FC}] \right) \right.$$
$$+ (1 - p) \cdot E \left[\frac{w'(\lambda_1)}{1 + w(\lambda_1)} \cdot \right.$$
$$\left. \left. \left(1 + \frac{\Pi_2}{(1 + w(\lambda_1)) \cdot (1 + i)} \right) \cdot \left(E[z] - z_1 \right) / no \ opportunity \right] \right]$$

An increase in the probability of an investment opportunity increases the weight of the first term, which is positive, hence everything else being equal, increases the optimal hedging ratio. Similarly, the optimal hedging ratio decreases if the probability of an investment opportunity decreases.

Consider now an increase in the slope of the cost of capital on the right of the minimum: $w'(\hat{\lambda}_1)$ is larger. Then, everything else being equal, the optimal hedging ratio increases.

Consider now the impact of correlation between investment opportunities and profitability. We have shown in Appendix 1.A.5 that:

$$cov(z_1, i) = (1 - p) \cdot \left(E[z] - E[z_1 / no \ opportunity] \right)$$

Then, everything else being equal, an increase in correlation increases the weight of the terms $w'(\lambda_1) < 0$ hence reduces the optimal hedging ratio. Similarly, a decrease in correlation leads to an increase in the optimal hedging ratio.

6.3 MONTE CARLO SIMULATIONS

In this section, we solve numerically for the optimal risk management strategy: we run Monte Carlo simulations (two million scenarios of profitability and investment opportunities) for different risk management strategies (λ_0, η), and determine the strategy that creates the highest value.[4]

6.3.1 Main inputs into the analysis

Cost of capital

As discussed above, the cost of capital is decreasing for leverage below a certain threshold, increasing afterwards. We model both segments differently.

Denote $w^-(\lambda)$ the cost of capital on the left of the minimum. Since the value of the debt varies with the value of the company, we use the Miles–Ezzell model discussed in Chapter 2:

$$w^-(\lambda) = E[r^*] - r_f \cdot \tau \cdot \lambda$$

where:

$$E[r^*] = r_f + \beta \cdot (E[r_M] - r_f)$$

We suppose our firm is such that $\beta = 1$. Then, with the risk free rate $r_f = 5\%$, the cash tax rate $\tau = 40\%$, and the market risk premium $E[r_M] - r_f = 5\%$, we have:

$$w^-(\lambda) = 10\% - 2\% \cdot \lambda$$

We suppose that the minimum cost is reached for leverage $\bar{\lambda} = 40\%$. Then $w(\bar{\lambda}) = 10\% - 0.8\% = 9.2\%$.

Denote $w^+(\lambda)$ the cost of capital on the right of the minimum. The probability of financial distress is no longer negligible, and debt holders and stock holders require an additional premium. The exact shape of the premium function has not been assessed empirically. This analysis uses a quadratic function. Since $w^-(\bar{\lambda}) = w^+(\bar{\lambda})$, we have:

$$w^+(\lambda) = 9.2\% + \alpha \cdot (\lambda - 40\%)^2$$

In the base case, we select $\alpha = 2$. This yields $w^+(50\%) - w^+(\bar{\lambda}) = +2\%$, which constitutes a "reasonable" penalty for higher leverage in the base case.

The impacts of a different β and penalties are examined in Section 6.4.

Profitability of initial invested capital
As discussed above, the magnitude of the initial invested capital is simply a normalisation factor. It is taken to be $I = US\$1\ billion$.

In the base case, the underlying profitability of initial invested capital is assumed to be normally distributed, with mean $E[z] = 10\%$, and standard deviation $\sigma_z = \sqrt{var(z)} = 4\%$. Normal distribution of profitability is consistent with many micro-models. Average profitability $E[z] = 10\%$ guarantees that the firm is slightly value-creating at its minimum cost of capital. Standard deviation $\sigma_z = 4\%$ of average profitability is consistent with for example commodity prices volatility. The impact of changes in profitability average and volatility is examined in Section 6.4.

Random investment opportunity
The investment opportunity i follows a binary distribution: with probability p an investment opportunity arises, with probability $(1 - p)$ none does. The size of the opportunity is constant. In the base case, we set the probability of a project at $p = 40\%$, and the size of the opportunity at $i = 20\%$ of initial invested capital. In other words, the firm has a 40% chance of facing a growth opportunity that would represent 20% of its size. It can either take it, or leave it. The impact of changing the investment's opportunity scale and probability of occurrence is examined in Section 6.4.

The profitability of the new investment is assumed to be normally distributed, with mean $E[y] = 12\%$, and standard deviation $\sigma_y = 4\%$. The new investment is very attractive for the firm, as it provides higher expected return, and proportionally lower volatility.

The correlation between the random investment opportunity i and z_1, the underlying profitability in period 1 is a critical parameter. In the base case, the correlation is assumed to be zero: the occurrence of an investment opportunity is unrelated to the level of profitability. The impact of changing the correlation is examined in Section 6.4.

6.3.2 No-uncertainty benchmark
It is helpful to start with the situation where the profitability and the investment opportunity are certain. In that case, there is no need for hedging, and the risk management strategy is simply the selection of the optimal initial leverage ratio λ_0. To facilitate comparison

with the base case, the no-uncertainty investment opportunity has a magnitude of 8% of invested capital, hence the same expectation as the random investment opportunity.

With the inputs selected for the base case, the investment opportunity is extremely attractive. The firm then selects its initial leverage to minimise its overall cost of capital, anticipating it invests for sure at date $t = 1$. The firm selects $\lambda_0^* = 40\%$, and the Value Created is $VC =$ US$15.2 *million*.

The Value Created is low (less than US$20 *million* for US$1 *billion* invested capital!), since we include only two periods in our analysis. However, the perpetual value created is in line with expectation: around US$200 *million* for US$1 *billion* invested capital. Taking perpetual values does not materially affect the insights from the analysis, since we are measuring relative changes in value created, and not absolute value creation levels.

6.3.3 Uncertain profits only

Suppose now the profitability is uncertain, while the investment opportunity is certain. Monte Carlo simulations show that the optimal risk management strategy is: $\eta^* = 100\%$; and $\lambda_0^* = 40\%$. Since the risk is hedged away, the firm finds itself in the previous situation, and selects the same leverage ratio. The Value Created is identical.

6.3.4 Uncertain profits and investment opportunities

Optimal strategy

The optimum strategy is characterised by an initial leverage ratio $\lambda_0^* = \bar{\lambda} = 40\%$ and hedging ratio $\eta^* = 90\%$. The firm executes the investment with 40% probability, ie, every time the investment opportunity arises: the firm is never financially constrained.

As illustrated in Figure 6.1, the average period-2 leverage ratio is $E[\lambda_1] = 35\%$ yielding the average cost of capital $E[w(\lambda_1)] = 9.36\%$. The distribution of leverage ratios is bimodal: if the investment is not financed (which happens 60% of the time), debt is repaid, and the leverage falls around 31%. If the investment is financed, then the leverage rises to 43%. In both cases, the cost of capital slightly lower than 9.4%, as illustrated in Figure 6.2. The Value Created is presented in Figure 6.3. The average Value Created is $VC =$ US$14.5 *million*. As expected, this value is lower

RISK MANAGEMENT STRATEGY

Figure 6.1 Base case: period-2 leverage

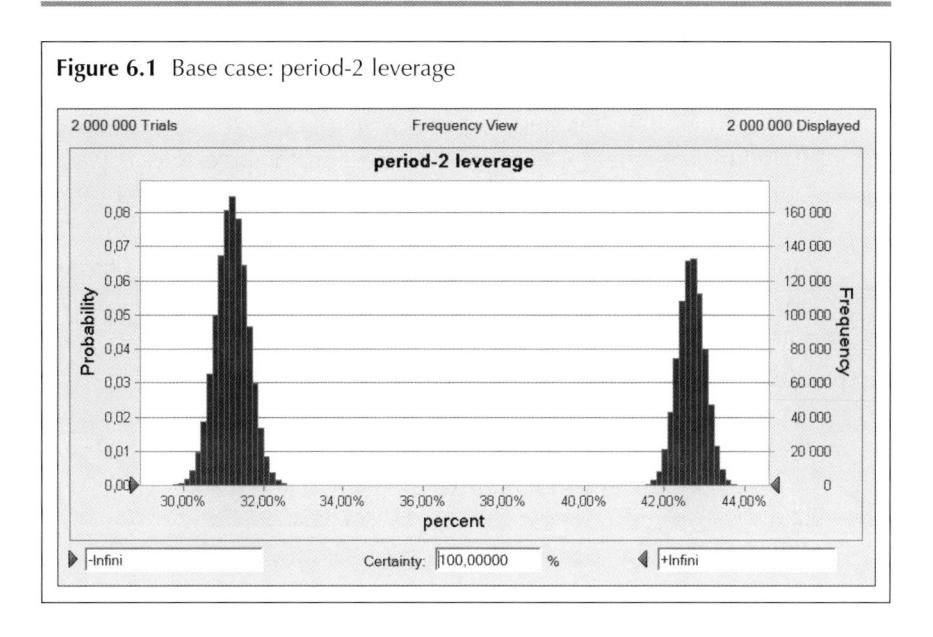

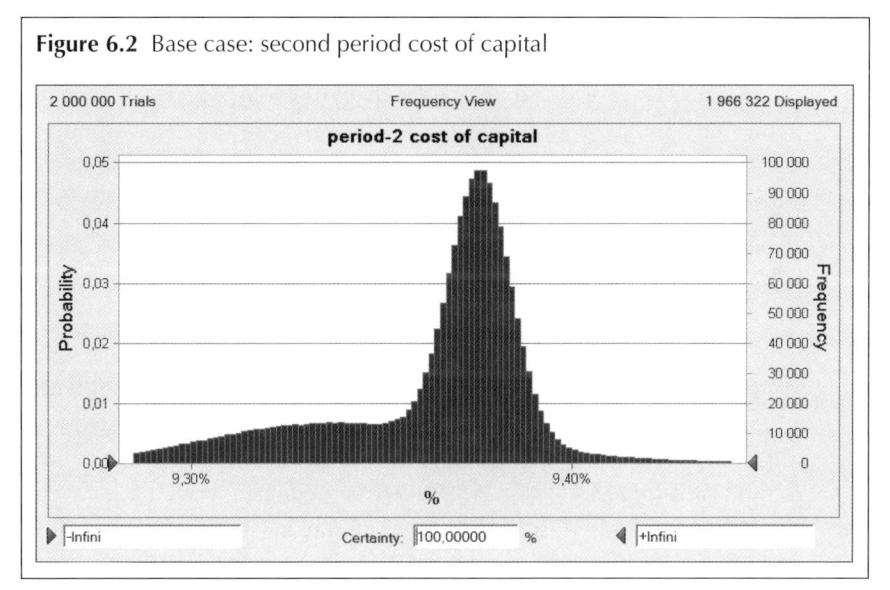

Figure 6.2 Base case: second period cost of capital

than in the no-uncertainty benchmark, due to the convexity in the profit function.

To understand why the strategy is optimal, it is helpful to examine what happens for different leverage and hedging ratios.

Figure 6.3 Base case: value created

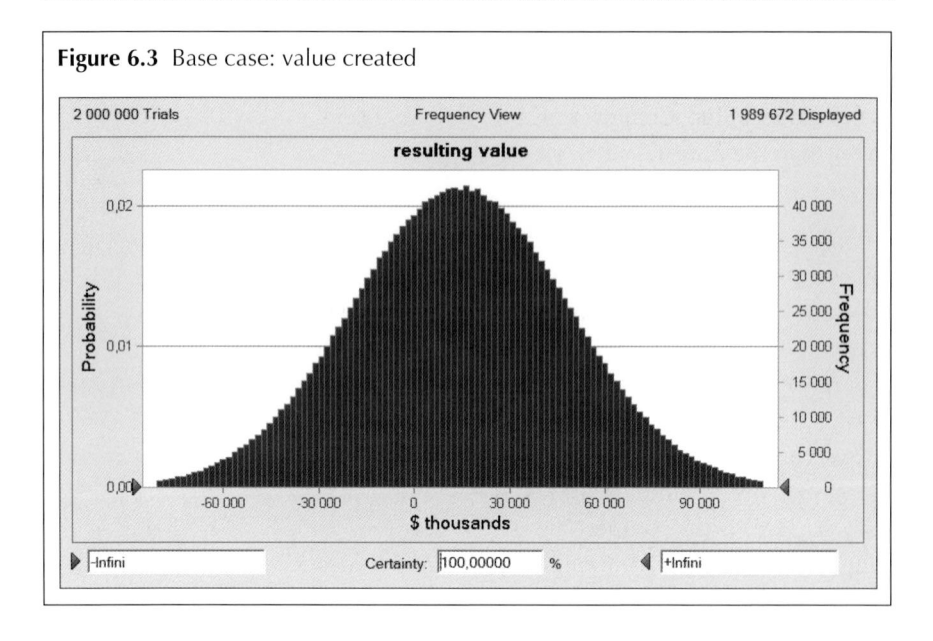

What is the impact of initial leverage?
Consider a lower initial leverage ratio, for example $\lambda_0 = 35\%$, with the same hedging ratio $\eta = 90\%$. The investment is still financed 40% of the time: in that case, a more conservative capital structure does not significantly increase the financial flexibility. However, it does increase the cost of capital in period 1 to $w(\lambda_0) = 9.30\%$. The average Value Created drops to $VC = US\$13.4\ million$.

Consider now a higher initial leverage ratio, for example $\lambda_0 = 45\%$, with the same hedging ratio $\eta = 90\%$. The investment is then never financed, as the incremental cost exceeds the marginal benefit. The average Value Created is only $VC = US\$8.8\ million$.

What is the impact of the hedging ratio?
Consider for example the case with $\lambda_0 = 40\%$, and no hedging: $\eta = 0\%$. The investment is financed only around 31% of the time: the firm is financially constrained around 25% of the instances an opportunity presents itself. While the average cost of capital remains roughly unchanged ($E[w(\lambda_1)] = 9.4\%$), there are too few opportunities captured. The average Value Created is then $VC = US\$14.1\ million$. Hedging therefore increases the probability of capturing the investment opportunity.

As discussed in Section 6.2, we also observe that full hedging is not optimal. If the firm selects $\lambda_0 = 40\%$, and full hedging: $\eta = 100\%$, the average Value Created is then $VC = $ US$14.4 *million* slightly lower than the optimal strategy.

What is the value of the optimal risk management strategy?
Of course, the answer depends on which reference point is selected. We adopt as a reference strategy the strategy that minimises the cost of capital in period 1, with no hedging: $\lambda_0 = 40\%$ and $\eta = 0\%$. The incremental value attributable to risk management is therefore $\Delta VC = $ US$0.4 *million*, or $\Delta VC/VC = 3\%$.

The value created is comparable to Tobin's Q, that measures the excess of market value of book value. Hence, the increase in Value Created is directly comparable to the increase in Tobin's Q used and estimated in the academic surveys discussed in Chapter 3. The magnitudes are also similar: we find around 3%, while the surveys indicate an average magnitude of 5.7%.

How does hedging substitute for equity?
Finally, one can quantify the substitution effect between hedging and equity. Suppose the firm does not hedge: $\eta = 0\%$. Numerical simulations show it then requires initial leverage $\lambda_0 = 30\%$ to achieve the same financial flexibility, ie, to finance the investment 40% of the time. The value created is then $VC = $ US$11.6 *million*. Substituting hedging for equity reduces the cost of capital, and increases the value created by $\Delta VC = $ US$2.9 *million*, or $\Delta VC/VC = 25\%$ of the initial value created.

6.4 CHANGES IN THE FIRM'S BUSINESS ENVIRONMENT

We now examine how changes in the business environment of the firm impact on its risk management strategy. We first examine the characteristics of the investment opportunity: correlations between profitability and investment opportunities, magnitude of the investment opportunity, and probability of occurrence. Then, we examine the characteristics of profitability: level and volatility. Finally, we consider the cost of capital environment. All results are summarised in Table 6.1.

Table 6.1 Impact of changes in the firm's business environment

	Optimal risk management strategy		Value created by risk management vs. reference strategy
Scenario	Leverage ratio (percent)	Hedging ratio (percent)	(percent)
Base case	40	90	+3
Investment opportunities			
Perfectly negatively correlated	40	180	+18
Perfectly positively correlated	40	−20	~0
Larger	29	80	+4
More likely	40	100	+7
Less likely	40	90	+1
Characteristics of profitability			
Lower average profitability	39	95	+5
Higher profitability volatility	40	100	+9
Lower profitability volatility	39	90	+1
Cost of capital environment			
Steeper cost of capital	39	95	+4

6.4.1 Characteristics of investment opportunities

Correlation with profitability

Suppose first investment opportunities are perfectly negatively correlated to profitability, ie, investment opportunities (are more likely to) arise precisely when profitability is lower. This is often the case in commodity industries, where the cost of new investment/acquisitions is positively correlated to the underlying commodity prices.

As one would expect, hedging is critical in that case. The optimal risk management strategy is: $\lambda_0^* = 40\%$ and $\eta^* = 180\%$. The firm maintains the same initial leverage ratio, and sells its profit forward 1.8 times. As a result, the firm is *short 0.8 times* its intrinsic profitability z_1. Then, its resulting profitability is positively correlated with the investment opportunities. The investment is financed 40% of time, and the resulting Value Created is $VC =$ US$15.2 *million*.

The performance of the firm is higher than in the no-correlation case, and (almost) as high as in the no-uncertainty case: the firm is able to take advantage of the correlation to increase the value created.

Risk management creates significant value. With no hedging, the firm finances the investment only 19% of the time, ie, captures less than half of the available opportunities. This yields a Value Created $VC = US\$12.9\ million$. Risk management therefore creates $\Delta VC = US\$2.3\ million$ of value, an 18% increase in value created.

Suppose now investment opportunities are perfectly positively correlated to profitability. The optimal risk management strategy is: $\lambda_0^* = 40\%$ and $\eta^* = -20\%$. The firm buys its profitability forward, and finds itself *long 0.8 times* its intrinsic profitability, which is exactly symmetric to the previous case.

The investment is undertaken 40% of the time, yielding a value created of $VC = US\$15.1\ million$. Risk management creates very little value, as the difference between value created using the optimal strategy and using other strategies is very small. This is not surprising: the positive correlation creates a natural hedge for the firm.

The optimal hedging ratio is therefore decreasing with the correlation between profitability and opportunities, as discussed in Section 6.2.

Magnitude

Consider now the firm faces an investment opportunity of larger scale, $i = 40\%$. The optimal risk management strategy is to adopt a very conservative capital structure $\lambda_0^* = 29\%$, and to reduce the hedging ratio to $\eta^* = 80\%$. The firm then captures the opportunity whenever it is available, ie, 40% of the time. However, this comes at a significant cost, as the value created is reduced to $VC = US\$13.0\ milllion$.

The value created is lower than when a smaller investment opportunity is available, due to the high cost of capital required to provide the necessary financial flexibility. This is partly an artefact of the model, as the value is captured for one period only, while in reality it is captured on multiple periods. However, the trade-off is real: a firm that limits itself to small (unplanned) investment opportunities can reduce its cost of capital, hence increase value created.

Selecting the optimal risk management strategy increases value creation by $\Delta VC = US\$0.4\ million$ or 3%: if the firm selects the reference strategy is captures the investment opportunity less than 4% of the time, and the value created is only $VC = US\$12.6\ million$. Creating the financial flexibility to capture the investment opportunity is so costly that the firm is almost as well off committing not to pursue the opportunity!

Probability of occurrence
Consider the case where the investment is much more likely to occur: $p = 80\%$. The firm reverts to the certain investment strategy: $\lambda_0^* = 40\%$ and $\eta^* = 100\%$. The opportunity is financed whenever it occurs, ie, 80% of the time. The value created is $VC = US\$16.9$ *million*. This is significantly higher than the reference strategy. In that case, the firm captures the opportunity only 63% of the time, and the value created is only $VC = US\$15.7$ *million*. The increase in value created from risk management is $\Delta VC = US\$1.2$ *million* or 7%.

Consider now the case where the investment is much less more likely to occur: $p = 20\%$. The firm reverts to the base case strategy $\lambda_0^* = 40\%$ and $\eta^* = 90\%$. The opportunity is financed whenever it occurs, ie, 20% of the time. The value created is $VC = US\$13.5$ *million*. In the reference strategy, the firm captures the opportunity only 16% of the time, and the value created is $VC = US\$13.3$ *million*. The increase in value created from risk management is $\Delta VC = US\$0.2$ *million* or 1%.

6.4.2 Characteristics of profitability

Profitability level
Consider now a less profitable firm. Specifically, assume the expected profitability of the initial invested capital is $E[z] = 9.5\%$. The firm is marginally value-creating, even at its minimum cost of capital.

The firm best risk management strategy is to adopt a conservative leverage: $\lambda_0^* = 39\%$. The optimal hedging ratio is $\eta^* = 95\%$. The probability of financing the investment is 40%, and the value created is $VC = US\$5.7$ *million*.

If the firm pursues the reference strategy, it captures the investment opportunity only 30% of the time, and the value creation is only $VC = US\$5.4$ *million*. Risk management increases the value created by $\Delta VC = US\$0.3$ *million*, or 5% of the initial value created.

Of course, if the firm is more profitable, risk management adds less value. For example, if the expected profitability of the initial invested capital is $E[z] = 10.5\%$, the incremental value creation attributable to risk management is less than 2%.

Profitability volatility
Consider a firm facing higher volatility of profitability: $\sigma_z = 80\%$. The optimal risk management strategy is $\lambda_0^* = 40\%$ and $\eta = 100\%$. The firm captures the opportunity 40% of the time, and the value

created is $VC =$ US$14.4 million. If the firm pursues the reference strategy, it captures the investment opportunity only 26% of the time, and the value creation is only $VC =$ US$13.2 million. Risk management increases the value created by $\Delta VC =$ US$1.2 million, or 9% of the initial value created.

Consider now a firm with lower volatility of profitability: $\sigma_z = 20\%$. The optimal risk management strategy is $\lambda_0^* = 39\%$ and $\eta = 90\%$. The firm captures the opportunity 40% of the time, and the value created is $VC =$ US$14.5 million. If the firm pursues the reference strategy, it captures the investment opportunity 39% of the time, and the value creation is $VC =$ US$14.3 million. Risk management increases the value created by $\Delta VC =$ US$0.2 million, or 1% of the initial value created.

These examples confirm the intuition that the value from risk management increases with the volatility of profitability: from 1% for low volatility ($\sigma_z = 20\%$) to 9% for high volatility ($\sigma_z = 80\%$).

6.4.3 Cost of capital environment

A higher beta moves the cost of capital curve upward, hence reduces the profitability. The analysis and the findings are identical.

Consider now that the firm faces a "steeper capital cost curve". Specifically, consider that the penalty coefficient is $\alpha = 3$. This will happen if the credit environment becomes tighter, and lenders require higher spread for lower quality credit. Continue to assume that $\bar{\lambda} = 40\%$ is the cost-minimising leverage ratio. Nothing has changed on the left of the minimum cost of capital. On the right of the minimum cost of capital, we now have:

$$w^+(\lambda) = 9.2\% + 3 \cdot (\lambda - 40\%)^2$$

The best risk management strategy is to adopt a slightly more conservative leverage at $\lambda_0^* = 39\%$. This is not surprising, as deviations from the minimum are more costly. The optimal hedging ratio is $\eta^* = 95\%$. The probability of financing the investment is 40%, and the value created is $VC =$ US$14.3 million, slightly lower than in the base case.

If the firm pursues the reference strategy, it captures the investment opportunity only 28% of the time (compared with 31% in the base case), and the value creation is only $VC =$ US$13.8 million. Risk management increases the value created by $\Delta VC =$ US$0.5 million, or 4% of the initial value created.

If the firm faces a less step cost of capital environment, for example $\alpha = 1$, risk management increases value created by around 2%.

6.5 CONCLUDING OBSERVATIONS

This chapter has presented a simple financial model where the optimal risk management strategy is determined, and the resulting value creation quantified. This simple analytical framework provides a blueprint for risk managers to apply to their own organisations.

The main finding from this chapter is that the value creation from risk management varies significantly depending on a firm's circumstances: it can be lower than 1% of the value created for a firm in a low-volatility environment, to up to 18% of the value created if the investment opportunities are perfectly negatively correlated to the profitability. The two main drivers of the value of risk management are the correlation between profitability and investment opportunities and the volatility of profitability. While the second is quite intuitive, the former is perhaps more surprising. Furthermore, the correlation has significant impact on the optimal hedging strategy.

Firms therefore need to carefully assess their circumstances before selecting their risk management strategy, in particular, they need to determine the correlation between profitability and investment opportunities. This is not a mathematical exercise, although some data analysis can provide supporting facts. Rather, it requires a strategic analysis of the industry dynamics.

As was discussed in Chapter 2, these findings must be reconciled with investors' expectations. For example, investors in commodity companies are likely to want some exposure to commodity prices (especially at the top of the cycle), and firms will not be able to extract the full value from risk management. However, a rigourous analysis such as the one presented here will quantify the trade-off, and support moving closer to the optimum.

I believe this type of modelling offers fertile ground for further analysis. On the theoretical front, one would like to expand on existing academic work to establish the general properties of these models, in particular the extension to multiple periods. On the practical front, one will need to test the results for a variety of distributions for profitability and investment opportunities.

APPENDIX

6.A DERIVATIONS OF THE OPTIMAL RISK MANAGEMENT STRATEGY

The firm's program is:

$$\max_{\lambda_0, \eta} VC = \frac{1}{1 + w(\lambda_0)} \cdot E\left[\Pi_1 + \frac{\Pi_2}{1 + w(\lambda_1)}\right]$$

6.A.1 First-order derivative with respect to initial leverage

We first show that:

$$\frac{\partial VC}{\partial \lambda_0} = -\frac{1}{1 + w(\lambda_0)} \cdot \left\{ w'(\lambda_0) \cdot (1 + VC) \right.$$

$$\left. + (1+r) \cdot \left(\frac{w'(\hat{\lambda}_1)}{1 + w(\hat{\lambda}_1)} \cdot \Pr(\Omega^{FC}) + E\left[\frac{w'(\lambda_1)}{1 + w(\lambda_1)} \left(1 + \frac{\Pi_2}{(1 + w(\lambda_1)) \cdot (1+i)}\right) \middle/ \Omega^{OC} \right] \cdot \Pr(\Omega^{OC}) \right) \right\}$$

Proof To simplify the notation, we introduce:

$$X_2 = \frac{\Pi_2}{1 + w(\lambda_1)}$$

the discounted value of second period value created. We have:

$$\frac{\partial VC}{\partial \lambda_0} = -\frac{w'(\lambda_0)}{1 + w(\lambda_0)} \cdot VC + \frac{1}{1 + w(\lambda_0)} \cdot (-w'(\lambda_0))$$

$$+ \frac{\partial}{\partial \lambda_0} E[X_2]$$

We need to consider two "regimes": the firm is either financially or opportunity constrained. Denote Ω^{FC} the event: "the firm is financially constrained", and Ω^{OC} the event: "the firm is opportunity constrained". Since a firm is either financially or opportunity constrained, Ω^{FC} and Ω^{OC} form a partition of the states of the world denoted Ω.

Denote $\hat{\lambda}_1$ the leverage ratio solution to the first-order condition (3), and $\hat{g}$ the corresponding growth rate. $\hat{\lambda}_1$ depends only on the cost of capital $w(\cdot)$ and the expected profitability of the new investment $E[y]$. We then have:

$$1 + \hat{g} = \frac{1 + \pi_1 - (1+r)\cdot \lambda_0}{1 - \hat{\lambda}_1}$$

The firm is financially constrained if and only if $\hat{g} < i$, which is equivalent to:

$$z_1 < \frac{(1-\hat{\lambda}_1)\cdot(1+i) + (1+r)\cdot\lambda_0 - \eta\cdot E[z_1]}{1 - \eta}$$

$$= \bar{z}_1(i;\lambda_0,\eta) \tag{6}$$

Since in our example z_2 and y are independent variables, and only their expectations matter for the analysis, we omit them in the notation, ie, all expectations are already taken with respect to z_2 and y. We then have:

$$\Omega^{FC} = \{(z_1,i) / z_1 < \bar{z}_1(i;\lambda_0,\eta)\}$$

and

$$\Omega^{OC} = \{(z_1,i) / z_1 \geq \bar{z}_1(i;\lambda_0,\eta)\}$$

Denote $f(z_1, i)$, the joint Probability Density Function of (z_1, i). We have:

$$E[X_2] = \int_i \int_{z_1 < \bar{z}_1(i;\lambda_0,\eta)} X_2 \cdot f(z_1,i) \cdot dz_1 \cdot di$$
$$+ \int_i \int_{z_1 \geq \bar{z}_1(i;\lambda_0,\eta)} X_2 \cdot f(z_1,i) \cdot dz_1 \cdot di$$

We then use the following result: Denote $a(x, t)$ a continuous and differentiable function, and $f(x, y, t)$ and $g(x, y, t)$ two continuous and differentiable functions such that $f(x, a(x, t), t) = g(x, a(x, t), t)$ and:

$$A(t) = \int_{-\infty}^{+\infty}\left(\int_{-\infty}^{a(x,t)} f(x,y,t)dy + \int_{a(x,t)}^{+\infty} g(x,y,t)dt\right)dx$$

We have:

$$A'(t) = \int_{-\alpha}^{+\alpha} \left(\int_{-\infty}^{a(x,t)} \frac{\partial f(x,y,t)}{\partial t} dy + \int_{a(x,t)}^{+\infty} \frac{\partial g(x,y,t)}{\partial t} dy \right) dx$$

$$+ \int_{-\infty}^{+\infty} \left(\begin{array}{c} f(x, a(x,t), t) \cdot \dfrac{\partial a}{\partial t}(x,t) \\ - g(x, a(x,t), t) \cdot \dfrac{\partial a}{\partial t}(x,t) \end{array} \right) dx$$

$$= \int_{-\infty}^{+\infty} \left(\int_{-\infty}^{a(x,t)} \frac{\partial f(x,y,t)}{\partial t} dy + \int_{a(x,t)}^{+\infty} \frac{\partial g(x,y,t)}{\partial t} dy \right) dx$$

since $f(x, a(x,t), t) = g(x, a(x,t), t)$.

Since (1) $\bar{z}_1(i; \lambda_0, \eta)$ is continuous and differentiable (except for $\eta = 1$), (2) $\Pi_2/(1 + w(\lambda_1)) \cdot f(z_1, i)$ and is continuous differentiable on Ω^{FC} and Ω^{OC}, and (3) $\hat{g}(\bar{z}_1(i; \lambda_0, \eta)) = i$, we can apply the previous result:

$$\frac{\partial}{\partial \lambda_0} E[X_2] = \int_i \int_{z_1 < \bar{z}_1(i; \lambda_0, \eta)} \left(\frac{\partial X_2}{\partial \lambda_0} \right)_{\Omega^{FC}} \cdot f(z_1, i) \cdot dz_1 \cdot di$$

$$+ \int_i \int_{z_1 \geq \bar{z}_1(i; \lambda_0, \eta)} \left(\frac{\partial X_2}{\partial \lambda_0} \right)_{\Omega^{OC}} \cdot f(z_1, i) \cdot dz_1 \cdot di$$

Consider first the case where the firm is financially constrained, $\lambda_1 = \hat{\lambda}_1$, and:

$$\left(\frac{\partial X_2}{\partial \lambda_0} \right)_{\Omega^{FC}} = \frac{1}{1 + w(\hat{\lambda}_1)} \cdot \left(E[y] - w(\hat{\lambda}_1) \right) \cdot \frac{d\hat{g}}{d\lambda_0}$$

$$= \frac{(1 - \hat{\lambda}_1) \cdot w'(\hat{\lambda}_1)}{1 + w(\hat{\lambda}_1)} \cdot \left(-\frac{1 + r}{1 - \hat{\lambda}_1} \right)$$

since $E[y] - w(\hat{\lambda}_1) = (1 - \hat{\lambda}_1) \cdot w'(\hat{\lambda}_1)$ by definition of $\hat{\lambda}_1$ and we can verify from Equation (1) that $d\hat{g}/\partial \lambda_0 = -(1 + r)/(1 - \hat{\lambda}_1)$. Then:

$$\left(\frac{\partial X_2}{\partial \lambda_0} \right)_{\Omega^{FC}} = -\frac{(1 + r) \cdot w'(\hat{\lambda}_1)}{1 + w(\hat{\lambda}_1)}$$

and:

$$\int_i \int_{z_1 < \bar{z}_1(i;\lambda_0,\eta)} \left(\frac{\partial X_2}{\partial \lambda_0}\right)_{\Omega^{FC}} \cdot f(z_1,i) \cdot dz_1 \cdot di$$

$$= -\frac{(1+r) \cdot w'(\hat{\lambda}_1)}{1 + w(\hat{\lambda}_1)} \cdot \Pr(\Omega^{FC})$$

Consider now the case where the firm is opportunity constrained. Then, $g^* = i$ and:

$$\lambda_1 = 1 - \frac{1 + \pi_1 - (1+r)\lambda_0}{1+i}$$

which yields

$$\frac{\partial \lambda_1}{\partial \lambda_0} = \frac{1+r}{1+i}$$

Then:

$$\left(\frac{\partial X_2}{\partial \lambda_0}\right)_{\Omega^{OC}} = \frac{1}{1 + w(\lambda_1)}(-X_2 - (1+i)) \cdot w'(\lambda_1) \cdot \frac{\partial \lambda_1}{\partial \lambda_0}$$

$$= -\frac{(1+r) \cdot w'(\lambda_1)}{1 + w(\lambda_1)}\left(1 + \frac{X_2}{(1+i)}\right)$$

and:

$$\int_i \int_{z_1 \geq \bar{z}_1(i;\lambda_0,\eta)} \left(\frac{\partial X_2}{\partial \lambda_0}\right)_{\Omega^{OC}} \cdot f(z_1,i) \cdot dz_1 \cdot di = -(1+r) \cdot$$

$$E\left[\frac{w'(\lambda_1)}{1 + w(\lambda_1)} \cdot \left(1 + \frac{X_2}{1+i}\right)/\Omega^{OC}\right] \cdot \Pr(\Omega^{OC})$$

Then:

$$\frac{\partial}{\partial \lambda_0} E[X_2] = -(1+r)$$

$$\cdot \left(\begin{array}{c} \dfrac{w'(\hat{\lambda}_1)}{1 + w(\hat{\lambda}_1)} \cdot \Pr(\Omega^{FC}) \\ + E\left[\dfrac{w'(\lambda_1)}{1 + w(\lambda_1)}\left(1 + \dfrac{X_2}{1+i}\right)/\Omega^{OC}\right] \cdot \Pr(\Omega^{OC}) \end{array}\right)$$

which then yield Equation (4).

6.A.2 First order derivative with respect to hedging ratio

We now show that:

$$\frac{\partial VC}{\partial \eta} = \frac{1}{1 + w(\lambda_0)}$$

$$\cdot \begin{pmatrix} \frac{w'(\hat{\lambda}_1)}{1 + w(\hat{\lambda}_1)} E\left[E[z] - z_1 / \Omega^{FC}\right] \cdot \Pr(\Omega^{FC}) \\ + E\left[\begin{array}{c} \frac{w'(\hat{\lambda}_1)}{1 + w(\hat{\lambda}_1)} \cdot \left(1 + \frac{\Pi_2}{(1 + w(\hat{\lambda}_1)) \cdot (1 + i)}\right) \\ \cdot (E[z] - z_1) / \Omega^{OC} \end{array}\right] \cdot \Pr(\Omega^{OC}) \end{pmatrix}$$

Proof We first have:

$$\frac{\partial VC}{\partial \eta} = \frac{1}{1 + w(\lambda_0)} \cdot \frac{\partial}{\partial \eta} E[X_2]$$

We can then apply the previous logic to the first-order derivative with respect to the hedging ratio, and take derivatives on both Ω^{FC} and Ω^{OC}. Consider first the financially constrained firm:

$$\left(\frac{\partial X_2}{\partial \eta}\right)_{\Omega^{FC}} = \frac{1}{1 + w(\hat{\lambda}_1)} \cdot \left(E[y] - w(\hat{\lambda}_1)\right) \cdot \frac{d\hat{g}}{d\eta}$$

$$= \frac{w'(\hat{\lambda}_1)}{1 + w(\hat{\lambda}_1)} \cdot \left(E[z] - z_1\right)$$

since

$$\frac{d\hat{g}}{d\eta} = \frac{E[z] - z_1}{1 - \hat{\lambda}_1}$$

Then:

$$\int_i \int_{z_1 < \bar{z}_1(i;\lambda_0,\eta)} \left(\frac{\partial X_2}{\partial \eta}\right)_{\Omega^{FC}} \cdot f(z_1, i) \cdot dz_1 \cdot di$$

$$= \frac{w'(\hat{\lambda}_1)}{1 + w(\hat{\lambda}_1)} E\left[E[z] - z_1 / \Omega^{FC}\right] \cdot \Pr(\Omega^{FC})$$

The expectation is positive, since it is conditioned by $z_1 < \bar{z}_1(i; \lambda_0, \eta)$.

Consider now the opportunity constrained firm:

$$\left(\frac{\partial X_2}{\partial \eta}\right)_{\Omega^{OC}} = -\frac{w'(\lambda_1)}{1+w(\lambda_1)} \cdot (X_2 + (1+i)) \cdot \frac{\partial \lambda_1}{\partial \eta}$$

$$= \frac{w'(\lambda_1)}{1+w(\lambda_1)} \cdot \left(1 + \frac{X_2}{1+i}\right) \cdot (E[z] - z_1)$$

since

$$\frac{\partial \lambda_1}{\partial \eta} = -\frac{\partial \pi_1}{\partial \eta} \cdot \frac{1}{1+i} = -\frac{E[z] - z_1}{1+i}$$

Then:

$$\frac{\partial}{\partial \eta} E[X_2] = \frac{w'(\hat{\lambda}_1)}{1+w(\hat{\lambda}_1)} E\left[E[z] - z_1 / \Omega^{FC}\right] \cdot \Pr(\Omega^{FC})$$

$$+ E\left[\frac{w'(\lambda_1)}{1+w(\lambda_1)} \cdot \left(1 + \frac{X_2}{1+i}\right) \cdot (E[z] - z_1) / \Omega^{OC}\right]$$

$$\cdot \Pr(\Omega^{OC})$$

which proves Equation (5).

6.A.3 Second order derivatives

We now derive the second-order conditions, and discuss necessary conditions for the extremum to be a maximum. However, we do not offer a rigourous mathematical proof that these necessary conditions are met. We therefore verify through the optimisation process that the optimum found is indeed a maximum. In addition, we examine the impact of the hedging ratio and the leverage ratios on $\Pr(\Omega^{FC})$.

We start from:

$$\frac{\partial VC}{\partial \lambda_0} = -\frac{w'(\lambda_0)}{1+w(\lambda_0)} \cdot (1+VC) + \frac{1}{1+w(\lambda_0)} \cdot \frac{\partial E[X_2]}{\partial \lambda_0}$$

We then have:[5]

$$\frac{\partial^2 VC}{\partial \lambda_0^2} = -\frac{w'(\lambda_0)}{1+w(\lambda_0)} \cdot \frac{\partial VC}{\partial \lambda_0} + \frac{1}{1+w(\lambda_0)} \cdot$$
$$\left(-w''(\lambda_0) \cdot (1+VC) - w'(\lambda_0) \cdot \frac{\partial VC}{\partial \lambda_0} + \frac{\partial^2 E[X_2]}{\partial \lambda_0^2}\right)$$
$$= \frac{1}{1+w(\lambda_0)} \cdot \left(\frac{\partial^2 E[X_2]}{\partial \lambda_0^2} - w''(\lambda_0) \cdot (1+VC)\right)$$

since $\partial VC/\partial \lambda_0 = 0$ at the extremum.

Similarly, we have:

$$\frac{\partial VC}{\partial \eta} = \frac{1}{1+w(\lambda_0)} \cdot \frac{\partial E[X_2]}{\partial \eta}$$

which the yields:

$$\frac{\partial^2 VC}{\partial \eta^2} = \frac{1}{1+w(\lambda_0)} \cdot \frac{\partial^2 E[X_2]}{\partial \eta^2}$$

and:

$$\frac{\partial^2 VC}{\partial \eta \partial \lambda_0} = \frac{1}{1+w(\lambda_0)} \cdot \frac{\partial^2 E[X_2]}{\partial \eta \partial \lambda_0}$$

The Hessian matrix at the extremum is then:

$$J = \frac{1}{1+w(\lambda_0)} \begin{pmatrix} \frac{\partial^2 E[X_2]}{\partial \lambda_0^2} - w''(\lambda_0) \cdot (1+VC) & \frac{\partial^2 E[X_2]}{\partial \eta \partial \lambda_0} \\ \frac{\partial^2 E[X_2]}{\partial \eta \partial \lambda_0} & \frac{\partial^2 E[X_2]}{\partial \eta^2} \end{pmatrix}$$

VC is locally concave if the matrix J is (locally) definite negative, which occurs if and only if:

$$\det(J) > 0 \quad \text{and} \quad Tr(J) < 0$$

We now introduce U the Hessian matrix of $E[X_2]$. By definition, we have:

$$U = \begin{pmatrix} \dfrac{\partial^2 E[X_2]}{\partial \lambda_0^2} & \dfrac{\partial^2 E[X_2]}{\partial \eta \partial \lambda_0} \\ \dfrac{\partial^2 E[X_2]}{\partial \eta \partial \lambda_0} & \dfrac{\partial^2 E[X_2]}{\partial \eta^2} \end{pmatrix}$$

We have:

$$\det(J) = \frac{1}{1 + w(\lambda_0)} \cdot \left(\det U - \frac{\partial^2 E[X_2]}{\partial \eta^2} \cdot w''(\lambda_0) \cdot (1 + VC) \right)$$

$$Tr(J) = \frac{1}{1 + w(\lambda_0)} \cdot (Tr(U) - w''(\lambda_0) \cdot (1 + VC))$$

Then, if $E[\Pi_2/(1 + w(\lambda_1))]$ is a (locally) concave function of (λ_0, η), since $w''(\lambda_0) \geq 0$, and assuming $1 + VC \geq 0$ around the extremum, we have $\det(J) \geq \det U/(1 + w(\lambda_0)) > 0$, and $Tr(J) \leq Tr(U)/(1 + w(\lambda_0)) < 0$. Constructing a rigourous proof that $E[\Pi_2/(1 + w(\lambda_1))]$ is (locally) concave for all possible distributions of (z_1, i) is somehow cumbersome, hence we resort to numerical simulations.

6.A.4 Impact of hedging ratio on $\Pr(\Omega^{FC})$

We can rewrite Equation (6) as:

$$\bar{z}_1(i; \lambda_0, \eta) = E[z] - \frac{E[z] - \bar{z}_1(i; \lambda_0, 0)}{1 - \eta}$$

where

$$\bar{z}_1(i; \lambda_0, 0) = 1 - ((1 - \hat{\lambda}_1) \cdot (1 + i) + (1 + r) \cdot \lambda_0)$$

We then have:

$$\frac{\partial \bar{z}_1}{\partial \eta} = -\frac{E[z] - \bar{z}_1(i; \lambda_0, 0)}{(1 - \eta)^2}$$

For "reasonable" values of the parameters, $E[z] - \bar{z}_1(i; \lambda_0, 0) > 0$. For example, we find that for the "base case" cost of capital, $\hat{\lambda}_1 = 41.2\%$. With $i = 0$, $r = 3\%$, and $\lambda_0 = 40\%$, we have:

$$\bar{z}_1(i;\lambda_0,0) = 1 - (1 - 0.412) + (1 + 0.03) \cdot 0.40 = 0$$

Then:
$$E[z] - \bar{z}_1(i;\lambda_0,0) = E[z] > 0$$

Then, since:
$$\frac{\partial(E[z] - \bar{z}_1(i;\lambda_0,0))}{\partial i} = -(1 - \hat{\lambda}_1) < 0$$

we have $E[z] - \bar{z}_1(i;\lambda_0,0) > 0$ for $i = 20\%$ and $i = 40\%$.
Therefore:

$$\frac{\partial \bar{z}_1}{\partial \eta} < 0 \quad \text{and} \quad \lim_{\eta \to 1} \bar{z}_1(i;\lambda_0,\eta) = -\infty$$

$\Leftrightarrow$

$$\frac{\partial \Pr(\Omega^{FC})}{\partial \eta} < 0 \quad \text{and} \quad \lim_{\eta \to 1} \Pr(\Omega^{FC}) = 0$$

Increasing the hedging ratio reduces the probability that the firm be financially constrained. At the limit, full hedging eliminates the risk of being financially constrained. As we have seen, this may not be optimal.

6.A.5 Impact of leverage ratio on $\Pr(\Omega^{FC})$

We have:
$$\frac{\partial \bar{z}_1}{\partial \lambda_0} = \frac{1+r}{1-\eta}$$

Hence, as long as $\eta < 1$, we have:
$$\frac{\partial \Pr(\Omega^{FC})}{\partial \lambda_0} > 0$$

Increasing the initial leverage raises the probability of the firm being financially constrained, since it increases interest payments, hence reduces the free cash flow available for investment.

1. Alternatively, the firm could maximise the perpetual value of the economic profits from the second period onwards, where $w(\lambda_1)$ is the perpetual discount rate: $E[\Pi_2/w(\lambda_1)]$ would replace $E[\Pi_2/1 + w(\lambda_1)]$. While this modifies the optimal risk management strategy, the main insights remain identical.
2. Since the profit, the borrowing, and the investment are after tax, the after-tax interest payment is the relevant quantity.
3. Alternatively, the firm could maximise the present value of the expected profitability: $E[\Pi_2/1 + w(\lambda_1)]$. Again, this slightly change the optimal investment decision (hence the risk management strategy) but not the main insights.
4. This simplified model runs on Crystal Ball, a commercially available Monte Carlo simulation software, that is simply added onto Excel. Crystal Ball has proven an effective tool as long as the number of random variables is less than 100. For larger simulations, other software solutions (eg, Matlab) can be used.
5. We ignore here technical issues of non differentiability, assuming they do not occur around the optimum.

7
Conclusion

This book started by introducing the risk management paradox: despite significant advances over the last decade, the value creation potential from risk management remains still largely untapped. This paradox has been attributed to two main factors: (1) most risk management programs are focused on risk measurement and control, not on value creation; and (2) a gap remains between clear(er) theoretical predictions on one side, and the frameworks and methodologies available to practitioners on the other side.

Chapter 2 proposed that risk management creates value primarily through three channels: (1) providing financial flexibility at minimum cost, (2) enhancing capital allocation and performance management, and (3) leveraging operational and strategic flexibility. These apply to financial and non-financial firms. Chapter 3 analysed three critical themes in corporate risk management: (1) managing with volatility – Enterprise Risk Management (ERM), (2) measuring volatility – from Value at Risk (VaR) to Economic Capital and (3) managing volatility – derivatives usage.

Hopefully, this book has also provided practitioners with practical tools to unlock the value creation potential from risk management: an approach to identify and quantify risks and estimate the distribution of future cash flows (Chapter 4), risk capital as a risk metric (Chapter 5) and a framework to develop an integrated risk management strategy, adapted to each company's circumstances (Chapter 6).

Each chapter has ended with concluding observations pertaining to its main theme. This brief concluding chapter discusses two issues of relevance to CROs: first, views on what makes a CRO successful, based on my experience (successes and failures), as well as numerous discussions with other CROs, secondly, a possible path forward for corporate risk management.

7.1 BEING A CHIEF RISK OFFICER

Most CROs agree that their main challenge is to show how the risk function effectively adds value to the firm, beyond the needed compliance tasks. The answer depends on each firm, its industry, and more importantly its culture and governance. However, I would like to offer a few lessons that have widespread applicability.

First, if we believe risk management intends to bring about a significant change in a firm's organisation, processes and governance, comparable with the adoption of Economic Value Added as a performance metric, or Continuous Improvement as a management principle, we must then remember the cardinal rule of change management:

Change does not happen when it is needed, but when it is possible.

Even though a firm could significantly benefit from risk management, until the board of directors and the very senior managers are supporting it, no substantial change can happen. The first challenge facing CROs is then to "convert" board members and senior managers. Creating a CRO position is a necessary first step, but it is not equivalent to fully embracing risk management as a core business process. As one CRO put it:

I have won their minds. I now need to win their hearts.

This requires CROs to clearly articulate the value creation levers from risk management, following a framework such as the one described in Chapter 2, and be evaluated on their performance against these levers.

Second, and somehow paradoxically, CROs have to *choose what they do not do*. In particular, they may have to relinquish some compliance responsibilities. For example at Alcan, the responsibility for SOX implementation, a significant and high-profile undertaking, was carried by the controller's group, and not by the risk management team, which could then devote its attention to value-creating activities.

Similarly, CROs may refrain from creating new risk management processes, and instead fit their needs into existing management processes. I have always been sceptical about risk management "grand' messes" where all managers are convened to discuss risk issues. Similarly, I have doubts about the effectiveness of risk inventories, where all risks are tabulated, and given a rating from green to red. While I fully appreciate their pedagogical value, and their role in energising a corporation around a new management theme, such as risk management, they appear to me as very costly, very intrusive, and contribute only marginally to value creation.

I prefer a more focused approach, where a few critical risks are identified, quantified, and effectively managed. I find this more cost-effective for the firm. At Alcan, we started by focusing on the core risks to the company: aluminium price and currencies, and progressively included other risks: other commodities, business conditions, pensions, etc. For each, we first developed a robust understanding of the true exposure, working with a few key personnel in the organisation. We then developed a risk management strategy, essentially following the blueprint presented in Section 2.5.

Throughout the process, the risk management team worked very closely with other functions such as treasury and controllership, as well as with the businesses. This teamwork had two benefits: (1) it reduced the cost of the risk management rollout, as it leveraged existing talent, knowledge and processes, and (2) it accelerated the diffusion of risk management thinking throughout the company, by rapidly reaching out "far and wide" in the organisation.

Similarly, CROs have to recognise – and advocate – that less hedging activity is sometimes better than more, even if it appears to lessen their personal contribution to the corporation. As mentioned in Chapter 4, many firms hedge their currency transaction exposure, or enter into interest rate swaps (92% according to a recent survey by the International Swap Dealers Association (ISDA)) that may in some instances increase the cash flow volatility. While of course some hedging can be beneficial, I am very sceptical of the value truly created by these programs. On the other hand, there can be no doubt that the costs of running these programs are significant. CROs may have to accept to reduce the scope of these programs and focus them on a few value-creating transactions.

Third, CROs need to introduce *fact-based, quantitative risk management in a few key decision-making processes*. Alcan selected the planning process and the capital allocation process as the main entry points for risk management. The risk management team worked very closely with the planning team (part of the controller's group) and the treasury team to develop a risk management strategy that was fully consistent with the strategic plan and the capital plan. Hard facts, based on Monte Carlo simulations, were the workhorses of the risk management strategy.

The risk management team was also responsible for risk analysis of all significant capital decisions, working closely with the businesses to understand the projects risks, but reaching its own independent conclusions on the severity and the cost of these risks, and on a recommended risk management strategy.

This does not imply that the risk management team is only a "quant shop". On the contrary, as discussed in Chapter 4, corporate risk management requires as much a robust understanding of the business as it does mastery of mathematical techniques. This simply recognises that the contribution of a risk management team is a robust fact-based discussion of risks facing the firm, and a quantification of various possible outcomes.

Finally, CROs must stand *ready to disagree with very senior executives*. If their independent analysis indicates that a business decision creates an unacceptable risk-reward trade-off, they have a responsibility to report their findings. Failing to do so would irremediably compromise the risk management process within the firm. This is probably the most challenging element of a CRO's role, as it often causes great personal stress. *Professional integrity is the most important quality of a successful CRO*.

7.2 THE PATH FORWARD

As discussed in Chapter 3, it took almost one hundred years for the Discounted Cash Flows (DCFs) rule to be widely adopted as the analytical framework of business decision making. I am confident that the adoption of risk management as *the* mindset for business decision making will be much faster. First, many of the required ingredients are already present (eg, theoretical foundations, computing capabilities, mathematical models, insurance and derivatives markets, etc). Also numerous practitioners, academics, consultants, bankers are actively involved in risk management, creating an environment fertile for widespread adoption.

However, a few major issues require additional analysis for risk management to reach its full value creation potential. A non-exhaustive list includes:

❑ *Stronger empirical evidence on value creation from risk management.* As reviewed in Chapter 3, multiple solid academic studies have attempted to ascertain the relationships between risk management activities, cash flow volatility, and value creation. While the evidence broadly suggests that risk management activities increase value of firms, mainly through an increase in the ability to capture growth options and a reduction in the cost of capital, many issues remain open. For example, one study found that hedging activities appear to have too small an impact on average to account for the incremental value reported by another study.

Additional work will clearly establish the causality chain between risk management activities and value creation. That will then enable CROs to more clearly articulate their contribution to value creation within their organisations, and firms to better communicate their risk management strategies to stakeholders.

❑ *A richer understanding of optimal risk management strategies.* Chapter 6 presented a simplified analytical framework to develop a firm's risk management strategy given its business environment. A more general model can be solved through numerical simulations (eg, including multiple periods, a more sophisticated financial model, etc).

Additional analysis is required to better understand the workings of the model, in particular how changes in the firm's business environment impact the risk management strategy. Additionally, the analysis should be applied to different industries, to develop general recommendations. This will then provide clear and practical guidance to firms as they set their risk management strategies.

❑ *Convergence on commonly accepted risk adjustment methodologies.* We have reviewed three mutually consistent approaches:

Economic Capital in Chapter 3, Risk Capital in Chapter 5, and the full risk management strategy in Chapter 6. Firms will need to develop common methodologies and criteria to apply each of these approaches.

❑ *Continued improvements in the quantitative toolkit.* As reviewed in Chapter 4, significant advances have been accomplished regarding price risk, in particular in the short-term, and counterparty risk.

Additional work is required to develop commonly accepted models of long-term price risk. Additionally, the analytical framework for business risks, such as Corporate Social Responsibility (CSR) needs to be upgraded. This means estimating the distributions that best capture the features of the different facets of business risk, as we now have distributions that capture the mean-reversion of commodity prices. "Spikes", ie, extremely unlikely yet highly damaging events, are likely to play a critical role in that modelling.

These issues cannot be resolved by academics or corporations alone. This will require exchanges and cooperations between academics, corporations, and professional services firms. This constitutes a second "S-curve" for risk management, as critical as the one already travelled.

Once progress has been accomplished on these issues, one can envision risk management progressively becoming a core business process, embedded in the fabric of firms. The value proposition will be clearly articulated. Practical frameworks will be taught in business schools, known to all senior executives, and as ingrained in corporate decision-making as the Net Present Value (NPV) rule is today. Risk analyses will be conducted routinely, following tried and true methods. Innovative risk transfer instruments will be developed, and widely used.

For risk managers, the best days are ahead!

Bibliography

Aid, R., A. Porchet, and N. Touzi, 2006, "Vertical Integration and Risk Management in Competitive Markets of Non-storable Goods", (Mimeo, Université Paris Dauphine CEREMADE).

Allayannis, G., U. Lel, and D. Miller, 2004, "Corporate Governance and The Hedging Premium Around the World", (Working Paper, University of Virginia School of Business), June.

Allayannis, Y. and J. Weston, 2001, "The Use of Foreign Currency Derivatives and Firm Market Value", *Review of Financial Studies*, **14** pp 243–76.

Altman, E. I., 1968, "Financial Ratios, Discriminant Analysis and the Prediction of Corporate Bankruptcy", *Journal of Finance*, pp 589–609, September.

Baldursson, F. M. and N.-H. V. der Fehr, 2006, "Vertical Integration and Long-Term Contracts in Risky Markets", November, Mimeo.

Bartram, S., G. Brown, and F. Fehle, 2006, "International Evidence on Financial Derivatives Usage", (Working Paper, University of North Carolina Business School), October.

Bernard, J.-T., L. Khalaf, M. Kichian, and S. McMahon, 2006, "Forecasting Commodity Prices: GARCH, Jumps, and Mean Reversion", (Working Paper 2006-14, Bank of Canada).

Bernstein, P. L., 1996, *Against the Gods: A Remarkable Story of Risk*, (New York: Wiley).

Bertrand M. and S. Mullainathan, 2001, "Are CEOs Rewarded for Luck? The Ones Without Principals Are", *The Quarterly Journal of Economics*, **116(3)**, pp 901–32.

Bessembinder, H. and M. L. Lemmon, 2002, "Equilibrium Pricing and Optimal Hedging in Electricity Forward Markets", *The Journal of Finance* **57(3)**, pp 1347–82.

Brown, G., 2001, "Managing Foreign Exchange Risk with Derivatives", *Journal of Financial Economics* **60**, pp 401–48.

Carter, D., D. Rogers, and B. Simkins, 2004, "Does Fuel Hedging Make Economic Sense? The Case of the U.S. Airline Industry", (Working Paper, Oklahoma State University).

Committee of Sponsoring Organizations of the Treadway Commission. Enterprise risk management – an integrated framework. http://www.coso.org/Publications/ERM, 2004.

Copeland, T. and V. Antikarov, 2003, *Real Options: A Practitioner's Guide,* (Texere, Revised Edition).

Copeland, T., T. Koller, and J. Murrin, 1995, *Valuation: Measuring and Managing the Value of Companies,* (New York: John Wiley and Sons, Inc.).

Copeland, T. E., J. F. Weston, and K. Shastri, 2003, *Financial Theory and Corporate Policy,* Fourth Edition, (Addison-Wesley).

Culp, C. L., 2002, *The ART of Risk Management,* (New York: Wiley).

Culp, C. L. and M. H. Miller (eds), 1999, *Corporate Hedging in Theory and Practice: Lessons from Metallgesellschaft,* (London: Risk Books).

Dev, A., (ed), 2006, *Economic Capital: A Practitioner Guide,* (London: Risk Books).

Dixit, A. K. and R. S. Pindyck, 1994, *Investment under Uncertainty,* (Princeton University Press).

Doherty, N., 2000, *Integrated Risk Management: Techniques and Strategies for Reducing Risk,* (New York: McGraw-Hill).

Donaldson, G., 1961, "Corporate Debt Capacity: A Study of Corporate Debt Policy and the Determination of Corporate Debt Capacity", (Harvard Graduate School of Business Administration).

Dowd, K. and D. Blake, 2006, "After VaR: The Theory, Estimation and Insurance Applications of Quantile-based Risk Measures", *The Journal of Risk and Insurance* **73(2)**, pp 193–229.

Drake, A., 1967, *Fundamentals of Applied Probability Theory,* (McGraw Hill, Inc.).

Foster, R. and S. Kaplan, 2001, *Creative Destruction: Why Companies That are Built to Last Underperform the Market – and How to Successfully Transform Them*, (New York: Doubleday), April.

Froot, K., D. Sharfstein, and J. Stein, 1993, "Risk Management: Coordinating Corporate Investment and Financing Policies", *Journal of Finance* **48**, pp 1629–58.

Froot, K. A. and J. C. Stein, 1998, "Risk Management, Capital Budgeting, and Capital Structure Policy for Financial Institutions: An Integrated Approach", *Journal of Financial Economics* **47**, pp 55–82.

Gates, S. and E. Hexter, 2005, "From Risk Management to Risk Strategy. Technical report", The Conference Board.

Geczy, C., B. Minton, and C. Schrand, 1997, "Why Firms Use Currency Derivatives?", *Journal of finance* **52**, pp 1323–56, September.

Graham, J. and D. Rogers, 2002, "Do Firms Hedge in Response to Tax Incentives?", *Journal of Finance* **57**, pp 815–39.

Green, R., 2006, "Carbon Tax or Carbon Permits: The Impact on Generators' Risk", (Mimeo, Institute for Energy Research and Policy, University of Birmingham), November.

Grinblatt, M. and S. Titman, 1998, *Financial Markets and Corporate Strategy*, (Boston: Irwin/McGraw-Hill).

Guay, W. and S. Kothari, 2003, "How Much do Firms Hedge with Derivatives?", *Journal of Financial Economics* **70**, pp 423–61.

Hamada, R. S., 1969, "Portfolio Analysis, Market Equilibrium and Corporation Finance", *Journal of Finance*, pp 13–31, March.

Haushalter, D., 2000, "The Role of Corporate Hedging: Evidence From Oil and gas Producers", *Journal of Finance* **55(1)**.

Holmström, B., 1979, "Moral Hazard and Observability", *Bell Journal of Economics* **10**, pp 74–91.

Holmström, B. and J. Tirole, 2000, "Liquidity and Risk Management", *Journal of Money, Credit and Banking* **32**, pp 295–319.

Hull, J., 2003, *Options, Futures, and Other Derivatives*, Fifth Edition, (Upper Saddle River, New Jersey: Prentice Hall).

Jin, Y. and P. Jorion, 2006, "Firm Value and Hedging: Evidence From U.S. Oil and Gas Producers", *Journal of Finance*, **61**, pp 893–919, April.

Jorion, P., 2001, *Value at Risk.* (New York: McGraw-Hill).

Kennedy, P., 1990, *The Rise and Fall of Great Powers*, (Random House), May.

Kim, Y., I. Mathur, and J. Nam, 2005, "Is Operational Hedging of Substitute For or a Complement to Financial Hedging?", (Working Paper, Southern Illinois University), July.

LaGattuta, D. A., J. C. Stein, M. L. Tennican, S. E. Usher, and J. Youngen, 2000, "CashFlow-at-Risk and Financial Policy for Electricity Companies in the New World Order", *The Electricity Journal*, pp 15–20, December.

Lee, I., S. Lochhead, J. Ritter, and Q. Zhao, 1996, "The Costs of Raising Capital", *Journal of Financial Research* **19(1)**, pp 59–74.

Leland, H., 1994, "Corporate Debt Value, Bond Covenants and Optimal Capital Structure", *Journal of Finance* **49(4)**, pp 1213–52, September.

Leland, H. and K. Toft, 1996, "Optimal Capital Structure, Endogenous Bank-Ruptcy, and the Term Structure of Credit Spreads", *Journal of Finance* **51(3)**, pp 987–1019.

Lewis, M. 1989, *Liar's Poker*, (Penguin).

Lowenstein, R., 2001, *When Genius Failed: The Rise and Fall of Long-Term Capital Management*, (Random House).

Markowitz, H., 1952, "Portfolio selection", *Journal of Finance* **7**, pp 77–91.

Marrison, C., 2002, *The Fundamentals of Risk Measurement*, (Boston, Massachusetts: McGraw-Hill).

Marshall, T., 2005, "Rating Methodology: Global Mining Industry", (Technical Report 94364, Moody's Investors Service), September.

Mayer, C., 1990, "Financial Systems, Corporate Finance, and Economic Development", in G. Hubbard (ed), *Asymmetric Information, Corporate Finance, and Investment*, (National Bureau of Economic Research, University of Chicago Press).

Merton R. and A. Perold, 1993, "Theory of Risk Capital in Financial Firms", *Journal of Applied Corporate Finance*, pp 16–32.

Merton, R. C., 2005, "You Have More Capital Than You Think", *Harvard Business Review*, November.

Miles, J. and J. Ezzell, 1980, "The Weighted Average Cost of Capital, Perfect Capital Markets, and Project Life: A Clarification", *Journal of Financial and Quantitative Analysis* **15(3)**, pp 719–30.

Miles, J. and J. Ezzell, 1985, "Reformulating Tax Shield Valuation: A Note", *Journal of Finance* **40(5)**, pp 1485–92.

Minton, B. A. and C. Schrand, 1999, "The Impact of Cash Flow Volatility on Discretionary Investment and the Costs of Debt and Equity Financing", *Journal of Financial Economics* **54**, pp 423–60.

Modigliani, F. and M. Miller, 1958, "The Cost of Capital, Corporate Finance and the Theory of Investment", *American Economic Review* **48(3)**, pp 261–97.

Modigliani, F. and M. Miller, 1963, "Corporate Income Taxes and the Cost of Capital: A Correction", *American Economic Review* **53(3)**, pp 433–92.

Myers, S. C. and N. Majluf, 1984, "Corporate Financing and Investment Decisions When Firms Have Information Investors Do Not Have", *Journal of Financial Economics* **13**, pp 187–221.

Nain, A., 2004, "The Strategic Motives for Corporate Risk Management", (Working Paper, University of Michigan).

Pettit, J., 2007, *Strategic Corporate Finance: Applications in Valuations and Capital Structure*, (Hoboken: Wiley Finance).

Rajan, R. and L. Zingales, 2003, "The Great Reverseals: The Politics of Financial Development in the 20th Century", *Journal of Financial Economics* **69**, pp 5–50.

Rochet, J.-C. and S. Villeneuve, 2006, "Liquidity Risk and Corporate Demand for Hedging and Insurance", (Mimeo, Institut d'Economie Industrielle), October.

Saunders, A. and L. Allen, 2002, *Credit Risk Measurement*, Second Edition(New York: Wiley Finance).

Schwartz, E. S., 1997, "The Stochastic Behavior of Commodity Prices: Implications for Valuation and Hedging", *Journal of Finance* **52**, pp 923–73.

Shimpi, P., (ed), 2001, *Integrating Corporate Risk Management*, (New York: Texere).

Slywotzky, J. and J. Drzik, 2005, "Countering the Biggest Risk of All", *Harvard Business Review*, pp 78–88, April.

Smithson, C. and B. J. Simkins, 2005, "Does Risk Management Add Value? A Survey of the Evidence", *Journal of Applied Corporate Finance* **17(3)**, pp 8–17, Summer.

Taleb, N., 2001, *Fooled by Randomness: The Hidden Role of Chance in the Markets and in Life*, (New York: Texere).

Tirole, J., 2006, *The Theory of Corporate Finance*, (Princeton University Press).

Tufano, P., 1996, "Who Manages Risk? An Empirical Examination of Risk Management Practices in the Gold Mining Industry", *Journal of Finance* **51**, pp 1097–37, September.

Index

A
Ahold 2
Aid *et al* (2006) 22
Air Liquide
 EBIT of 111
 ROCE of 111
Airbus currency exposures 137
Allayannis and Weston (2001) 22, 100–1, 104
Allayannis *et al* (2004) 104
Altman (1968) 144
Aluminium prices
 arbitrage power vs 49, 78
 average annual 94
 versus CAD/USD exchange rates 21–2
Aluminium producer, example of 183–6
Aluminium smelter 159
Amaranth 1
Anderson–Darling test 161

B
Baa1-rated bonds 88
Baldursson and von der Fehr (2006) 22
Barings 1
Barrick, on hedging programme 57
Bartram *et al* (2006) 104
Basel Committee on Banking Supervision 3, 65, 87, 96
Bernard *et al* (2006) 161
Bernoulli example 161, 168, 173–4, 179–83, 190
Bernstein (1996) 22

Bertrand and Mullainathan (2001) 81
BHP-Billiton 6
Binary distribution 190
Black–Scholes–Merton option pricing model 43, 121, 146
Black swan paradox 157
Brown (2001) 104
Brownian diffusion 121
Business environment, changes in firm 209–14
Business risk 29, 149

C
Capital allocation 43–6
 and performance management 41–8
 on risk-adjusted basis 44, 59
 risk management strategy and 59
Capital Asset Pricing Model (CAPM) 41, 43, 62, 166
 logic underlying 42
Capital structure
 as financial flexibility lever 39
 irrelevance of 60–61
Carter *et al* (2004) 104
Cash Flow at Risk (CFaR) 86
Cash flows, distributions for 57, 39
Certified Financial Analyst (CFA) 2
Chevron invested capital growth 122
Chi-square 161
Chief Executive Officer 52, 84
Chief Financial Officer 52, 84

Chief Risk Officers (CROs) 9, 52, 226
Committee of Sponsoring Organisations (COSO) 103
Conditional probability and independence 12
Conservative, as risk management strategy 54
Constant volatility, profitability 112–13
Contango 57
Continuous random variables 17–18
Copeland and Antikarov (2003) 22
Copeland *et al*
  (1995) 67–8
  (2003) 69, 73, 82, 189
Corporate risk management, advances in 1
Corporate Social Responsibility (CSR) risk 29, 230
Correlation coefficients, meaning of 20
Correlations 146
  on cash flows and investment opportunities 55
  hunting for 154
Cost of capital 70–73, 194–5, 213–14
  distribution of 58
  resulting 170–73
  U-shaped 33–4, 64
"Counterparty" risk 28–9, 142–7
Covariance
  and correlation 15
  revisited 19–20
"credit" risk 29
Culp (2002) 22, 81
Cumulative distribution function (CDF) 17
Currency choice, reduce risks 40
Currency risk exposure 134–8

D
Debt, market value of 182
Default per credit rating, probabilities of 89

Dev (2004) 81, 104
Diffusion-like profitability 121
Direct exposure 134
Discounted Cash Flows (DCF) 67, 228
  to value projects/investments 43
Discrete random variables 12–17
Distribution, invariance of 109
Diversifiable risk 42
Dixit and Pindyck (1994) 22
Doherty (2000) 60, 64-5, 80
Donaldson (1961) 81
Dowd and Blake (2006) 104
Drake (1967) 22

E
Economic Capital 95–6
  with margin calls 96
  measure of net assets 96
  to measure risk 186–8
  on VaR 96
"Economic exposure" 136
Economic mean reversion 115
Economic Profit (EP) 67, 73
Emission regulation risk 150
Emission trading, coal-fired plant profit under 159
Enron 2
Enterprise risk analysis, specificity of 156–8
Enterprise Risk Management (ERM) 2, 83–5
  objective of 84
Equity holders, in trading business 175
Expectation 14, 18
  conditional 14
Exposure
  determination of 143–4
  investors' appetite for 55
Exposure map 126
  aluminum producer aluminum 129
  aluminum producer price 128, 136
  gold producer revenue 128, 135

F

FASB 133, accounting rule 48
Financial distress, probability of 204
Financial flexibility
  examples of value of 36–8
  levers of 38
  modelling 31–6
  providing, at minimum cost 29–30
  risk transfer instruments on 54
  understanding 29–31
  value of 5
Financial metrics, for valuation 67–70
"Financial" risk 28
Financial Risk Manager (FRM) 2
Firm, expected value of 182, 195–6
Firm-specific risk, investors' views on 55
Foster and Kaplan (2001) 161
Free Cash Flow (FCF) 68–9, 73
Froot and Stein (1998) 23
Froot *et al* (1993) 22, 191, 198, 202

G

Gates and Hexter (2005) 22
Geczy *et al* (1997) 97, 104
Global Association of Risk Professionals (GARP) 22
Graham and Rogers (2002) 82, 104
Green (2006) 133, 159
Grinblatt and Titman (1998) 60, 65, 80-1
Guay and Kothari (2003) 100-1

H

Hamada (1969) 71
Haushalter (2000) 104
Hedging, and value creation 99
Hedging ratio
  first order derivative with 219–20
  impact of 208, 222–3
"Hidden" price exposures, in purchasing costs 131

Holmström and Tirole (2000) 22, 202
Hull (2003) 22, 108

I

IAS 39, accounting rule 48
Idiosyncratic risk 55
Incremental volatility reduction 100
Initial leverage, impact of 208
Inside-out risk analysis 126–54
Insurance asset, expected return on 189
Insurance payments, discount rate for 166–7
Internal funds, availability of 31
International Swap Dealers Association (ISDA) 2, 97, 227
Invariance, of distribution 109
Invested capital growth 121–4
Invested capital, profitability of initial 205
Investment opportunity
  characteristics of 210–12
  uncertain 77

J

Jin and Jorion (2006) 104
Joint probability density function 17
Joint probability mass function 12
Jorion (2001) 65, 81, 103-4
JP Morgan, free RiskMetrics service 87

K

Kennedy (1990) 161
Kim *et al* (2005) 104
KMV credit risk measurement approach 179
Kolmogrov–Smirnov tests 161

L

LaGattuta *et al* (2000) 104
Lee *et al* (1996) 81
Leland (1994) 80
Leland and Toft (1996) 80

239

Leverage ratio, impact of 223
Lewis (1989) 104
Long-Term Capital Management (LTCM) 1, 91
Long-term strategic risk 29
Long vs short, for firm 129
Loss Given Default (LGD) 143
Lowestein (2000) 104

M
Managing risks, theoretical foundations for 1
"Market" risk 28
Markowitz (1952) 103
Marrison (2002) 65, 81, 103-4, 108
Marshall (2005) 161
Mayer (1990) 81
Mean-reversion, rationale for 113–17
Mean-reverting assumptions 117
Mean reverting profitability 113–21
Merton (2005) 81
Merton and Culp (1999) 80
Merton and Perold (1993) 22, 81, 190
Mettallgesellschaft 1
Miles and Ezzel model 204
 (1980) 72
 (1985) 73
Minton and Schrand
 (1997) 81
 (1999) 80
Misaligned incentives, example of 46
Modern finance theory 27
Modigliani and Miller
 (1958) 60
 (1963) 60, 64, 72
Modigliani-Miller irrelevance propositions 27
Modigliani-Miller results, limitations to 64
Monte Carlo simulations 203–9
Myers and Majluf (1984) 81

N
Nain (2004) 104

Net exposure 129–32
Net Operating Profits Less Adjusted Taxes (NOPLAT) 67–8
Net present value rule, for project valuation 4
No-uncertainty benchmark 205–6
"Noise"-adjusted performance 47

O
Observed volatility, impact of growth on 110
One-period project valuation 173–6
Operating Cash Flow (OCF) 109
 distribution of future 124–6
 weakness of 110
Operational and strategic flexibility, maximising 48–51
Operational flexibility 49–50
Operations management, critical volatility-reduction tool 40
Operations risk 147–9
 plant risk 29
 process risk 29
Optimal hedging ratio 201–3
Optimal risk management
 strategy, derivations of 215–19
 value of 209
Option value 80
Outside-in risk analysis 108–26
Overseas Shipholding Group (OSG) 108, 112, 119, 125, 126
 profitability as constant volatility 113
 profitability, cumulative distributions of 120
 profitability, distributions of 119

P
Parmalat 2
Payoffs, in different cases 165
"pecking order hypothesis" 32–3, 81
Performance management, risk management enhances 46

INDEX

Pettit (2007) 67, 81, 191
Portfolio composition 39
Price correlation, for corporate risk analysis 21
Price exposures, in contract clauses 131
Price risk 28, 127–42
Probability density function, for continuous random variable 17
Probability mass function (PMF) 12
Probability of default (PD) 143, 144–6
Probability of occurrence 212
Probability theory 79
Professional Risk Managers' International Association (PRMIA) 22
Profitability
  characteristics of 212–13
  volatility of 212

Q
Quantitative credit scores 144

R
Rajan and Zingales (2003) 81
Random investment opportunity 32–3, 205
Random variable 11
Random walk process 121
RARoC (Risk-Adjusted Return on Capital) 42, 86
Return On Invested Capital (ROIC) 74, 193
Risk-adjusted performance 46–7
Risk-adjusted profit determination 45–6
Risk adjustment, alternative approach to 43
Risk aggregation 154
Risk-based capital allocation 76
Risk capital 43
  derivation of 164
  investment capital and 169–73
  on investment cost 165
  for multi-period firm 176–86

source and adequacy of 169–70
Risk correlated with market 63
Risk management
  definition 51–2
  on firms 7
  integrated approach to 51–9
  to leverage operational flexibility 5
  paradox of 1–4
  process of 52
  tools of 50
  value creation from 27
  value of 4–7, 38
Risk management analysis framework, simplified 192–9
Risk management committee 51
Risk management model, ingredient of 31
Risk management practices, review of 83–104
Risk management products, usage of 2
Risk management strategy 51, 78
  drivers of 6, 53
  example of 57
  and growth aspiration 7
  optimal 199–203
  typology of 52–7
  updating 57–9
Risk management team, role of 59
Risk measurement 51
Risk transfer 185
  irrelevance of 61–4
  short- to medium-term volatility management tool 40
Risk typology 65
Risks
  cash flow at 92–5
  categories of 28, 41
  channels for 40
  defining 28
  universe of 28–9
Rochet and Villeneuve (2006) 22, 191
RoRAC (Return on Risk-Adjusted Capital) 42

241

S

"S-curve", for risk management 2, 230
Sample space 11
Sarbanes–Oxley Act
  for public companies 3, 101
Saunders and Allen (2002) 108
Schwartz (1997) 159, 161
Shimpi (2001) 22, 65, 81
Short-term risk 29
Slywotzky and Drzik (2005) 103
Smithson and Simkins (2005) 104
Special Purpose Vehicle (SPV) 7
Spread risk 132–4
"square root of time rule" 18–19
Standard corporate finance approach, implementing 42
Strategic flexibility 50–51
Student-t distribution 161
Sumitomo (1996) 1

T

Tirole (2006) 22, 31, 66, 80-1
Tobin's Q 104, 209
Trading losses, series of 1
Transaction exchange rate exposure 137
Tufano (1996) 104

U

Uncertain profits, and investment opportunity 206–9

V

Value at Risk (VaR) 42, 83, 86–92
  and CFaR concepts 95
  computation of 88–90
  definition of 87–8
  estimation, accuracy of 91
  history of 86–7
  limitations of 90–92
Value creation mechanisms, for non-financial firms 85
Variance 15
Volatility
  managing 96–103
  measuring 85–96
Volatility management technology 76–7
Volatility metric 109–10

W

Weighted Average Cost of Capital (WACC) 70
Wharton/Canadian Imperial Bank of Commerce survey, of financial risk management 2
WorldCom 2

Z

Z-score model 144